BLACKFEET

Beaverhead River

Montana

Wyoming

Bannock Peak

Bannock Trail

Shoshone River

Big Horn River

Yellowstone Lake

Fort Lemhi

Henry Fork

Jackson Hole

Wind River

Fort Hall

Blackfoot River

Portneuf River

Bannock Creek

NOCK COUNTRY

Green River

Battle of Bear River

Bear River

SHOSHONI

Bear Lake

Corinne

great Salt Lake

Weber River

Fort Bridger

Wyoming

Utah

Salt Lake City

UTE

THE BANNOCK OF IDAHO

THE BANNOCK
OF IDAHO

By

Brigham D. Madsen

Illustrated by

MAYNARD DIXON STEWART

THE CAXTON PRINTERS, LTD.

CALDWELL, IDAHO

1958

© 1958 BY
THE CAXTON PRINTERS, LTD.
CALDWELL, IDAHO

Library of Congress Catalog Card No. 57-5248

Printed, lithographed, and bound in the United States of America by
The CAXTON PRINTERS, Ltd.
Caldwell, Idaho
79520

To my mother and father
Lydia Cushing Madsen
Brigham Madsen

Preface

THE Bannock are a branch of the Northern Paiute who, in historic times, inhabited the region of Fort Hall, Idaho. Although they lived in the midst of numerous Shoshoni and probably never exceeded two thousand in population, the Bannock persistently maintained their tribal entity and language. In the eighteenth century they acquired the horse and developed a culture similar in many ways to that of the Plains Indians. Possessed of an aggressive and warlike spirit, these people soon achieved the reputation of being skillful horse thieves and courageous warriors.

The first white explorers and fur traders to reach the country of the Bannock left many accounts of their difficulties with these haughty and turbulent Indians. The inauguration of overland travel brought greater white penetration and, unfortunately for the Bannock, the California and Oregon trails passed through the heart of their tribal country. As emigrants came in increasing numbers, Indian pasture lands were impoverished and, occasionally, members of the tribe were killed by the whites.

Taking retaliatory action, Bannock warriors soon became the scourge of the western roads from Fort

Bridger on the east to Humboldt Sink and Fort Boise on the west, until General Patrick E. Connor's California Volunteers, in 1863, defeated a combined force of Shoshoni and Bannock at Bear River. Thereafter, the Bannock pursued a less hostile course, signed the Treaty of Fort Bridger in 1868, and moved to the Fort Hall Reservation.

Aloof and independent, proud of their tradition as hunters and warriors, the Bannock found it difficult to adapt themselves successfully from their former nomadic existence to a sedentary, agricultural life. They despised farming as women's work and steadfastly blocked most attempts to civilize them. As their great chief, Taghee, said to Governor D. W. Ballard in 1867, "I do not know where to go nor what to do." Their unyielding opposition to white intrusion and their propensity for inciting surrounding Indian nations to revolt have given them a distinctive place in the history of the West.

In writing the story of these people I have used the commonly accepted spelling of their name with an *o,* even though, throughout most of the 1800's, they were known more generally as the "Bannack." I have attempted to limit the number of footnotes which include additional text material but have cited extensively the sources used in the preparation of the book.

A number of people and organizations have been very kind in directing me to original materials and in giving criticisms which have helped make this study more profitable. To the staff of the Bancroft Library and to Dr. George P. Hammond of the University of California, I am most grateful. The initial research on this project was begun there. The Latter-day Saints Church Historian's Office in Salt Lake City contributed generously to the materials for the chapter on the Lemhi Mission. Various officials at the Fort Hall Agency gave helpful assistance in locating copies of the old Letter Books which have proved invaluable. The Idaho Historical Museum at Boise has an excellent file of old state papers and letters which were very helpful on the period of the establishment of the Fort Hall Reservation. The various newspapers used were a veritable gold mine of current attitudes and information concerning the entire period after 1850. Special mention should be made of the kindness of staff members at the offices of *The Idaho Statesman, The Pocatello Tribune,* and *The Idaho Falls Post-Register.* Dr. S. Lyman Tyler and his staff at Brigham Young University Library were very generous in granting me the use of their microfilm facilities. Mr. Albert C. Todd, Jr., proved a tireless and painstaking researcher in Bannock materials at the National Archives in Washington, D.C. Idaho State College officials took a special interest in this project, and my special thanks are due Dr. Sven Liljeblad. His extensive knowledge of the Bannock language and customs should be given recognition here.

Above all I am grateful to Dr. Lawrence Kinnaird, Professor of History at the University of California, for his encouragement, kindness, and patience in helping me in this study. The original research was begun under his guidance, and I should like to acknowledge the debt that his students owe this outstanding teacher.

Without the constant encouragement of my wife, Betty McAllister Madsen, this work would not have been possible. She accompanied me on all visits to archives and libraries, typed the manuscript, gave helpful criticism, and, in many ways, helped to make the preparation of this book a fine experience.

BRIGHAM D. MADSEN

SALT LAKE CITY, UTAH
May 1, 1955

Table of Contents

List of Illustrations

THE BANNOCK OF IDAHO

Cultural Heritage

THE Bannock Indians have occupied the area around Fort Hall, Idaho, since prehistoric times, sharing the region with a tribe of horse Shoshoni known to modern anthropologists as the Fort Hall Shoshoni. Linguistically, the Bannock are related to the Northern Paiute of eastern Oregon but, within the realm of recorded history, have been separated from the parent group by two hundred miles.[1] The Paiute Wada-Eaters of eastern Oregon have the tradition that the Bannock migrated east across the Snake River when buffalo withdrew from Oregon; and this may very well be the logical reason for the location of the Bannock within the linguistic area of the Shoshoni.[2] Early writers who recognized the linguistic similarity of the Northern Paiute (Paviotso) and their eastern kin often referred to the former erroneously

---

[1] Julian H. Steward, *Basin-Plateau Aboriginal Sociopolitical Groups* *(Bulletin 120, Bureau of American Ethnology)* (Washington, 1938), quoted above, and Steward, *Culture Element Distributions, XXIII: Northern and Gosiute Shoshoni* ("Anthropological Records," Vol. VIII, No. 3 [Berkeley, Calif.: University of California Press, 1943]), have been used as the chief bases for this chapter. Dr. Steward has not only made a study of the records and diaries of early travelers who observed the Bannock, but he has also checked these findings against a culture element list compiled by talking to aged members of the tribe. These informants provided the key for unlocking many of the mysteries about the early culture of the Bannock.

[2] Verne F. Ray, "Tribal Distribution in Eastern Oregon and Adjacent Regions," *American Anthropologist*, XL (Menasha, Wis., 1938), p. 405.

as the Western Bannock.[3] In fact, many of the first travelers into the Pacific Northwest placed the "Bannock Indians" in eastern Oregon, thus failing to identify them as a group distinct from the Shoshoni with whom they lived.

Although the word Bannock has been defined as of Shoshoni origin meaning ". . . 'Bamp,' 'hair,' and 'nack,' 'a backward motion,' alluding to the manner in which the tribe wore a tuft of hair thrown back from the forehead," a more probable explanation is that these Indians called themselves Banakwut (ba, "water," plus nakwut, possibly a nominal ending).[4] Fort Hall Shoshoni called them Ba naite, translated as "people from below."[5] In substantiation of this origin of the name, the Bannock at Fort Hall in recent times have reported the tribal tradition that, originally, their ancestors migrated from a great distance "across the water." From this historic incident these people called themselves "Pah'ahnuck" (pah, "water," plus ahnuck, "over" or "across"). The name might well refer to the movement of the tribe from eastern Oregon across the Snake River to southeastern Idaho.[6] There was much confusion among the earliest travelers concerning the status of the Bannock, and the tribe was often classified as Shoshoni or Snake, the latter term being a very general one used to in-

---

[3] Omer C. Stewart, *The Northern Paiute Bands* ("Anthropological Records," Vol. II, No. 3 [Berkeley, Calif.: University of California Press, 1939]), p. 128.

[4] John E. Rees, *Idaho Chronology, Nomenclature, Bibliography* (Chicago, 1918), p. 53.

[5] Steward, *Basin-Plateau Groups, op. cit.*, p. 198.

[6] *Idaho Statesman* (Boise, Idaho), March 13, 1938, p. 8.

clude most of the tribes in the Snake River drainage basin.[7]

The first visitors to the Fort Hall region were likewise in disagreement concerning the size of the Bannock tribe; but a conservative estimate would number them, within historic times, as slightly in excess of 1,000.[8] The Fort Hall Shoshoni with whom they wintered and hunted numbered about 1,500. In physical appearance the Bannock resembled more closely the Shahaptian Nez Perce than they did the Shoshoni. They were tall, slender, and of a lighter complexion than the Shoshoni, the men being among the finest looking of their race. Possessed of strong physical courage, they were warlike, and only their small number kept them from gaining a reputation commensurate with that of the Blackfeet, their traditional enemy.[9]

The Bannock culture was strongly stamped with

---

[7] Most writers agree that the name Snake came to be applied to the Indians of southern Idaho as a result of misinterpretation by the first explorers of the sign language employed by the Indians. When asked the name of his tribe, the native would extend his hand slowly forward with a waving motion from side to side. Rees therefore concluded that the Indians meant to convey that they were called "grass weavers," while Bailey affirmed that they should have been known as "Salmon Indians." Rees, *op. cit.,* p. 113; Robert G. Bailey, *River of No Return* (Lewiston, Idaho, 1935), p. 152.

[8] Grace Raymond Hebard, *Washakie; an Account of Indian Resistance to the Covered Wagon and the Union Pacific Railroad Invasion of their Territory* (Cleveland, 1930), p. 119. Hodge quotes James Bridger as saying that the Bannock, in 1829, numbered 1,200 lodges or about 8,000 people. In 1868, Chief Taghee and 800 Bannock met at Fort Bridger to sign a treaty for a reservation. It is improbable that the tribe ever numbered 8,000, as estimated by Bridger. Frederick Webb Hodge (ed.), *Handbook of American Indians North of Mexico* (Smithsonian Institution, Bureau of American Ethnology, Bulletin 30 [Washington, 1912]), I, 129-30.

[9] Rees, *op. cit.,* p. 53; Chittenden says the Bannock ". . . had the reputation of being a sort of lawless banditti. . . ." Hiram Martin Chittenden (ed.), *The American Fur Trade of the Far West* (2 vols.; New York, 1935) II, 871.

Plains traits. Ownership of horses and the hunting of buffalo distinguished them from the foot Shoshoni found along the Snake River below American Falls. These "Digger Indians" were, by contrast, impoverished, primitive in culture, and unorganized. Few of them owned horses.[10]

The home area of the Bannock near Fort Hall was an arid, sagebrush-covered plain, broken only by the green of lush bottom lands along the Snake, Portneuf, and Blackfoot rivers. Wild game included some antelope and deer, a small number of mountain goat, sheep, and bear, and two species of rabbit. The important food item in the region was the salmon, obtainable below Shoshone Falls on Snake River.[11] Buffalo were numerous in the Fort Hall vicinity until 1840, after which they were hunted near the headwaters of the Yellowstone and Missouri rivers.[12]

With such barren country for a home, it was necessary for the Bannock to travel a large part of the year through near-by areas in search of food stocks to tide them over the winter months. The necessity for these continuous movements in search of food made the horse the most valuable contribution to Bannock economy. It is improbable that the Bannock had horses

---

[10] Bancroft, in typical prose, well described these people: "Lying in a state of semi-torpor in holes in the ground during the winter, and in spring, crawling forth and eating grass on their hands and knees, until able to regain their feet: having no clothes, scarcely any cooked food, in many instances no weapons, with merely a few vague imaginings for religion, living in the utmost squalor and filth, putting no bridle on their passions, there is surely room for no missing link between them and brutes." Hubert Howe Bancroft, "Wild Tribes," in *Native Races* (5 vols.; San Francisco, 1882), I, 440.

[11] John C. Fremont, *Memoirs of My Life* (Chicago and New York, 1887), I, 218.

[12] Steward, *Basin-Plateau Groups, op. cit.*, p. 200.

before the New Mexican Pueblo Revolt of 1680, when southern Indians got large herds from the farms around Santa Fe. By 1700 the Bannock and Shoshoni probably possessed some horses and acted as middlemen in trading the animals to such tribes of the Northwest as the Nez Perce and Cayuse.[13]

The horse revolutionized Bannock economy by enabling people to live in large and permanent groups.[14] New methods of hunting gave greater wealth in food and hides and allowed increased mobility so that small bands were not tied to the vicinity of their food caches. When buffalo began to disappear from the upper Snake River Valley prior to 1840, the Bannock and Fort Hall Shoshoni, either alone or with Nez Perce, and sometimes in company with Flathead, Lemhi, or Wyoming Shoshoni, made annual fall hunting trips through the Yellowstone region into Montana. This route across the Divide was followed for so many years by the Bannock that it has been known ever since as the Great Bannock Trail. It was neces-

---

[13] Francis D. Haines, *Red Eagles of the Northwest* (Portland, Ore., 1939), p. 19; Berreman claims that the original position of the Bannock (1750) was the upper Salmon River region, and that the pressure of Blackfeet from the east drove them to their present location. There may have been a few scattered bands of Bannock in this area at that time, but Steward is probably correct in claiming that the Fort Hall area has been the Bannock home in historic times. As recently as the late 1800's, a few Bannock were found in the mixed band of Lemhi Indians under Chief Tendoy in the Salmon River country. Joel V. Berreman, *Tribal Distribution in Oregon* ("Memoirs of the American Anthropological Association," No. 47 [Menasha, Wis., 1937]), p. 64; Steward, *Basin-Plateau Groups, op. cit.*, p. 200.

[14] On the other hand, Shimkin points out some of the disadvantages that the horse brought to the Plains Indians: "As I see it, the principal effect of the horse was to create a life of extreme cyclicity, of ups and downs to an incredible degree: there were gorging and starvation, great assemblies and complete solitude, elaborate ermine tippets and the crudest of basketry." D. B. Shimkin, *Wind River Shoshone Ethnogeography* ("Anthropological Records," Vol. V, No. 4 [Berkeley, Calif.: University of California Press, 1947]), p. 281.

sary for these various tribes to combine in a sort of armed neutrality in order to protect themselves and their wealth in horses from the marauding Blackfeet and other Plains groups.[15]

Seasonal movements in search of subsistence became quite regularized for most members of the Bannock tribe. After wintering in the neighborhood of Fort Hall, groups of six or more related families would start down the north bank of Snake River to Shoshone Falls and sometimes as far as the Boise, Payette, and Weiser rivers. The main purpose was to procure salmon, which did not get above the falls. After a few weeks spent in fishing and drying the catch, during which the small groups might also barter for fish from the Snake River Shoshoni, the Bannock families then moved on to Camas Prairie, to the north of the Snake River in central Idaho. Here they scattered out to gather roots and seeds. Camas root was the most important of vegetable roots, but there were also *pasigo,* yamp, and tobacco root. The camas was an integral part of the Bannock diet and, during the treaty period of the 1860's, Chief Taghee insisted that Camas Prairie be set apart as a section of the proposed reservation.

From time to time during this harvesting the scattered groups would assemble with the Nez Perce and local Shoshoni to dance and barter. With the Nez Perce they exchanged buffalo robes for war horses, the ownership of which continually involved the Bannock in fights with the Blackfeet. Toward late summer,

---

[15] Steward, *Basin-Plateau Groups, op. cit.,* pp. 201-2; Shimkin, *op. cit.,* p. 280.

the related groups with their stores of salmon, roots, and seeds, would begin to drift back to Fort Hall to prepare for the fall buffalo hunts. The greater efficiency of communal hunting, plus the fear of the Blackfeet, compelled the Bannock to travel as a tribal unit under the direction of their chiefs during the trek to Montana and back. In the vicinity of Yellowstone they usually stopped to gather pine nuts which they stored in caches to be picked up on the return trip. Continuing then over the Great Bannock Trail, they came into the buffalo country near the headwaters of the Missouri River.

The hunting of the buffalo was under the direction of a special chief who might also be the tribal chief. He appointed temporary scouts to find the herd; and the men would then ride after the animals, shooting three or four apiece with bow and arrow. After the kill, the dried buffalo meat and robes were loaded on horses, and the tribe returned to Fort Hall for the winter. During the late fall, large groups might leave the tribal home for short hunting excursions on Bear River, or to go to other near-by areas where deer and antelope were taken. Deer were killed by individuals in small parties, while antelope were usually obtained in communal hunts featuring shamanistic ritual. The horse relay was also used to take the animals. Other animals used for food were bear, mountain goat, bighorn sheep, and beaver.

The constant movements, necessitated by the search for subsistence, involved contacts with other Indians and the concomitant of wars and the danger of hostile raiding parties. The Blackfeet were the perennial enemy, while relationships with the Crow seem to have alternated between friendship and enmity. The Utes engaged in intermittent strife with the Bannock but rarely ventured north of the Salt Lake region. With the Nez Perce and Flathead the Bannock maintained an armed neutrality, although there was some war with the Nez Perce in the 1820's. The few fights which occurred with the Flathead were usually a result of horse-stealing raids by one tribe or the other.[16]

The Fort Hall Shoshoni were friendly to the white man most of the time, but here the Bannock differed sharply from their neighbors, being much more aggressive and looking upon all whites as fair game for raids. The most important battles were defensive and led by the band chief, although well-planned attacks and numerous horse-stealing raids were organized and led by either the band chiefs or other prominent men. Before leaving for battle or a raid, the warriors carried a buffalo robe through camp, holding its edges and beating it. Others joined in the ceremony, singing, offering needed food and equipment, and shaking hands with the departing braves. The war paraphernalia consisted of a lance, bow and arrows, and war bonnet if desired; the warriors themselves wore only a breechcloth and paint. Equal war honors included: the first four braves touching a dead enemy with the hand or spear, stepping in an enemy's blood, stealing a horse, and stealing other property. A return-

---

[16] Teit relates an incident in which the Bannock, Crow, and Flathead were involved in a short war over some stolen horses. James A. Teit, "The Salishan Tribes of the Western Plateaus" (*Forty-Fifth Annual Report, Bureau of American Ethnology*) (Washington: Government Printing Office, 1928), p. 361.

ing war party, whether victorious or not, was met by an escort from the village, and the entire group then engaged in a scalp or victory dance. During times of peace the Bannock held drill parades on horseback as a means of training for battle.

Political organization consisted of the direction of subsistence and other activities by certain strong individuals whose control varied from season to season and over a period of years. The Bannock and Fort Hall Shoshoni were politically distinct, each having its own band chief and maintaining its own political organization. The band chief became more important as the buffalo retreated from Snake River Valley to the plains area of Montana. He had an announcer who also served as messenger, and a new chief might choose a different announcer. Subject to community approval, succession was patrilineal, but a forceful personality outside the chieftain line might be chosen to lead the tribe. The duty of the chief in winter was to supervise the supply of food and fuel, and he made the decision to move camp when necessary. The Bannock and Fort Hall Shoshoni set up a few camps on Lincoln Creek, some near the mouth of Blackfoot River, a few more on the Portneuf River upstream as far as Lava Hot Springs, and some on Ross Creek. The greatest number, however, wintered along the bottom lands of the Snake River above American Falls.[17]

---

[17] Rees' description of petroglyphs found along Blackfoot River would indicate that the tribe had occupied this area for many years: "The writings are carved, here and there, along the course of the stream for a distance of some two miles and have the appearance of being quite old as the eroding elements of heat, cold and moisture have dimmed and given them a glazed aspect wholly different from the work of

During other seasons of the year the band chief directed movements in search of food. Disputes in camp did not concern him, and the participants settled these affairs in their own way. He had no obligation to entertain visitors, but he might do so on special occasions. Buffalo hunting gave him more power, and the annual trip to and from Montana was under his supervision. The chief might appoint another leader to direct such events as the communal antelope hunt. The band chief had the special function of leading war parties in battle, and he wore an eagle-feather bonnet and carried a spear on these occasions. But many raiding expeditions were headed by brave and experienced men who organized and led parties without the chief's permission. After the arrival of the white man the tribal council gained in importance, its principal function being to advise the chief in his dealings with the whites. The band chief directed the Scalp Dance and the Grass Dance in the fall; but, with these two exceptions, other dances were directed by men recognized as being specially skilled in their particular dance. The Sun Dance is a late-comer to the Bannock, having been imported from the Plains Indians since 1900. Although the tribal chief directed the activities already mentioned, his authority was never complete, and small groups might branch off under some younger leader to pursue independent courses.

Relations with the Fort Hall Shoshoni included

a few years. . . . They were made by the Bannock Indians whose dragon-fly totem appears quite often interspersed with the other carvings." John Rees, "Bannock Petroglyphs Along the Blackfoot River" (Unpublished MS, Public Library, Blackfoot, Idaho), p. 134.

wintering together at Fort Hall and uniting in the annual buffalo hunts. When the two tribes traveled together, leadership of the combined groups went to the chief who had initiated the project, and this was especially true of communal hunting expeditions. Otherwise, the Bannock chief was customarily in authority, except in certain dealings with the white man. The Fort Hall Shoshoni's friendly inclination toward the white man caused the main dissension between the two bands; but the Bannock, in some instances, were successful in drawing the Shoshoni into raids and battles against the whites.

In time of danger or for special festivities, a camp circle was organized. After the chief had pitched his tipi, the others pitched theirs to form a circle, with an opening to the east, opposite the chief. When enemy raids threatened, tree limbs were placed between the tipis to form a corral, and the horses were taken inside. Guards were posted at such times, but they usually fell asleep before morning.

Whether traveling or in winter camp, the Bannock pitched a tipi as his dwelling. A small one required seven or eight smoked buffalo hides sewed together; a large one might take as many as twenty hides. The man of the family often painted his exploits over the doorway. Other dwellings used occasionally were domed willow houses for summer use, conical grass houses for winter, and caves for traveling war parties.[18]

---

[18] A Fort Hall Shoshoni related an interesting experience of one of his tribesmen who used a cave for temporary shelter while on a raid: "A war scout once sought refuge in a cave after dark. He suspected someone else's presence, and in the morning saw a Crow enemy. By sign language, they agreed to gamble for the other's scalp. The Shoshoni won and scalped the Crow." Steward, *Northern and Gosiute Shoshoni, op. cit.*, p. 367.

In addition to the tipi, another important structure was the domed, willow sweat house, covered with a rabbitskin blanket, grass, and earth. Heated by hot rocks placed inside, the sweat house was used for cleansing the body and also for religious purposes. During the bathing process the individual offered up prayers of thankfulness to Nature. The sweat house was individually owned, but was used by anyone in the community.

Fire was made by igniting artemisia bark tinder with sparks from two pieces of flint, or by the use of a compound drill, about two feet long, that was manipulated by two men. A bark bundle slow match was carried on journeys; its composition of tightly wrapped sagebrush (three inches in diameter and three or four feet long) retained a smoldering fire for a long time.

As with most Indians of the region, the chief weapon of the Bannock was the bow and arrow. Two types of bow were manufactured: a sinew-backed bow about three feet in length with a buckskin-wrapped grip; and a mountain sheep horn bow made of two horns set end to end and overlapping, secured by a process of wrapping with sinew. Arrows were constructed with and without foreshafts, three eagle feathers five inches in length being fastened in non-spiral fashion at the end. A quiver of young antelope or deer fur held the arrows, while the bow was carried in a special compartment. When in use the bow was held in a vertical position, and the arrows were pulled under the arm.

Miscellaneous weapons included a wooden thrusting spear some six or seven feet long with a stone point, a rawhide or buffalo bullneck shield, a war ax, flint, dagger, and a pogamoggan or war club. The war horse was decorated with a bunch of feathers tied on the head and with white clay painted in various patterns. A buffalo-scrotum rattle had a special use in wartime, being:

> . . . used as club by men called wiyagit (singers), who were foolhardy in war. They wore no special dress. No more than 2 men might be wiyagit at once. Such men slept all day and sang all night, even when there was no danger, thus guarding the camp at night. They did no hunting. They were always up to mischief, e.g., they might take an old man's pipe and break it or pour the tobacco out on the ground. But they were tolerated because people understood their condition. They were invulnerable in war except for some small spot, such as the little finger. Going to war they both rode the same horse. They lagged on the way but when the enemy was ambushed, they rushed out ahead of other people. Unusual war bravery absolved them of their condition and they became normal again. If one was killed, the other became normal. Then there might be no wiyagit for a time until two men decided to become this way.[19]

Although a horse people, the Bannock did navigate the streams of their country by hide-covered log rafts and balsa rafts. These latter held as many as five persons and were constructed of three bundles of tules, side by side, with pointed prow and square stern. They were propelled by means of poles or by a horse driven along the bank of the stream.

Despite the ubiquitous horse, some Bannock transportation was accomplished by packing for short dis-

---

[19] *Ibid.*, p. 372.

tances. A pack strap, for braves and squaws, passed over the head and across the shoulder and chest. The travois was in common use both for horse and dog; one stick was slightly shorter than the other so that both would not bounce at the same time in rough country, the poles being held together by rope laced back and forth between them. Infants' cradles were constructed of a basketry framework covered by buckskin. The child was wrapped in a fawnskin or wildcat hide blanket, and the cradle was carried by a strap across the breast.

Although Bannock women did not fabricate basketry and pottery of ornate or ornamental design, they did produce substantial everyday utensils of willow and clay. Among the basket forms were a seed beater, a fan-shaped winnowing basket, a fishing basket, basket bowls, and a water jug with a handle and lid of buckskin. Pottery jugs were constructed of clay mixed with pitch, formed and baked in holes in the ground. The women of the tribe also made fur blankets, wove feather blankets of duckskins, and manufactured fish nets of bark. Miscellaneous implements included spoons, dippers, and plates made of horn from mountain sheep and moose, knives of flint, salmon-skin bags for berries, buckskin bags for seeds, and wooden awls.

In the art of dressing skins the Bannock became very proficient; that is, the Bannock women did; the only men who practiced the art were the bachelors of the tribe.[20] After a skin had been soaked, it was twisted dry and then tanned with brains, bear fat,

---

[20] Thomas H. Leforge, *Memoirs of a White Crow Indian*, as told by Thomas B. Marquis (New York, 1928), p. 199.

The travois was in common use

or liver, the tanning agent being boiled and stored in a piece of intestine. The hide was again soaked in warm water, grained by being pulled across a sinew rope, and finally smoked on one side. Leather intended for moccasins was smoked on both sides. The leather shirts and dresses prepared from the tanned buckskin were noted for their utility and beauty.

Various decorations of the person were employed by both sexes. Women wore necklaces of elk teeth and bone tubes, bracelets of claws or teeth, and belts of buckskin or otter fur. The men used eagle-feather fans at home, and carried them during festivals or gatherings. Over a coat of grease, black, white, red, and yellow paints were distributed on the body according to any pattern desired by the individual. The front lock of hair might be painted either yellow or white on special occasions. Paints were also used to prevent the skin from darkening in summer, and they were applied around the eyes as a protection against sun and snow blindness. The morning after a particularly bad dream it was often applied as a counteragent. Dressing of the hair was accomplished with a porcupine-tail brush and a rough comb. Men wore their hair in two braids, one over each shoulder, and occasionally a third braid was formed which hung down the back of the head. The front lock stuck up, some warriors wearing it short and tied to stand erect. Women parted their hair with a braid over each shoulder, each braid being wrapped with fur. The Bannock men wore an eagle feather sticking out at an angle from the crown of the head. Depilation of the beard was accomplished by using the fingernails.

A man's cap, worn winter and summer, was constructed of a single piece of deer rawhide, with a visor in front and back and the center cut in strips which were bent up. This frame was then pulled down over the head and the top wrapped with a band of coyote fur. Men also wore a headband of buckskin, weasel, or otter fur. Woven fur robes were worn by both sexes: wildcat, beaver, buffalo, elk, and other pelts being used in their manufacture. Beaver fur was not considered warm because the animal lived in cold water. A man's buckskin shirt was made of two deerskins (or antelope or mountain sheep skins) sewed together, with an inset on the sides. The sleeves were wrist-length and fringed; the shirt was tied at the neck, and the bottom was fringed. Decorations of scalps along the fringe and small, round holes on the breast were further enhanced by the varied patterns of red, yellow, and black painted on the shoulders. The breechcloth for men was of buckskin. Leggings for man and woman varied only in their length; the man's reached from the hip to the ankle with a strip tied to the belt for support, while the woman's knee-length legging was secured by a garter. Fringe on the outside of the legging was decorated with scalps and quills. The woman's long gown was made in much the same fashion as the man's shirt, differing chiefly in the triangular insert which was sewed into the front at the neck for ornamental purposes. Skin moccasins were either one-piece or two-piece affairs, with ankle flaps and tongues added for further protection. Besides quill decorations, red paint might be rubbed on the instep to show that the owner had stepped in the blood of the enemy—provided he had actually killed an enemy and stepped close enough to get blood on his moccasins. Elliptical snowshoes, laced with thongs of leather, and with the toe slightly bent up, provided foot mobility in winter.

Various games were used by the Bannock to while away their leisure hours. Ball races in which the ball was kicked from one point to another, a game of shinny, and rock quoits provided physical exertion as well as fun. Other sports were horse racing, archery, arrow tossing at a target, diving and swimming meets, gang fights, and shot-putting. Wrestling matches were held in which a man chose his opponent from the circle formed around him. When any part of a man's body above the knee touched the ground, he resumed his place in the circle and a new opponent was chosen by the victor. Although betting took place in most contests, it became sharper and was more common when such games as four-stick dice, the four-stick guessing game, and other hand games were played. Women engaged in juggling matches (with three stones) and ran races while performing this feat.

The use of tobacco was common. The leaf was gathered wild, dried, crushed, mixed with other leaf, and carried in a buckskin bag with the pipe. The pipe was either tubular, of some five inches in length with a stem of four inches, or L-shaped with a stem of about eight inches. They were both made of a greenish or bluish stone that glowed red when lighted. There was some community smoking at gatherings and camp circles; but usually it was an individual matter, indulged in mostly by old men at bedtime only. The shamans, of course, used tobacco and smoking in some of their ceremonies.

Various musical instruments in use in camp circles were hoof rattles, musical bows, and notched sticks and rasps. A deer-foot bone tied to a string became a buzzer. Two-headed drums were suspended from four stakes for use in the different dances, while a special one-headed drum furnished music for the Scalp Dance. Whistles made of eagle-wing bones were used by war parties in time of danger. Young swains courted the maidens of their choice with elderberry flutes.

The Bannock prohibited any marriage between blood relatives, and preferred a match between a man and his mother's brother's stepdaughter or the daughter of any female relatives of the mother's brother's wife. True cross-cousins called one another "brother" and "sister." In ordinary marriage a man would persuade a girl whom he met at a gathering to accompany him to his father's camp. The girl's family was not consulted and, if she chose to go with the man and remained with him, the marriage was considered consummated. Marriage by inducement occurred when a girl's family asked someone, usually her uncle, to tell the young man whom they considered a good hunter that they would like him for a son-in-law. He was offered no presents; but if he went to the girl's house for a few days and slept with her, he was considered to be her mate. A third type of marriage—by abduction—took two forms: capture and rape. If a Bannock man saw a woman, married or unmarried, whom he desired, he summoned his blood relatives or those related by marriage and set out to steal her. The husband likewise summoned his friends and relatives, and a gang fight ensued. Although there was no intent to kill on either side, deaths and severe injuries did occur. Deaths were not avenged, being considerd as legitimate hazards of abduction. The husband took no steps to recover his wife, although she might return to him of her own accord. In the case of adultery, the husband ordinarily gave his wife a severe beating and killed one or more of the paramour's horses. If a couple separated, it was the husband who took the initiative; a woman who left her husband was nearly always sent back by her family. If not, the mother took the children. Polygyny was practiced among the Bannock, with the wives usually being sisters because the first wife might object if the second were not her sister. Premarital intercourse was forbidden; in such instances, the girl was reprimanded and the man was beaten.

The closest friends of a Bannock brave were his cousins. These men went on sexual escapades together, borrowed one another's property, and helped one another. So-called joking relatives included brothers-in-law and sisters-in-law.

Birth customs involved the construction of a special birth house in which the new mother was confined thirty days after the child arrived. Any experienced woman acted as midwife, and a nurse was provided to attend to the mother during the first few days.

At the end of confinement, the mother was given new clothes and had her face painted. The husband provided firewood for the birth house although, during the five days following the birth, he, too, was confined to a special house, after which he was given a cold bath and new clothing. For this five-day period the father could not eat meat and could not gamble. After thirty days, the infant was placed in the customary basket cradle.

After death, a corpse prepared for burial was washed, dressed in the best clothes, and then wrapped in a blanket and tied. Burial took place in any convenient spot in the rocks, with the body extended and the head toward the west. Chief Pocatello of the Bannock Creek Shoshoni was wrapped in a blanket, tied with a rope, and pushed feet down into a spring by means of a tipi pole, the pole being left as a marker. But this type of burial was not common. Gifts were made to the deceased, and his best horse was killed, the remaining horses being distributed to relatives. The sorrowing relatives cut the manes and tails of the animals. The mourning customs included cropping of the hair, gashing the legs, refraining from participation in all dances for twelve months, and observing a ban against remarriage for twelve months.

Either men or women could become shamans. There was a family tendency toward shamanism, and a person usually inherited the power from a relative. Dreams, either sought or unsought, were the source of power, although the latter were more efficacious. During administration to the sick, the shaman used the patient's house or his sweat house, other people accompanying him as he sang. The doctor might talk and smoke as his assistant repeated everything said and passed a pipe to the audience. The actual curing process consisted of sucking from the patient's body such things as blood, a stone, a snake, a small animal, a worm, or a ghost. It was then regurgitated, exhibited to the audience, and thrown away. Other practices were to blow water on a patient, sprinkle water with a piece of sagebrush, put ashes on the patient, or touch him with a heated antler. The shaman frequently went into a trance during which he supposedly restored the patient's soul. Among special powers possessed by the shaman-doctor, the handling of fire was considered quite awe-inspiring: he might walk on fire, put live coals in his mouth, or hold his hands in the flames. He also handled rattlesnakes, and he could cure snake bites by sucking out the poison. His weather control power consisted of bringing rain, stopping rain, or bringing warm winds. An unsuccessful shaman demanded no fee and ceased to practice.

Individual Indians prayed to "Father," the Sun, or Nature, and offered prayers at mealtime. The Bannock believed that the soul resided in the head and that, at death, the soul went west along the Milky Way to "Father." A person would be transformed into a bird if killed by a bullet, and reincarnation as a human being was expected at some future date. There was a branching trail to the afterworld, with a fork to the bad people's land and a guide at the forks to direct people.

Of the many dances performed, the Circle Dance

was perhaps the most common. It could be held at any time, although the favorite seasons were spring and summer. The general purpose was to make the seeds grow and to bring rain. Special singers furnished music, offering prayer songs in which everyone joined. The men encircled the camp before the dance, and the sexes alternated in dancing in the circle around the fire. With a side-shuffle step, the group moved clockwise around the circle while clowns cavorted in additional supplication for good fortune. A Bear Dance or Back and Forth Dance was for pleasure only, and generally lasted four days. A pre-Columbian dance that suggests Bannock culture before the advent of the horse or of buffalo hunting was the Rabbit Dance, in which the participants dressed to represent rabbits. A musician and a doctor were stationed in the center, and the men dancers pretended to shoot people while dancing around in the circle. The dancers were paid by the onlookers.

A very important ceremony was the Scalp Dance, of which there were at least seven varieties. All were danced after the return of a war party. In one dance, men and women in a circle (the men grasping the women's waists) would jump, bow, blow while facing the center, and then hop as the circle moved clockwise. Other dances were those in which presents were exchanged, and a war dance which was limited to valorous warriors.

The Bannock man probably had at least three names during his lifetime. At birth his parents named him from a relative's great deed. Also, he acquired a secret nickname by which he was known to close friends while a young man. As he approached maturity, he was given a new name from some valorous deed which he had performed.

Perhaps the outstanding characteristic of Bannock culture was its persistent survival in the midst of numerous Shoshoni. Although both tribes were similarly influenced by the introduction of the horse and by the adoption of buffalo hunting as the basic economy, the Bannock maintained their singular customs and language until the late nineteenth century, when confinement on a reservation began to break down the old ways and traditions.

Fur Trade Era

THE first mention of the Bannock in recorded history may have been made by Meriwether Lewis, in his journal for August 20, 1805.[1] At the time, the Lewis and Clark expedition was encamped in the Salmon River area near a group of Shoshoni. There, an old man of the tribe warned Captain Clark that it would be dangerous to travel to the south because that area was held by a fierce and warlike people called the "broken mockersons or mockersons with holes." From the description of the country inhabited by these Broken Moccasins, Hodge concluded that they were the Bannock.[2] Another writer, however, once questioned Chief Tendoy of the Lemhi Indians concerning the identity of the Broken Moccasins.[3] The chief said they were not the Bannock but a mythical race that had been destroyed many years ago by a huge flood that had inundated their land. There is, thus, considerable doubt that Lewis and Clark ever learned of the existence of the Bannock or that these Indians were identical with the Broken Moccasins.

---

[1] Reuben G. Thwaites (ed.), *Original Journals of the Lewis and Clark Expedition 1804-1806* (New York, 1904), II, Part II, 381.

[2] Frederick W. Hodge (ed.), *Handbook of American Indians North of Mexico* (Smithsonian Institution, Bureau of American Ethnology, Bulletin 30 [Washington, 1912]), I, 129.

[3] DeCost Smith, *Indian Experiences* (Caldwell, Idaho, 1943), p. 286.

Following the explorations of Lewis and Clark, American fur traders began to penetrate the Rocky Mountain area. As far as present knowledge goes, the first white man to enter the homeland of the Bannock was John Colter who, in 1807, crossed the Teton Range from the east and descended into Pierre's Hole near Henrys Fork of the Snake River before turning back to the Yellowstone Park area.[4] Three years later, Andrew Henry of the Missouri Fur Company established Fort Henry on the upper Snake River and a number of trappers spent the winter of that year in the region, finally abandoning the trading post in the spring of 1811.[5] Unfortunately, these early explorers and traders were more interested in trapping beaver than in recording travel experiences or in writing descriptions of the country and its native inhabitants.

It was not until the fall of 1811, and the coming of Wilson Price Hunt's party of Astorians, that any written account was made of the Indians living in the Fort Hall region. Hunt kept an extensive journal of his travels across the country to Oregon and noted on October 23, 1811, that "a band of Snakes and Chochonis fled at seeing us."[6] The expedition was then just below the forks of Snake River, in the heart of the Bannock country. It is possible that Hunt's reference to "Snakes and Chochonis" was an indication

---

[4] Stallo Vinton, *John Colter, Discoverer of the Yellowstone* (New York, 1926), p. 59.

[5] Hiram M. Chittenden (ed.), *The American Fur Trade of the Far West* (2 vols.; New York, 1935), I, 143.

[6] Phillip A. Rollins (ed.), "Wilson Price Hunt's Diary of His Overland Trip Westward to Astoria in 1811-12," in *The Discovery of the Oregon Trail, Robert Stuart's Narratives* (New York, 1935), p. 291,

that he realized there were two distinct tribes living in the region.

When Robert Stuart passed through the area in the summer of 1812, carrying dispatches from Fort Astoria in Oregon back to New York, he followed the precedent already set and referred to all the Indians he met as Snakes. On August 20, the Stuart party met four hunters who had left Hunt the previous year to trap in the upper Snake River Valley. They told of trapping on Bear River where they had met "a southern band of 'Snakes.' " Phillip Ashton Rollins, editor of the Stuart papers, is of the opinion that these Indians were "probably either Bannocks or else Shoshonis proper. . . ."[7] Again, this is merely conjecture, although apparently the first travelers through the region did recognize differences among the Snake Indians.

A final party of Astorians became involved with the Indians of Snake River during the winter of 1812. John Reed was sent out from Fort Astoria as leader of a small group of fur hunters and established a post on Snake River as a base for trapping operations. In January, 1813, a band of Indians attacked the post and killed nine of the men. The Indian wife of Pierre Dorian escaped with her two children and eventually made her way back to Walla Walla to report that a band of "bad Snakes, called the Dogrib tribe" had committed the murders.[8] The exact

---

[7] *Ibid.*, pp. 86, 105.

[8] Alexander Ross, *Adventures of the First Settlers on the Oregon or Columbia River* [London, 1849], reprinted in *Early Western Travels, 1748-1846*, ed. by R. G. Thwaites (Cleveland, 1904), VII, 265, 270; Ross Cox, *Adventures on the Columbia River, including the Narrative of a Residence of Six Years on the Western Side of the Rocky Mountains* (New York, 1832), pp. 136-38.

identity of the guilty Indians remained a mystery until Donald McKenzie made his first Snake River expedition for the British Northwest Company in 1819.

One of the purposes of McKenzie's expedition was to ensure that the "Snakes" would adhere to a treaty of peace which he had arranged between them and the Nez Perce and other Columbia River Indians. In order to exploit the fur resources of the Snake River Basin it was paramount that the Indian tribes be at peace so that the Northwest trappers could work the area. During the initial stages of the expedition it became necessary to send most of the party back to Fort Walla Walla for supplies. While McKenzie was thus left with only three men to help him, "a very suspicious party of the mountain Snakes appeared" at their camp. The Indians at first accepted some gifts presented to them by McKenzie but, later, they became bolder and attempted to get behind the breastwork which the four whites had built for defense. At this juncture, McKenzie sprang over the breastwork, placed a keg of gunpowder between himself and the Indians, lighted a match, and dared them to renew their threats. Taken by surprise, the mountain Snakes retreated and then left in a hurry when about two hundred Flathead Indians rode up on the other side of the river.[9]

By the early 1820's, perhaps no one knew more about the Indians of Snake River than did Alexander

---

[9] As explained later in the Ross narrative, the "mountain Snakes" were the "Ban-at-tees." Alexander Ross, *The Fur Hunters of the Far West; A Narrative of Adventures in the Oregon and Rocky Mountains* (2 vols.; London, 1855), I, 219.

McKenzie placed a keg of gunpowder between himself and the Indians

Ross, the chronicler of the adventures of Donald Mc-Kenzie, and himself a leader of one of the Snake expeditions. He was able to catalogue the "Snake" tribes as follows: The Sherry-dikas, or Dog-eaters; the War-are-ree-kas, or fish-eaters; and the Ban-at-tees, or robbers. According to his classification, the Sherry-dikas were the real Shoshoni, the buffalo-hunting Plains Indians. The War-are-ree-kas were the Shoshoni or "Digger" Indians of the lower Snake River: those who lived chiefly on salmon and did not hunt the buffalo. The third group, the Ban-at-tees, was found in small bands living a predatory and wandering life in the mountains. The real Shoshoni, said Ross, looked upon them as outlaws. From this description, Ross apparently had learned that the Bannock were a warlike people but did not recognize them as a tribe associated with Plains traits. It is also possible that he attached the name, Ban-at-tee, to just a few of the tribe who were always going on raids, and included the majority of the Bannock with the Sherry-dikas or "real Sho-sho-nees." He acknowledges that:

> With all their experience our friends possessed but a very confused idea of the Snakes, both as to their names or numbers. One would call them Ban-nacks, and another Warracks, while a third would have them named Dogs! Nor was it till I had subsequently gone to their country, travelled, traded and conversed with them that I could learn anything like facts to be depended upon, and even after all I can state, it cannot be relied upon as entirely correct.[10]

Eventually, McKenzie was able to gather the Snakes together to discuss the treaty of peace signed with

---

[10] *Ibid.*, pp. 249-51.

the Indians to the West. Ross recorded that the mighty encampment stretched seven miles on both sides of the river and contained over ten thousand Indians. The Sherry-dikas, presided over by the chiefs Pee-eye-em and Ama-qui-em, took the lead in the conference, while the War-are-ree-kas and Ban-at-tees held subordinate positions. In fact, the Ban-at-tees were not allowed to take part in the meetings until the last two or three days. Pee-eye-em declared that it was the Ban-at-tees "who disturbed and waged war with the Nez Perces, and plunder the whites when in their power." He continued:

". . . for us to run after and punish the Ban-at-tees every time they do evil would be endless. It would be just as easy for us to hunt out and kill all the foxes in the country as to hunt out and punish every Ban-at-tee that does mischief. They are like the mosquitoes, not strong but they can torment. . . ."[11]

Then Ama-ketsa, a chief of the War-are-ree-kas, denounced the Ban-at-tees as a "predatory race, and the chief cause of all the Snake trouble with the Nez Perces."

After the Ban-at-tees had been thus arraigned, four of their chiefs were called before the council and told by Ama-qui-em that if their people did not observe the peace, all of them would be punished with death by the Sherry-dikas.

In uttering these words, Ama-qui-em got quite enthusiastic. "Yes," said he to the trembling Ban-at-tees, "you are robbers and murderers too! You have robbed the whites;

---

[11] *Ibid.*, pp. 252-55.

you have killed the whites." After this declaration, he made a pause, as if regretting what he had said.[12]

After the conference was over, McKenzie asked the chief what he had meant by his reference to the killing of whites. Ama-qui-em explained that it was the Ban-at-tees who had plundered and murdered the Reed party in 1813. As if to live up to the reputation they were acquiring among the whites, the Ban-at-tees assumed a haughty tone and began to plague the trappers as soon as the Sherry-dikas had gone.

McKenzie and Ross were not alone in their denunciation of the Bannock. Peter Skene Ogden, leader of the Snake expeditions from 1824 to 1829, joined his voice in the chorus of condemnation. He recorded in his journal for June 8, 1826, that during the preceding ten months the Snakes had stolen 180 traps from the American traders and killed thirteen whites. He said, "The Americans swear to make an example of them; I do hope from my soul they may."[13] While he condemned all the Snakes impartially, Ogden did attempt to classify them. He divided them into the

---

[12] Hebard concluded that the Ban-at-tees of Ross's narrative were the Bannock, but quite incorrectly added, "Though often referred to as a separate tribe or sub-tribe, it seems safer to regard them as an outlaw band, hardly distinguishable except in their propensity to treachery and violence, from the 'real' Shoshones. From time to time the more lawless spirits among the other bands would join them. . . ." Grace R. Hebard, *Washakie; an Account of Indian Resistance to the Covered Wagon and the Union Pacific Railroad Invasion of their Territory* (Cleveland, 1930), p. 34.

[13] T. C. Elliott (ed.), "The Peter Skene Ogden Journals, Snake Expedition, 1825-1826," *Oregon Historical Society Quarterly*, X, No. 4 (December, 1909), 357, 362; T. C. Elliott (ed.), "The Peter Skene Ogden Journals, Snake Expedition, 1827-1828," *Oregon Historical Society Quarterly*, XI, No. 4 (December, 1910), 365; Washington Irving, *The Adventures of Captain Bonneville* (New York, 1885), pp. 105-06.

Plains Snakes, of 1000 warriors, and the Lower Snakes, of 1,500 warriors. Evidently the Lower Snakes were the Bannock because, during the Snake expedition of 1827-28, Ogden met the chief of that tribe, "The Horse," who was later definitely identified by Captain Benjamin L. E. Bonneville, in 1833, as chief of the Bannock.

The American trappers referred to by Ogden were members of the Rocky Mountain Fur Company, a firm which had been established in 1822 by General William H. Ashley. They, too, had shared in troubles with the Bannock. During the winter of 1825, the Ashley party, with their families and Indian friends, settled down at the mouth of Weber River near the present Ogden, Utah. One stormy night shortly after the encampment had been established, a party of Bannock stole eighty horses. Although Weber River was far to the south of their wintering ground, apparently the Bannock could not resist the temptation offered to enrich themselves in horses and glory. The following morning, forty trappers under Thomas Fitzpatrick and James Bridger set out to regain their animals. After a pursuit of five days, the whites arrived at the Bannock camp and spotted their horses in the Indian herd. The trappers decided to split their forces: while Fitzpatrick led an attack on the village of some four or five hundred people, Bridger's party stampeded the horses and succeeded in getting away with 120, or forty more than had been stolen. Six Bannock were killed in the short engagement, but Fitzpatrick's force escaped unharmed. Upon returning to Weber River, the trappers discovered that

in their absence a Shoshoni group of six hundred
lodges, or about 2,500 people, had set up winter
quarters next to the Ashley camp. James P. Beckwourth said, "They were perfectly friendly, and we ap-
prehended no danger from their proximity."[14] While
it is not always safe to rely on the statements or
statistics of the redoutable Beckwourth, his observation concerning the friendly attitude of the Shoshoni
was apparently correct.

Again, in the following year, the Rocky Mountain
Fur Company trappers had to deal with a portion
of the Bannock tribe. Beckwourth was again the
narrator and ascribed the success of the affair to his
own innate ability. The whites were camped at the
junction of Salt River and Snake River near a village
of "Snakes." It was soon learned that two miles away
there were 185 lodges of "Pun-nocks . . . a discarded
band of the Snakes, very bad Indians, and very great
thieves." Captain William Sublette, commanding the
trappers, advised the friendly Shoshoni to warn the
Bannock that if any horses were stolen from the
whites he would "rub . . . out" the entire Bannock
tribe. One evening shortly after, two of the trappers
and a Shoshoni strolled down to visit the adjoining
camp and were set upon, the Shoshoni being killed
and the two whites seriously wounded. Determined
to fulfill his promise, Sublette the next morning sent
215 of his men after the Bannock, who had hurriedly
broken camp and departed as soon as they learned
of their comrades' attack on the Americans. After a

---

[14] T. D. Bonner (ed.), *The Life and Adventures of James P. Beckwourth* (New York, 1931), pp. 60-61.

chase of forty-five miles, the Indians reached Green
River and fortified themselves on an island in the
stream. Beckwourth's story to this point seems entirely
credible, but his account of the attack on the island
fortress is so similar to one that occurred about ten
years later that it is entirely possible that he became
confused about the two battles and allowed his propensity for embellishment to make up for his poor
memory of the affair. Nevertheless, he recorded that
when the Americans reached the river, James Bridger,
leader of the group, said,

> "What shall we do now, Jim?"
> "I will cross to the other side with one half the men," I
> suggested, "and get abreast of the island. Their retreat will
> be thus cut off, and we can exterminate them in their trap."
> "Go," said he, "I will take them if they attempt to make
> this shore."[15]

Having thus modestly outlined a plan of attack, Beckwourth carried out his share of the venture, and the
two groups practically annihilated the Bannock tribe,
taking 488 scalps. Only six or eight squaws were
saved, and these were given to the Shoshoni. The
latter were delighted at the victory and immediately
held a Scalp Dance in honor of the defeat of the "very
bad Indians." There is little doubt that Beckwourth's
estimate of the number of Bannock killed was greatly
exaggerated, and it is highly improbable that most
of the tribe was wiped out, as he claimed.

Only a year after the Bannock were supposedly
all killed, Peter Skene Ogden met the "Lower Snakes,"

---

[15] *Ibid.,* pp. 87-88.

or Bannock, on Camas Prairie and estimated their numbers at 300 lodges, or 1,500 people. They had about 3,000 horses with them at the time. Ogden had, perhaps, a better knowledge of the subsistence activities of the Bannock than any of the other early traders. He described quite accurately the relation between their camas gathering, their fishing, and their annual treks to the buffalo country in Montana. On November 25, 1827, the Bannock head chief, "The Horse," visited Ogden and carried an American flag to the meeting. The British trader gave the Indian leader a number of presents and seemed to get along very well with him. About a week later the chief restored a stolen trap to the Hudson's Bay men.

Despite this congenial relationship, the Bannock continued to attack many white trappers, and the Americans suggested to the British traders that an all-out war be waged against the tribe. Ogden was bound by his company's policy of friendship toward all Indian tribes, but in this one instance he regretted having to sustain it:

Acting for myself, I will not hesitate to say I would willingly sacrifice a year or two to exterminate the whole Snake tribe, women and children excepted. In so doing I could fully justify myself before God and man. Those who live at a distance are of a different opinion. My reply to them is: Come out and suffer and judge for yourselves if forbearance has not been carried beyond bounds ordained by Scripture and surely this is the only guide a Christian sh'd follow.[16]

In an entry for January 26, 1828, Ogden estimated

---

[16] Elliott, "Peter Skene Ogden Journals, Snake Expedition, 1827-1828," *op. cit.*, pp. 362-72.

that the Bannock had four hundred guns which they had obtained in war excursions against the Blackfeet and as a result of forays against white trappers. Apparently secure under the protective policy of the Hudson's Bay Company, the Bannock continued their depredations, and many another British trader would have joined with Ogden in saying that "threats are of no avail among the Snakes."

One of the last of the Snake expeditions entered the Snake River Valley in the fall of 1830, under the direction of John Work. If this leader had any trouble with the Bannock, he failed to record it in his journal, although he mentioned that the "Bannock Snake" had driven off the elk in the vicinity of Lost River. In December, 1830, he recorded a visit of the "Snakes" to his camp at the lower end of "Blackfoot Hill." This group displayed the scalps of two Blackfeet whom they had killed during a battle with that tribe on December 19. Later, in March, a chief—"The Horn" —paid a visit to the British camp, and this is, no doubt, Chief The Horse, whom Ogden had met in 1827.[17]

The next traveler to leave a written account of his contact with the Bannock was W. A. Ferris, a trapper in the employ of the American Fur Company. At the end of February, 1832, Ferris and some companions were near Lost River on their way to the confluence of Blackfoot and Snake rivers. Here, the white hunters met about two hundred "Ponacks . . . or Po-nah-ke as they call themselves." From this time

---

[17] T. C. Elliott (ed.), "Journal of John Work, Covering Snake Country Expedition of 1830-31," *Oregon Historical Society Quarterly*, XIII, No. 4 (December, 1912), 369-71.

until the end of the year, there were frequent meetings between the Ferris party and the Bannock. Ferris must have met the tribe during a period of poor hunting, for his descriptions leave the picture of dirty and unkempt Indians, endeavoring only to keep from starving or freezing to death. In comparison with their "handsome and well clad neighbours, the Flatheads," the Bannock appeared to be the most wretched beings Ferris had ever seen. A party of Rocky Mountain Fur Company trappers visited with the Ferris group in November of 1832 and described a recent battle that had been fought between the Bannock-Shoshoni and the Blackfeet, near Big Lost River. One hundred and fifty Blackfeet had attacked the Bannock and Shoshoni village but were driven off into a thicket of willows. The defenders then fired the prairie and, when the scorched Blackfeet broke from cover, the combined Bannock and Shoshoni pursued them three miles across the plain to a forest edging the base of the mountains. The Blackfeet lost forty men and five women in the battle; the opposition, only nine warriors. However, among them was the "famous Horned Chief, remarkable for his lasting friendship to the Whites."[18]

Only two months later, Captain Benjamin L. E. Bonneville, United States Army, entered the Portneuf River area for the first time and came upon the Bannock mourning the loss of their chief. After commenting on the remarkable control exercised in the past by Chief The Horse to keep his people from

---

[18] W. A. Ferris, *Life in the Rocky Mountains*, ed. by Paul C. Phillips (Denver, 1940), pp. 132, 185-90.

committing too many depredations on the whites, Bonneville said:

> . . . This chief was said to possess a charmed life, or rather, to be invulnerable to lead; no bullet having ever hit him, though he had been in repeated battles, and often shot at by the surest marksmen. . . . His fall in nowise lessened the faith of his people in his charmed life; for they declared that it was not a bullet which laid him low, but a bit of horn which had been shot into him by some Blackfoot marksman; aware, no doubt, of the inefficacy of lead.[19]

As was usually the case after a strong chief died, there ensued a period of confused disturbance while subordinate chiefs vied for the vacant position. Bonneville described the lack of control over the young men who became troublesome and "dangerous neighbors," ready to pounce upon any small party that ventured into Bannock territory.

With the end of 1833 approaching, Captain Bonneville decided to head for the Portneuf-Snake River confluence to set up his winter camp, so that his horses would have good pasturage in the open river bottoms of the area. On Portneuf plain, his company met a group of twenty-five Bannock hunters who proposed that the two parties combine to hunt the herds of buffalo grazing only a few miles away. The white men agreed, and the chase was on. Washington Irving has left a stirring picture of this buffalo hunt, which was typical of most of the hunts staged by buffalo Indians. His description of the horsemanship of the Bannock leaves no doubt concerning their skill as hunters or their bravery. A huge feast climaxed

---

[19] Irving, *op. cit.*, p. 106.

the successful kill. In the course of the celebration, the Bannock braves became quite boastful of their prowess as warriors and dared their absent enemies, the Blackfeet, to come and do battle. After many hours of thus taunting shadows, they all went to sleep without leaving a single guard "so that, had the Blackfeet taken them at their word, but few of these braggart heroes might have survived for any further boasting."[20]

After the buffalo hunt, Bonneville left his new-found Indian friends and went in search of a party of trappers that had become lost from the main group. When the reunited whites appeared at the mouth of the Portneuf River on December 4, 1833, they found the Bannock village in the midst of a great victory celebration. Some scouts had discovered a band of Blackfeet approaching and had been able to warn the encampment in time for the Bannock warriors to set up an ambush. The unsuspecting Blackfeet had fled in panic from the attack, leaving behind many buffalo robes and a dead companion. The scalp of the victim had been fastened to a pole in the village, and the whole Bannock tribe had entered into the spirit of the Scalp Dance.

Not wishing to make an encampment too close to his Indian friends, Bonneville was forced to move some three miles away to the edge of the river bottom land where his horses did not have the luxuriant forage that the Indian animals had. Gradually, through various gifts to the chiefs, Bonneville was able to establish very good relations between his trappers and

---

[20] *Ibid.*, pp. 173-74.

the Indians. Occasionally, the whites were obliged
to turn their weakest horses out to forage for themselves among the Indian herd, and if any happened
to stray to the Bannock camp, they were always
brought back.

. . . It must be confessed, however, that if the stray horse
happened, by any chance, to be in vigorous plight and good
condition, though he was equally sure to be returned by
the honest Bannecks, yet it was always after the lapse of
several days, and in a very gaunt and jaded state; and always
with the remark, that they had found him a long way off.
The uncharitable were apt to surmise that he had, in the
interim, been well used up on a buffalo hunt; but those
accustomed to Indian morality in the matter of horseflesh,
considered it a singular evidence of honesty that he should
be brought back at all.[21]

The Bonneville party was left with a strong impression of the honesty and bravery of the Bannock, in
contrast to other travelers who admitted their bravery
but condemned them in nearly every other respect.
    Shortly after Captain Bonneville and his men de-
parted from the region, an event occurred which was
to have profound significance in the later history of
the Bannock. In 1832, Nathaniel J. Wyeth had crossed
the continent from Boston with the purpose of entering the Oregon fur trade. His first venture had failed,
but he was back in the Snake River area again in
the summer of 1834 with a large amount of trading
goods and he built Fort Hall as a post which he could
use as an agency for selling his goods. Because of
Wyeth's intimate knowledge of the area and his reputation as an accomplished writer, Henry R. School-

---

[21] *Ibid.*, pp. 178-79.

craft asked him to contribute an article on the "Shoshone or Snake Nation" for the *Archives of Aboriginal
Knowledge.* Wyeth described the Pawnack, Bonack,
or Paunaque Indians, as he variously called them, as
being "more intelligent and better supplied with all
the means of Indian independence" than the Shoshoni.[22] He attempted to discover the difference between the Bannock and Shoshoni; but, invariably,
whoever was questioned would answer that the other
tribe was bad and would murder the whites and that
his own tribe was always good and always friendly to
the whites.

Included among the members of Wyeth's second
expedition was John K. Townsend, whose narrative
of his overland trip is one of the classics among early
Oregon travel accounts. On August 12, 1834, the
Townsend group came to a large, recent encampment
of the Bannock near the Lost River Mountains. The
trappers afterward learned that a battle had been
fought at this spot between the Bannock and the
Blackfeet. The latter was the larger party, but was
handicapped by being afoot on an open plain. The
Bannock pressed their advantage of being mounted
and won a bloody victory, killing forty of the enemy
and taking about thirty-six scalps. Townsend remarked thankfully, "This was not the first time that
we narrowly escaped a contest with this savage and
most dreaded tribe."[23]

---

[22] Archer B. Hulbert (ed.), *The Call of the Columbia* (Denver, 1934), p 136; Henry R. Schoolcraft, *Archives of Aboriginal Knowledge* (Philadelphia, 1860), I, 206, 207.

[23] John K. Townsend, *Narrative of a Journey Across the Rocky Mountains to the Columbia River,* reprinted in *Early Western Travels, 1748-1846,* ed. by R. G. Thwaites (Cleveland, 1905), XXI, 242.

A few days later the whites did run into a Bannock village of some thirty lodges while approaching the Boise River region. The chief urged that they stop awhile to trade, and the trappers finally concluded to do so, although they had an abundance of supplies. Captain Wyeth indicated to the chief that they were in a hurry and wanted to get the trading over; but that individual insisted on smoking the pipe and holding a council meeting. After an hour or so of such deliberations, the white men's patience was exhausted, and they prepared to mount and ride away. Thereupon, the chief sent several squaws to fetch about a dozen fried fish, which the women threw on the ground in front of Wyeth's men. The Indians asked exorbitant prices for the few fish, so the trappers mounted their horses and started away. This aroused the anger of the Bannock, and several loosened their bows from their shoulders in evident preparation for a fight. A young brave struck Townsend's horse on the head with a stick and, in return, received Townsend's whip several times across the shoulders. The whites narrowly averted a battle and, as they rode off, the Indians gave them "a scornful, taunting laugh, that sounded like the rejoicings of an infernal jubilee."[24] Two other white men, one a Wyeth trapper, were not so hospitably received by the Bannock chief. They left openly and unsuspectingly, only to be ambushed and killed by their hosts. None of the Wyeth group was able to account for the sudden change in the Indian attitude toward the Americans.

Another member of the second Wyeth expedition

---

[24] *Ibid.*, pp. 262-63, 326.

proved to be one of the most literate of those "mountain men" who engaged in the trapping of beaver. This man, Osborne Russell, became so enamored of the wild life of the Rockies that he soon left Wyeth to pursue the career of a free trapper. Russell first became acquainted with the Bannock during his stay at Fort Hall as an employee of the Wyeth firm. About 250 lodges of these people encamped near the fort in October, 1834, and engaged in a brisk trade with the trappers. In the autumn of 1835, Russell and Wyeth were traveling with Jim Bridger from western Wyoming to Fort Hall, and Russell was sent ahead to procure horses so that it would not be necessary to depend upon Bridger's horses. While thus traveling alone, Russell came upon the entire Bannock tribe engaged in a buffalo hunt on the Snake River plains. The ground was covered with the slain animals, approximately one thousand having been killed by the Indian hunters. The Bannock village consisted of 332 lodges and averaged six persons to each lodge. In addition, there were fifteen lodges of "Snakes" in the bustling community. Russell was very kindly received by the old Bannock chief, who was a brother of "the celebrated Horn Chief" and was called Aiken-lo-ruckkup, or the "Tongue Cut with a Flint." The next morning the chief informed Russell that the two Indians who had only recently killed two of Wyeth's trappers were in the village, and asked what the white men would do about it. Russell replied that the two culprits would be hung if they were caught at the fort; whereupon the old chief said they deserved death.

I believe they have murdered the two white men to get their property, and lost it all in gambling, for . . . ill gained wealth often flies away and does the owners no good. But . . . you need not be under any apprehension of danger whilst you stop with the village.[25]

A few days later, Russell left the Indian camp and soon reached Fort Hall, having been hospitably treated while among the Bannock.

Early in the spring of 1836, Osborne Russell left the employ of Wyeth and went to work as a trapper for Jim Bridger. The main camp of the mountain men was on Bear River at the time, situated near four hundred lodges of Bannock and Shoshoni and one hundred lodges of Nez Perce and Flathead. The congenial relations between the whites and the Bannock continued until a horse-stealing episode led to another pitched battle between the two groups. According to the biographers of Jim Bridger and Joe Meek, the incident occurred in 1836; but Russell's more reliable personal observation places the affair in June, 1837. While on Green River awaiting supplies from the East, the trappers were visited by sixty lodges of Bannock who displayed horses and traps stolen from some Nez Perce trappers the previous spring. When the Bannock refused to give up the plunder, a few of the whites and two Nez Perce hunters entered their village and regained the stolen horses while the warriors were away. That afternoon thirty Bannock rode into the white camp and demanded the return of their horses, saying that they did not desire war with the Americans. The trappers

---

[25] Osborne Russell, *Journal of a Trapper; or, Nine Years in the Rocky Mountains, 1834-1843* [2nd ed.; Boise, Idaho, 1921], pp. 14, 40-41.

chose to defend the property of the Nez Perce hunters and refused to deliver up the animals. Most of the Bannock thereupon began to leave the camp, but one warrior rode toward Jim Bridger, who was holding one of the stolen horses by the bridle. The Indian, paying no heed to the cocked rifles aimed at him, seized the bridle and tried to take it away from Bridger by force. His bravery was his undoing for, as soon as his hand touched the bridle, two rifle balls ended his life. His comrades wheeled to run but, before they could escape, twelve more were shot from their horses. The whole body of trappers then mounted and charged the Bannock village, plundered it, and drove the entire tribe of men, women, and children before them for three days before agreeing to listen to the proposals of peace which the Bannock had been pressing on them. Russell said, "We granted their request and returned to our camp, satisfied that the best way to negotiate and settle disputes with hostile Indians is with the rifle." The evidence does not seem to point out that either the Bannock or the Americans had the weight of justice on their side. The results of the battle merely emphasize the age-old principle that "might makes right."[26]

---

[26] *Ibid.*, pp. 45, 62-63; Stanley Vestal, *Jim Bridger: Mountain Man* (New York, 1946), pp. 122-24; Frances Fuller Victor, *The River of the West* (San Francisco, 1870), pp. 197-98.

Overland Travelers

A S THE decade of the 1840's approached, interests other than trapping began to draw Americans to and through the Rocky Mountains. The founding of Indian missions in Oregon brought some of the first permanent settlers to that region, and a significant indication that the fur trade era was nearing an end came with startling suddenness when white women began to appear on the overland trail to Oregon. Mary Richardson Walker was among the first to travel through the Snake River area, and her diary suggests a very early fear of the Bannock on the part of emigrants. On July 21, 1838, she recorded that the approach of ten lodges of Bannock caused keen apprehension among the members of the expedition. She described the Indians as "more savage than any we have seen in their appearance."[1] The following year Asahel Munger and his wife met a large camp of "Ponack Indians" at Fort Hall and noted, "They are said to be very bad Indians."[2]

By 1839 the Bannock had established a reputation

---

[1] Mary Richardson Walker, "The Diary of Mary Richardson Walker, June 10-December 21, 1838," ed. by Rufus A. Coleman, in *Sources of Northwest History No. 15,* ed. by Paul C. Phillips, as reprinted from *The Frontier,* XI, No. 3, 8.

[2] Asahel Munger, "Diary of Asahel Munger and Wife," *Oregon Historical Society Quarterly* (Portland, 1907), VIII, 400.

which became almost traditional, and which still colors most thinking and writing about the tribe. Thomas J. Farnham, a traveler of that year, met a portion of the "Bonak" nation in the Boise River area. He spoke of them as "a fierce, warlike and athletic tribe . . . [that] speak a language peculiar to themselves . . . and one regarded by the whites as a treacherous and dangerous race."[3] Amid growing fears that the small group of white men would all be killed, Farnham and a comrade were able to induce several of the warriors to guide them to Fort Boise. During the entire journey, many other Bannock joined the expedition, and all kept up a continued wailing which Farnham judged was a part of the process of mourning for some deceased member of the tribe. Many of the Indian horses had recently had their tails shorn in the "most uncouth manner." The copious tears and the sincere sympathy of the mourners for each other convinced Farnham that the Bannock possessed much of "the social affection," despite the current belief to the contrary. Two years after this affair, Joseph Williams met the "Ponock" near Fort Hall and said, "They seemed to show some dislike to us," but he was assured by the captain of the emigrant company that the Indians would not approach openly if they were not for peace.[4]

The Jesuit, Father P. J. DeSmet, had an opportunity to observe the Bannock when his Flathead con-

---

[3] Thomas J. Farnham, *Travels in the Great Western Prairies, the Anahuac and Rocky Mountains, and in the Oregon Territory* (New York, 1843), p. 76.

[4] Joseph Williams, *Narrative of a Tour from the State of Indiana to the Oregon Territory in the Years 1841-2* (New York, 1921), p. 45.

verts met them during the autumn of 1841. Although the two tribes camped side by side on apparently amicable terms, the Flathead Chief Ensyla, or "Little Chief," refused to smoke the pipe with his Bannock friend. The two Indian leaders had met some time previously, when two hundred Bannock warriors had paid a visit to Chief Ensyla's camp of twenty Flathead braves. After smoking a pipe of peace, the Bannock had retired to their camp and then had determined to annihilate the little Flathead band. Chief Ensyla learned of this intention and was able to ward off the attempt, killing nine of the aggressors in the action, among whom was the brother of the Bannock chief. According to DeSmet's account, more of the attackers would have been killed, had not the Flathead chief stopped his warriors at the height of the pursuit, announced that it was the Sabbath, and knelt with his men in prayer. During the meeting of the two tribes the Jesuit attempted to preach Christianity to the Bannock chief, and the Indian leader promised to use all his power to persuade his people to adopt religious sentiments. Later on, DeSmet wrote that "many . . . Banacs" were baptized, along with members of the Flathead, Nez Perce, Kootenai, and Blackfeet nations.[5]

Because the travelers to Oregon did not always meet with hostility from the Bannock, trading between the two peoples was quite common. The com-

---

[5] DeSmet described the Bannock as "the most perfidious nation after the Blackfeet." P. J. DeSmet, S.J., *Letters and Sketches: with a Narrative of a Year's Residence Among the Indian Tribes of the Rocky Mountains* [Philadelphia, 1843], reprinted in *Early Western Travels, 1784-1846*, ed. by R. G. Thwaites (Cleveland, 1906), XXVII, 278, 280, 289, 319, 327-28, 353.

pany of Medorem Crawford camped near a Bannock village in 1842 and obtained a number of horses from the Indians on "reasonable terms."[6]   Early in the spring of 1843, "Old Bill" Williams and a group of trappers met the Bannock on Blackfoot River and traded for furs. Williams remarked that they were skillful in the collection of fine furs and also expert in the manufacture of pemmican. His account is not too reliable in some respects; his story of a battle between the group of whites and the "Bannock" at "Camas Prairie," later in the year, is apparently much confused. He placed the Camas Prairie in Oregon near Walla Walla, which would indicate that the Indians involved were probably the Northern Paiute, close relatives of the Bannock, who spoke a similar language. This was only one of many instances in which travelers mistook the Paiute for Bannock, sometimes calling the Paiute of Oregon "Western Bannock."[7]

Not only were horses and furs popular articles of trade with the Bannock, but salmon also was highly prized by the emigrant whose food supply was usually rather low by the time the Snake River was reached. The overland traveler, Theodore Talbot, left an interesting description of the control of the fisheries near Shoshone Falls. The Bannock held a monopoly in the late spring while the fish were in the best condition. After the departure of this, the

---

[6] Medorem Crawford, "Journal of Medorem Crawford, an Account of His Trip Across the Plains with the Oregon Pioneers of 1842," ed. by F. G. Young, in *Sources of the History of Oregon* (Eugene, Ore., 1897), I, No. 1, 15.

[7] William T. Hamilton, *My Sixty Years on the Plains,* ed. by E. T. Sieber (New York, 1905), pp. 115, 124-27.

most powerful tribe, various bands of Shoshoni appropriated the fishing stations until late summer, when the poor and miserable Diggers finally were allowed to catch what fish they could. Talbot said of the Bannock in 1843, "I believe [they] are rather disposed to be treacherous but are at present on good terms with the whites."[8]

A company of emigrants, two years later, did not find the Bannock so friendly. A member of the party, Joel Palmer, did not mention the name "Bannock," but divided the Indians of the Fort Hall area into two groups, "Shoshonee" and "Snake." If it is assumed that his Snake Indians were the Bannock, some members of that tribe certainly displayed hostile intent upon this occasion. Several warriors came upon an advance scout of the emigrants and chased him for about two miles before abandoning the pursuit. The man arrived at the wagon train so paralyzed with fear "that it was with difficulty we obtained from him the cause of his alarm."[9] The whites prepared for an

[8] Theodore Talbot, *The Journals of Theodore Talbot, 1843 and 1849-52; with the Fremont Expedition of 1843 and with the First Military Company in Oregon Territory, 1849-1852,* ed. by Charles H. Carey (Portland, Ore., 1931), pp. 46, 49, 56-57.

The frontiersman, James Clyman, also met fishing parties of Bannock on Snake River in September, 1844. They were not catching salmon but "small fish of the Sucker mouthed kind." James Clyman, *James Clyman, American Frontiersman, 1792-1881,* ed. by Charles L. Camp (San Francisco, 1928), pp. 99-101.

[9] Joel Palmer, *Journal of Travels Over the Rocky Mountains to the Mouth of the Columbia River, 1845 and 1846,* reprinted in *Early Western Travels 1748-1846,* ed. by R. G. Thwaites (Cleveland, 1906), XXX, 84, 247.

About this time (1846), a descriptive pamphlet of Oregon Territory listed the "Boonacks" as being an Indian tribe of the region. Of all the varied spellings of the tribal name, this one certainly occupies a unique place. S. Augustus Mitchell, *Accompaniment to Mitchell's New Map of Texas, Oregon, and California, with the Regions Adjoining* (Philadelphia, 1846), p. 19.

attack but evidently were too many in number, because the Indians left them alone for the remainder of the trip through the Snake River country.

Throughout the period of increasing migration to Oregon, survivors of the old era of the mountain men occasionally appeared to grace the later pages of history with their exploits. One of them, Jim Baker, became quite friendly with the Bannock and Shoshoni and was finally adopted into the Shoshoni tribe in 1847. In the latter part of 1859, after some years' absence from the Indians, Baker returned to visit the Bannock and married into the tribe.[10] Another old trapper, Joe Meek, last encountered the Bannock when he made a trip from Oregon to the States in 1848. Before starting out, he decided to adopt the red belt and Canadian cap of the employees of the Hudson's Bay Company in order to assure a safe conduct among the Indians of Snake River Basin. Three days' travel beyond Fort Boise he met a village of Bannock who immediately made warlike demonstrations, but they agreed to a "talk" when they noticed the costume he was wearing. Meek explained to the chief that he was going on the business of the British company to Fort Hall, and that Thomas McKay was only a day's march behind with a large trading party. The American was allowed to go on his way and chose to travel day and night until he reached the safety of Fort Hall.[11]

Throughout 1849 the Bannock were, on the whole,

---

[10] Nolie Mumey, *The Life of Jim Baker 1818-1898: Trapper, Scout, Guide and Indian Fighter* (Denver, 1931), pp. 50, 160-61.

[11] Frances Fuller Victor, *The River of the West* (San Francisco, 1870), p. 434.

friendly to the whites who were traveling across the tribal area to Oregon. The forty-niner, John E. Brown, recorded that one day a man came running into the emigrant camp shouting at every step, "Indians!" Immediately, about forty rifles were leveled at a lone Bannock who came galloping up. The Indian had wanted only to shake hands with the white man, but he narrowly escaped with his life. Most of the white travelers were not so considerate and preferred to shoot first and investigate afterward.[12]

An outstanding example of Bannock friendliness is recorded in the journals of J. Goldsborough Bruff, who spent considerable time with these Indians during 1849 and has left nothing but praise for their considerate attitude toward him. While traveling on Bear River, he met two Bannock men and a middle-aged squaw. In very broken English the men attempted to trade the squaw for a copper powder flask, but the whites declined the offer. About a week later, Bruff and his companions came upon two Indian villages situated approximately two miles apart. Three Indians rode out from the first camp to meet the travelers, and one brave traded a pair of half-boot moccasins for a looking glass. Another wished to barter away a dressed deerskin but was not satisfied with the articles offered in exchange. Bruff left an interesting description of their dress:

One of those first met, had on a tolerably decent black summer-cloth frock coat, a blue-striped cotton shirt, blue

---

[12] John E. Brown, *Memoirs of a Forty-Niner*, ed. by Mrs. Katie E. Blood (New Haven, 1907), p. 21.

nankeen pants, and cotton *suspenders*, with an old black hat,—decorated with a broad red worsted band. The 2d was attired in deer skin—frock, leggings, & mocasins; and the 3d wore a very tall straw hat, a tatter'd Marsaile's vest, no shirt, & leggings, with mocasins.[13]

He noted that "Many of the mean [men] wear the common plaid Scotch bonnet, such as sailors use; given them by the Hudson Bay Compy."

Bruff was able to trade for a horse, and then accepted the services of an old "Panak" to guide the party to Cantonment Loring. This military post, named in honor of an overland party of Mounted Riflemen, had been established in July of 1849, about five miles above Fort Hall, to give protection and succor to emigrants. It was abandoned on May 6, 1850, because it was located too far north. While being entertained at the post, Bruff asked permission to grant his old Bannock guide a seat at the table. The old fellow behaved with perfect propriety, and the colonel in charge explained his civilized conduct by informing Bruff that the Indian had once visited in St. Louis.

Beginning in 1850, as the tide of immigration increased, a growing hostility was noticeable among all the Indians of the Snake River area. Henry J. Coke recorded that he was very much annoyed by two "Bonock" Indians at one of his camp sites because they attempted to steal his provisions.[14] A group

---

[13] Joseph Goldsborough Bruff, *Gold Rush; The Journals, Drawings, and Other Papers of J. Goldsborough Bruff, 1804-1889;* ed. by Georgia Willis Read and Ruth Gaines (2 vols.; New York, 1944), I, 88-110.

[14] Henry J. Coke, *A Ride Over the Rocky Mountains to Oregon and California* (London, 1852), p. 220.

of fifteen California traders encountered more tangible resistance from the Bannock while traveling along the upper Humboldt River. The little expedition first came upon the body of a white man and, as they were speculating about the reason for his death, three Bannock rode up and engaged them in conversation. Next day it was discovered that the trio had been a reconnaissance unit for a large band of Bannock which attacked the travelers. After one Indian had been killed, the whites decided to sue for peace, but the man sent out on the mission had his horse shot from under him and was forced to return in a hurry. The Californians eventually lost most of their horses and all of their provisions, but they were fortunate enough to escape with their lives.[15]

With the increased animosity manifested by the Snake River Indians in the early 1850's came also, for almost the first time, official recognition on the part of the United States government that such tribes existed. As early as 1842, the Commissioner of Indian Affairs had reported that the Snake Indians numbered two hundred lodges or one thousand "souls" and were a "poor tribe, in the Rocky Mountains"; but, beyond this, little was known about them.[16] During the 1850's and early 1860's the Indian Office administered affairs in the West by dividing the area into superintendencies according to territorial boundaries. At first the territorial governors acted as *ex officio* super-

---

[15] H. S. Beatie, "The First in Nevada" (Bancroft MS, dictated in 1884), p. 5.

[16] U.S. Congress, Senate, *Report of the Commissioner of Indian Affairs,* Ex. Doc. No. 10, 27th Cong., 3rd Sess., Serial No. 414 (Washington, 1842), p. 433.

intendents, but, after the government had become well established, separate superintendents were usually assigned.

The Bannock and Shoshoni were first under the technical jurisdiction of the Oregon Superintendent of Indian Affairs, until the admission of Oregon as a state in 1859 placed them in Washington Territory. The great distance of the Bannock from Oregon and Washington headquarters resulted, for the most part, in rather desultory supervision over the tribe. The creation of Idaho Territory in 1863 finally placed a Superintendent of Indian Affairs in the Boise area. While most of the Oregon and Washington officials sincerely tried to direct affairs in the upper Snake River region, the great distance and the lack of funds prevented them from establishing agencies among the Bannock and neighboring tribes, and it was only on rare occasions that a traveling agent made a short visit to these Indians.

Joseph Lane, Superintendent of Indian Affairs for Oregon in 1850, was able to report on the Bannock only because he had in his employ as agent the mountaineer, Robert Newell. This man described the "Ponashta" as "divided into small bands, and . . . so intermarried with the Shoshonees that it is almost impossible to discriminate between them. The Ponashtas predominate, however. They are a warlike people . . ."[17]

Increasing cognizance was taken of the Snake River Indians in 1851 when reports began to come in of

---

[17] U.S. Congress, Senate, *Report of the Commissioner of Indian Affairs.* Ex. Doc., 31st Cong., 2nd Sess., Serial No. 587 (Washington, 1850), p. 158.

depredations upon emigrant groups. Governor John P. Gaines of Oregon wrote President Millard Fillmore in June asking for troops "to keep in check all the tribes upon Snake and Upper Columbia, some of whom are of very uncertain temper and well-disposed to theft and insolence. . . ." He mentioned that some emigrant trains had been followed by "Snake" Indians and, although these people had suffered no losses, they "ascertained a spirit to exist which may create much trouble and difficulty later in the season when broken and exhausted trains shall arrive from the states."[18] Again, John Holeman, at Fort Laramie, reported to the Indian Commissioner that the overland travelers were being forced to band together to ward off Indian attacks. Agent Holeman also pointed out the obvious fact that the emigrants could not distinguish among the tribes and could not tell whether the Indians they met were peaceful or warlike. As a result the tendency was to take forceful action first, and even peaceful tribes were thus being turned against the whites.[19]

Many of the emigrants provoked hostilities among their red brethren by rash action in situations where caution should have been followed. In answer to the charge that thirty-two whites had been killed during the summer of 1851 by "Snake" Indians, one of the Oregon Indian agents ascribed the attacks to the fol-

[18] Governor John P. Gaines of Oregon to President Fillmore, Oregon City, Oregon Terr., June 13, 1851. U.S. Congress, Senate, *Military and Indian Affairs in Oregon*, Ex. Doc., I, No. IV, No. 11, 32nd Cong., 1st Sess., Serial No. 611 (Washington, 1851), 144.

[19] U.S. Congress, House of Representatives, *Report of the Commissioner of Indian Affairs*, Ex. Doc., 32nd Cong., 1st Sess., Serial No. 636 (Washington, 1851), p. 444.

lowing incident. A train of emigrants under a Dr. Patterson was proceeding along Snake River, in the vicinity of Rock Creek, when Patterson, with some others, rode ahead to pick a camp site for the night. Finding a band of Indians camped at the best spot in the area, he peremptorily ordered them off. When the Indians refused to move, perhaps because they did not understand his commands, Patterson fired his shotgun over their heads, and he and his men pursued them on horseback to see how fast they could run. The next day, as a result, three of the whites were shot by the Indians. One died of his wounds. John N. Davis, a member of the Patterson party, later testified that this incident was the cause of "the whole trouble with the Bannock tribe of Indians that year."[20] Superintendent Anson Dart of Oregon Territory recognized his inability to cope with the situation along Snake River and wrote to the Indian Commissioner:

Having no agents or sub-agents to locate in the Rogue River and Snake countrys, and the improbability of visiting them in person this season will prevent me from having that control over them that is desirable.[21]

Although instructed by Superintendent Dart to visit the Indians around Fort Hall, Agent Elias Wampole of Utilla Agency likewise found it impossible to make the trip. From emigrant reports, however,

---

[20] T. W. Davenport, "Recollections of an Indian Agent," *Oregon Historical Society Quarterly* (Portland, Ore., 1907), VIII, 363.

[21] Anson Dart to Commissioner of Indian Affairs, Oregon City, Oregon Terr., May 7, 1851. U.S. National Archives, Records of the Bureau of Indian Affairs, Oregon Superintendency, No. 3, Copies of Letters Received and Sent, 1850-1853, p. 119.

he was able to compile a long list of depredations perpetrated by the Indians of that area. Near Bear River, the "Snakes & Pannocks" stole eight horses and four head of cattle from travelers. At Fort Hall, the Snakes stole seventy-four oxen from three wagon trains. Eight oxen were lost to the Indians near American Falls and, near Shoshone Falls, four horses were taken. A wagon train was attacked at Black Rock Creek; four people were killed, a woman was wounded and abused, and twenty-two horses were taken. The Snakes stole twenty-six horses from travelers north of Fort Hall, and the Bannock took three valuable horses from a Dr. Newsome. Near Fort Hall also, four men were killed and thirteen horses stolen by Bannock. Wampole concluded that "the Emigrants state that they were in dread of their lives and property throughout the limits of these nations." He attributed most of the Indian unrest to the activities of white traders who plied the natives with whisky and sold them guns and ammunition:

. . . it is my opinion this whole Band of lawless squatting traders, the country swarms with, should be removed. There can be no peace to Emigrants while white men are left in the country having Indian women and Indian sympathy and a burning thirst for gold.[22]

It should be added that, only a month later, Agent Wampole himself admitted to charges of accepting a bribe of four horses for favors extended to four white traders.[23]

---

[22] Elias Wampole to Anson Dart, Utilla, Oregon Terr., September 22, 1851, *ibid.*, pp. 190-91.

[23] Anson Dart to Commissioner of Indian Affairs, Oregon City, Oregon Terr., October 21, 1851, *ibid.*, p. 194.

Corroboration of the charge that traders were inciting the Indians came from the 1853 report of Agent
J. H. Holeman of Utah Territory. He said that the
road from Salt Lake City to California was lined with
traders who usually had nothing to barter but whisky.
Through unkind treatment of neighboring Indians,
they were slowly making the natives hostile to all
whites. In addition, the traders themselves committed
many depredations which they were able to ascribe
to the Indians. Some of these lawless whites even
offered to buy any cattle and horses that the Indians
could steal from the emigrants. When Agent Holeman warned these men that the laws would be enforced against them, he found them disdainful of any
threatened governmental action. He wrote: "They
laughed at me: they defied me and the laws; they told
me there were so many of them that they could and
would do as they pleased, law or no law."[24]

Contrary to the reports of Wampole and others,
Holeman found that many of the Bannock were disposed to be friendly to the whites. He met a band
of six hundred under a Chief Te-ve-re-wera ("the
long man") at Humboldt Sink. This portion of the
tribe was on a hunt at the time and assured the Indian agent that they would not disturb any Americans.

During the year 1842 a traveler to Oregon added another interesting
version of the Bannock name when he noted, "Parvekee indians plenty."
See James Akin, Jr., "The Journal of James Akin, Jr.," ed. by Edward
Everett Dale, *University of Oklahoma Bulletin*, New Series No. 172,
University Studies No. 9 (Norman, Okla., 1919), p. 20.

[24] U.S. Congress, Senate, *Report of the Commissioner of Indian Affairs*,
Ex. Doc., 33rd Cong., 1st Sess., Serial No. 690 (Washington, 1853), pp.
444-46.

Although the Indian depredations along Snake River during the years 1851 to 1853 had caused the Indian Office some concern, an attack by "Diggers" on a wagon train near Fort Boise in August, 1854, finally aroused the Oregon Superintendency to military action. Robert R. Thompson of Utilla Agency reported to his superior that a party of emigrants under a Mr. Ward had been almost completely wiped out, only two of the twenty-one people escaping with their lives. Many of those killed were women and children who were tortured to death in the most brutal fashion. Also, forty-one head of cattle and about three thousand dollars in money were taken. The guilty Indians were a band of thirty "Winnestah" Snakes residing east of Fort Boise. Shortly after the Ward Massacre, three other whites were shot to death near the fort, and several more were killed on Camas Prairie, seventy-five miles from the post. To add to the general apprehension caused by these killings, Thompson also learned that the Snakes were determined to rob and kill all those who came into their country:

They say the Americans have been continually telling them that unless they ceased their depredations an army would come and destroy them, but no such thing has been done, and that the Americans are afraid of them, and say that if we wish to fight them to come on.[25]

---

[25] Robert R. Thompson to Joel Palmer, Utilla Agency, Oregon Terr., August 26, 1854. U.S. National Archives, Records of the Bureau of Indian Affairs, Oregon Superintendency, No. 10, D, Letter Books, pp. 10, 12; Thompson to Palmer, Grand Ronde, Oregon Terr., September 3, 1854, *ibid.*, pp. 29-31; Thompson to Palmer, Utilla Agency, Oregon Terr., September 6, 1854, *ibid.*, pp. 28-29.

In answer to the challenge, a force of sixty-five men under Major G. A. Wallan was sent to capture the Ward party murderers. After killing one or two hostile Indians, the advance party reached Fort Boise and made prisoners of six men of the "Bonac Tribe" who happened to be at the post. When the prisoners, with their captors, reached the army camp, two of the Bannock became so frightened at the sight of the regular troops, who were on parade at the time, that they broke and ran. One made his escape, but the other, less fortunate, was shot down. Agent Thompson held a council with some Bannock whose chief, "Oete," professed friendship for the whites. Indeed, Chief Oete was reported by the Hudson's Bay Company men "as being a good Indian for this locality."[26]

A few days later, Thompson questioned three other Bannock at Fort Boise concerning their attitude toward the whites. They maintained that although the Winnestah Snakes were bad Indians, they themselves were good. But Thompson recorded his opinion that "I am very much deceived in Indian Character, if they are not arrant hypocrites, and as much to be dreaded as the Win-nes-tahs who committed the massacre."[27] Why the agent should have expected any other answer to his questions is hard to determine. On the way back to The Dalles, the Wallan party met a Charles Ogden of Fort Boise who reported that he had come upon three Bannock warriors only a very short time before. After holding Ogden for

---

[26] Thompson to Palmer, Boise River, Oregon Terr., September 14, 1854, *ibid.*, p. 56.

[27] Thompson to Palmer, The Dalles, Oregon Terr., October 11, 1854, *ibid.*, p. 66.

some time, the Indian trio had decided in lengthy conference that they had been mistaken in thinking he was an American and so had let him go.

As a result of the Ward Massacre, Superintendent Joel Palmer instructed Special Agent Nathan Olney to investigate reports that British traders at Fort Boise were selling guns and ammunition to the Indians and accepting money in return. Palmer intimated that it was common knowledge that the Britishers were influencing the natives against the Americans and said that if the charges were substantiated, he would close the doors of the fort as a trading post for the Hudson's Bay Company. At the same time the Oregon superintendent notified Thompson to investigate rumors that the Nez Perce were acting as middlemen in trading arms to the Indians of Snake River and to use his influence to stop such illegal and dangerous intercourse.[28]

Further information about Indian affairs in the Snake River area came from an unexpected source. Neil McArthur, a former employee of Hudson's Bay Company, and three other white men wrote from Salmon River to Agent Olney, explaining that the "Snakes" and Bannock disavowed the acts of the "Diggers" near Fort Boise. The letter explained that the Bannock were perfectly friendly toward the whites but were concerned about the stoppage of the trade in ammunition, an article that they must have because they lived entirely by hunting. McArthur also informed the American agent that the Nez Perce and

---

[28] Palmer to Nathan Olney, Dayton, Oregon Terr., September 28, 1854, *ibid.*, p. 175.

other Indians were spreading the rumor that it was the intention of the "white chiefs to kill off all the Bannocks and Snakes next Summer."[29] Despite the efforts of McArthur and his friends to convince them otherwise, these two tribes believed the rumor. Therefore, the Britisher suggested that Olney visit the Indians at Fort Hall to quiet their fears, and he added that it would be unwise to bring an escort of troops along because the natives would probably run for the mountains at the sight of the regulars.

Contrary to the advice of the British mountain men, Olney took along a guard of six soldiers the following summer (1855) as he traveled toward Fort Hall. At Camas Prairie he had the opportunity to learn something about the Indians of Snake River and sent in one of the first official reports of these people. According to his information, the Snakes numbered about 3,000 and were divided into three groups: the Green River Snakes, numbering 1,500; the Fort Hall Snakes, numbering 1,200, of whom 200 were Bannock; and the Too-koo-ree-keys or Sheepeaters, numbering 300. The "Wineptas" of the Boise River area numbered about 400 and were looked down upon by the Snakes and Bannock as inferior people. Olney noted that the Bannock spoke an entirely different language from the other tribes of Snake River and also recorded that they claimed Camas Prairie as part of their country.[30]

The Indian authorities of Utah Territory were also

[29] Neil McArthur et al. to Olney, Salmon River, Oregon Terr., December 23, 1854, ibid., p. 160.

[30] Olney to Palmer, Camas Prairie, Oregon Terr., July 30, 1855, ibid., No. 10, F, pp. 57-59.

Renegades continually attacked emigrant parties

cognizant of the dangers that hostile Bannock and Shoshoni might bring to the settlers along their northern border. Agent Garland Hunt pointed out in September, 1856, that the emigrant road from Bear River to the Humboldt was neutral ground lying between the Bannock, Shoshoni, and "Cum-i-um-has." Renegades from the three tribes continually attacked emigrant parties with a growing disregard for any threatened retaliatory action by United States troops. Hunt warned that unless steps were taken to stop the depredations "their [Indian] success will encourage others to adopt their practices and in a short time . . . their merciless deeds may exceed anything known to the history of Indian barbarity."[31]

The very nature of tribal organization, with its loose control over the individual, allowed leeway for small groups of Bannock to take short excursions on the warpath in search of horses and scalps. Even the veteran Indian fighters, Kit Carson and Jim Bridger, failed in one instance to interpret aright the attitude of a party of Bannock warriors. In 1857 the two mountain men and several companions were traveling from Virginia City, Montana, to Fort Hall. Sighting an Indian village ahead, the two leaders examined it through field glasses and then thanked their good fortune because it was a "friendly" Bannock village, and not a camp of hostile Blackfeet or Crow. But, much to their chagrin, fifty of the Bannock warriors attacked them the next day, apparently for no other reason than that here was a chance for battle and

---

[31] U.S. Office of Indian Affairs, *Annual Report of the Commissioner of Indian Affairs, 1856* (Washington, 1857), p. 230.

plunder. A providential rainstorm freed the whites from their attackers, but not before Kit Carson had received a painful shoulder wound. The hostile action was even more surprising because the Bannock at the same time were harboring in their country on Lemhi River a settlement of Mormon pioneers with whom they had been on friendly terms for over two years.[32]

---

[32] William F. Drannon, *Thirty-One Years on the Plains and in the Mountains* (Chicago, 1900), pp. 322-23.

Mormon Mission at Lemhi

THE American Indian has always been of significant interest to the Church of Jesus Christ of Latter-day Saints. Through its prophet, Joseph Smith, the church received the Book of Mormon, accepted as a record of a branch of the house of Israel which fled from Jerusalem about 600 B.C. and finally found a home in the western portion of the Americas.[1] The natives of the Western Hemisphere, according to this ancient narrative, were thus literal descendants of the Israelites. In September, 1830, a revelation announced by Joseph Smith gave the Saints a direct obligation to carry the message of the Book of Mormon to the Indians.[2] The first missionaries to carry out these instructions left New York State in October, 1830, and eventually preached Mormon doctrine to the Wyandots in Ohio and to the Delaware Nation in Missouri.[3] Missions were sent to other tribes in the Mississippi region during the following years; and, after the removal of the church to Utah, the work was taken up among the natives of the Great Basin.

---

[1] John M. Sjodahl, *An Introduction to the Study of the Book of Mormon* (Salt Lake City, 1927), pp. 92-93.

[2] Church of Jesus Christ of Latter-day Saints, *Doctrine and Covenants* (Salt Lake City, 1920), Sec. 28, vs. 8.

[3] Joseph Smith, *History of the Church* (Salt Lake City, 1902), I, 181.

The second President of the Church, Brigham Young, recognized the necessity of maintaining friendly relations with the surrounding Indian nations and, under his direction, the missionaries to the western tribes became Indian agents as well as conveyors of a gospel of salvation. The practical attitude of the Mormons toward the Indians was expressed by Governor Brigham Young in a message to the Utah Legislature on December 11, 1854:

I have uniformly pursued a friendly course towards them [Indians], feeling convinced that independent of the question of exercising humanity toward so degraded and ignorant a race of people, it was manifestly more economical and less expensive to feed and clothe than to fight them.[4]

An indication of the religious motive is found in a letter of instructions to Jacob Hamblin upon his appointment as president of one of the Utah missions. Brigham Young wrote:

Continue the conciliatory policy toward the Indians which I have ever commended and seek by works of righteousness to obtain their love and confidence. Omit promises where you are not sure you can fill them; and seek to unite the hearts of the brethren on that mission, and let all under your direction be united together in holy bonds of love and unity.[5]

During the initial period of settlement in Utah the Saints were not unaware of the northern tribes in adjacent Oregon Territory. As early as 1851, Mormon traders were active among the Bannock and Sho-

---

[4] *Deseret News,* December 14, 1854, p. 3.

[5] James A. Little, *Jacob Hamblin* (Salt Lake City, 1881), p. 44.

shoni in the Snake River area. Agent Elias Wampole of Utilla Agency reported to Superintendent Anson Dart of Oregon Territory that a Mormon trader by the name of Johnson was living two miles east of Fort Hall. According to emigrants who had passed through the area, Johnson openly boasted of his influence with the two tribes. One traveler reported that, after some Indians had stolen sixteen horses from a wagon train camped west of the fort, the owners of the stolen animals offered Johnson a reward of $260 —and within ten hours all the horses were brought in.[6]

The activities of such traders, with their unofficial missionary work, no doubt had some influence in bringing about a meeting between a delegation of Bannock chiefs and Brigham Young on May 21, 1853. The "Journal History" of the Mormon church merely records that "the Bannock Indians had a talk with the Superintendent of Indian Affairs at his office," and does not indicate the subject of discussion.[7]

The establishment of several Utah missions by 1855 cleared the way for consideration of a religious delegation to these tribes on the northern border of Utah. At a General Conference of the church held in Salt Lake City, April 6, 1855, President Brigham Young appointed twenty-seven men to conduct missionary work among "the buffalo-hunting Indians of Washington Territory." The Mormons were directed to settle at a spot chosen by themselves within the coun-

---

[6] Elias Wampole to Anson Dart, Utilla Agency, Oregon Terr., September 22, 1851. U.S. National Archives, Records of the Bureau of Indian Affairs, Oregon Superintendency, No. 3, Copies of Letters Received and Sent, 1850-1853, p. 191.

[7] Church of Jesus Christ of Latter-day Saints, "Journal History" (MS in L.D.S. Church Historian's Office, Salt Lake City), May 21, 1853.

try of the Bannock, Shoshoni, or Flathead nations. After founding a settlement, the missionaries were to teach the Indians the principles of civilization, convert as many as possible to Mormonism, and promote peace among the several tribes.[8]

The expedition to the northern mission got under way from Farmington, Utah, on May 15, 1855. It consisted of eleven wagons loaded with wheat, corn, flour, and other provisions, and sufficient tools to begin farming operations. By May 27 the little party had reached the Portneuf River near its confluence with the Snake. The mission secretary recorded for that day that two Bannock came to the camp for a visit and chose to accompany the group for the next three days. On the third day the two Indians were joined by another Bannock with his wife and child. G. W. Hill of the missionary party preached to the visitors, explaining the Book of Mormon to them. After the discussion the three Indian men offered themselves for baptism, so the entire camp met in religious services during which Elder Hill baptized the Bannock braves. The squaw refused baptism at that time but allowed the missionaries to bless her twelve- or fourteen-months-old son, Ion-ish. The child's father was named Warra-hoop. The other two men bore the names of Jock-ick and Chu-mi. The mission journal for the following day reported: "The three Bannocks are still in camp. They seem in the

---

[8] Joseph Parry, Robert McQuarrie, and Joseph Hall, "Report of the Committee on Pioneers" (MS in L.D.S. Church Historian's Office, Salt Lake City), p. 2.

best of spirits and very much pleased with the principles of 'Mormonism.' "[9]

On June 4 another group of five Bannock under
one Mattigan joined the expedition and, after accompanying it for three days, pushed on ahead. The
Mormon party finally reached a branch of Salmon
River on June 12 and named it the Limhi, after a
Nephite king in the Book of Mormon.[10] Shortly after
a camp had been established at this spot, the head
chief of the Bannock rode up. The Mormons always referred to the chief as Sho-woo-koo, but he
was more widely known as "Le Grand Coquin (The
Great Rogue) ," having been so named by the French-
Canadian trappers because of his early reputation as
an efficient horse stealer.[11] The chief had been told
by Mattigan of the coming of the new missionaries
and, leaving the main camp of his tribe, had traveled
seventy-five miles to welcome the whites to the Bannock country. In a council meeting the Grand Coquin
expressed his pleasure at the intention of the Mormons to settle in the Salmon River region and assured
them that they could have any land they wished for
farming purposes. He explained that his people were
suffering and in want because the traders were not
allowed to sell them any ammunition. After expressing a hope that the Mormons would show the Indians

---

[9] David Moore, "Salmon River Mission Record" (MS in L.D.S. Church
Historian's Office, Salt Lake City), pp. 7-8.

[10] John E. Rees, *Idaho Chronology, Nomenclature, Bibliography* (Chicago, 1918), p. 74. The spelling of "Limhi" was later changed to "Lemhi."

[11] U.S. Congress, House of Representatives, "Report of C. H. Miller,"
in *Report of the Secretary of the Interior on Pacific Wagon Roads*, Ex.
Doc. 108, 35th Cong., 2nd Sess., Serial No. 1008, March 1, 1859 (Washington, 1859), p. 71.

how to farm and raise crops, the chief tried to induce the missionaries to found a settlement on the
Lemhi River, instead of going farther north toward
the country of the Flathead and Nez Perce. He stayed
on in the camp until definite plans were made by
the Saints to remain on the Lemhi, after which he
left to rejoin his people.[12]

With the decision made to found a settlement in
Lemhi Valley, the pioneers began construction of a
stockade on June 15, 1855, selecting a site about two
miles north of the present town of Tendoy.[13] Fort
Lemhi was well located for the proposed missionary
work, being in one of the areas of the Snake River
Basin where the Bannock, Shoshoni, Flathead, and
Nez Perce tribes were accustomed to meet in early
summer of every year to gamble and to trade for
horses. Only six days after the settlement was started,
twenty-two lodges of Nez Perce came in from the
east and camped near the fort. By this time also,
the Grand Coquin and some of his Bannock were
situated near by, and they soon began a brisk trade
of buffalo robes for some of the three or four hundred horses the Nez Perce had brought along. On
June 23, the mission secretary wrote:

When the brethren met for prayers, the old chief (Nez
Perce) and the Bannock Chief (Shoo-woo-koo) also met with
them and united their voices in keeping time with the tune
of the hymn sung, and during the time of prayer they observed the utmost attention and silence.[14]

---

[12] Moore, "Salmon River Mission Record," *op. cit.*, pp. 11-17.
[13] Cornelius J. Brosnan, *History of the State of Idaho* (New York,
1935), p. 104.
[14] Moore, "Salmon River Mission Record," *op. cit.*, pp. 22-24.

While the Saints were engaged in constructing their new settlement, they were impressed with the orderly and friendly manner of the many Bannock camped near by. The Indians were quiet and peaceable, preparing for the annual buffalo hunt, and on July 15 the majority of the tribe left for the Montana plains in search of the winter's meat supply. Throughout the remainder of the first year the Indians around the fort continued their friendly attitude; and one of the Mormons, William Burgess, Jr., was so struck with the integrity of the natives that he wrote George A. Smith, a church official in Salt Lake City, commenting on this characteristic:

The Indians are very honest here or have been so far. When we wash we sometimes let our clothes hang days, let our tools lay around anyway, and Indians coming and going daily. Not one thing has been stolen yet. I wish Christians were this honest. They abhor a thief, comparing him to a wolf, and they think a wolf is the meanest animal there is.[15]

After the majority of the Indians had gone, the missionaries settled down to the hard work of building and farming, but they did not neglect the chief purpose of the mission. A definite program of study was arranged for the purpose of learning the Shoshoni language. The "brethren" held three sessions of school a week and were soon able to converse with the Indians. With the return of many of the Bannock and Shoshoni in October, meetings were held frequently and, on October 21, fifty-five Indians were baptized into the church. Thomas S. Smith, president

---

[15] William Burgess, Jr., to George A. Smith, Fort Lemhi, Oregon Terr., Oct. 9, 1855, in Moore, "Salmon River Mission Record," *op. cit.*, p. 38.

One of the missionary party explained the Book of Mormon to them

of the mission, wrote to Brigham Young, in July of 1856, that "everything is write with the indiens and a good spirit prevails there has been 100 baptised. . . ."[16] Most of those accepted into the Mormon church were Bannock, the members of this tribe apparently having a greater interest in the gospel taught by the white missionaries. Although few of the leading Bannock men were converted, Tio-van-du-ah (Snag), chief of the local band of Shoshoni, was baptized November 11, 1855.[17]

To maintain their successful mission among the Indians of the Oregon Country, the Mormons found it necessary at first to rely on the home base of Salt Lake City for supplies. Frequent trips were made between the two settlements and, in November of 1855, the first reinforcements came to the small group when five women and six children made the difficult 379-mile journey to Fort Lemhi.[18] By the spring of 1857, the mission showed signs of becoming a prosperous settlement, and it was with an air of some pride that the inhabitants made preparations to receive a visit from their president and prophet, Brigham Young. Governor Young and a large party of Saints left Salt Lake City on April 24, 1857, "to visit the settlement on Salmon River, to rest their minds, to invigorate their bodies, and to examine the intermediate country." The company consisted of 115 men, 22 women, 5 boys, with 168 horses and mules, 54 wagons and carriages, and 2 light ferryboats. Upon his arrival

---

[16] Thomas S. Smith to Brigham Young, Fort Lemhi, Oregon Terr., July 26, 1856, in Moore, "Salmon River Mission Record," op. cit., p. 60.

[17] Ibid., p. 40.

[18] Parry, McQuarrie, and Hall, op. cit., p. 3.

at Fort Lemhi, one of the first acts of Brigham Young was to distribute presents of blankets and other goods to some Bannock who were camped near the settlement.[19]

At one of the meetings held with the local Saints during the visit, two of the church leaders, Heber C. Kimball and Daniel H. Wells, urged the young men of the mission to marry native women because "the marriage tie was the strongest tie of friendship that existed."[20] This advice indicated an abrupt departure from the long-standing policy of the Mormons to discourage such unions between whites and Indians. Brigham Young modified the instructions by cautioning the men to marry only young girls "because . . . if the brethren were to marry those old vanigadoes they would be off with the first mountaineer that came along."[21] In accordance with this counsel, several young men later made overtures to the "dusky maidens," but the parents "refused to let their daughters go, or at least seemed not willing."[22] Only a few such marriages were made during the period of the mission.

Although Brigham Young could congratulate the Salmon River missionaries upon their accomplishment in founding a settlement and upon their conversions among the Indians, he could not give equal praise to their efforts at promoting peace among the

[19] *Deseret News,* June 10, 1858, p. 108.

[20] Moore, "Salmon River Mission Record," *op. cit.,* p. 113.

[21] W. H. Daines, "Journal" (MS in L.D.S. Church Historian's Office, Salt Lake City).

[22] David Moore, "Salmon River Mission, Journal" (MS in L.D.S. Church Historian's Office, Salt Lake City), I, 7.

several tribes. Ancient animosities and the strong urge of the young men to distinguish themselves in the arts of horse stealing and war led to constant raids and skirmishes between the tribes. As early as July 22, 1855, the mission secretary recorded that a group of Blackfeet stole fifteen horses from the other Indians near the fort. The Bannock spent the winter of 1855-56 at "Horse Prairie," in the Montana Beaverhead country, and information of their troubles with the Nez Perce during that season eventually came to Fort Lemhi. Chief Grand Coquin appeared at the post on February 21, 1856, received some presents from the missionaries, and left " his brother-in-law at the Fort on the hands of the brethren." On March 19, the Shoshoni Chief Snag, coming in to settle at Lemhi, reported on the winter activities among the Indians. He said that the Bannock and Nez Perce had gambled all winter on amicable terms until a Bannock stole two horses from the Nez Perce. In retaliation, the Nez Perce stole two from Chief Grand Coquin and planned to go to war against the Bannock but had been dissuaded through the efforts of Snag. According to the story, Chief Snag preached to both tribes "the words that Brigham Young had told him, that it was not good to fight, that the Lord was not pleased with those that wanted to fight, and . . . that it was good talk."[23]

Early in the spring of 1857 reports reached the mission that the Pend d'Oreille and Bannock had had a fight in the buffalo country during which six Bannock were killed. In confirmation of this engage-

---

[23] Moore, "Salmon River Mission Record," *op. cit.,* pp. 49, 59.

ment, two Indians arrived at the fort from Horse
Prairie in June with the news that twenty-two of the
Bannock were on their way to the Pend d'Oreille
country for the purpose of stealing horses in retaliation for horses stolen from them by the Pend d'Oreille.
A few days later, five Nez Perce arrived at the fort
and announced that sixty horses had been stolen from
them. Chief Snag held a conference and told the
Nez Perce about the plan of the twenty-two Bannock
to steal horses from the Pend d'Oreille.

Disturbed by the unrest among the Indians, President Smith of the Salmon River Mission wrote to
Major John Owen, at Fort Owen in Bitter Root Valley, asking the major to persuade the Pend d'Oreille
to return the stolen Bannock horses. At the same time
Smith promised to get the Bannock to return the
sixty horses stolen from the Nez Perce.[24] As early as
April of 1857, Major Owen had had to counsel the
Nez Perce under his charge against the preparations
they were making for war on the Bannock. Shortly
after receipt of the letter from Fort Lemhi, Owen
received news that the Nez Perce had lost a number
of horses to Bannock raiding parties in the Big Hole
country.[25]

Throughout this period of unrest, and amidst the
rumors of hostilities between the various tribes, the
Mormons continued to retain the friendship of the
Indians. The Bannock, especially, maintained congenial relations with the missionaries. Chief Grand

---

[24] Ibid., pp. 64, 71-72.
[25] John Owen, The Journals and Letters of Major John Owen, Pioneer
of the Northwest, 1850-1871, ed. by Seymour Dunbar and with notes by
Paul C. Phillips (2 vols.; New York, 1927), I, 160, 167, 169.

Coquin visited Fort Lemhi in October of 1856 and appeared very friendly toward the whites. As late as June, 1857, the mission secretary noted that ten Bannock who arrived from the Soda Springs area exhibited the friendliest of feeling toward their brethren of the church.[26]

Despite the atmosphere of peace which pervaded the Lemhi Valley settlement, the Mormons realized that the maintenance of their position in the heart of the Indian country was dependent solely upon the rather fickle nature of a people whose chief glory was war and conquest. And now the situation of the white settlement was made even more precarious by developments of an entirely different nature.

Relations between the Mormon leaders in Utah and the national government had become increasingly worse in the years following the California gold rush. By the spring of 1857, it had been established by the government, supposedly on sufficient evidence, that federal officials had been driven from Utah, that one of the federal judges had been threatened with violence, and that the records of one of the courts had been destroyed or concealed.[27] President James Buchanan, therefore, determined to suspend Brigham Young as governor and to send a military force to Utah Territory to sustain the authority of his successor.

On the twenty-fourth of July, 1857, the Mormons heard for the first time of the approach of a federal army of six thousand men whose mission, they supposed, was to drive them from their homes at the

---

[26] Moore, "Salmon River Mission Record," *op. cit.*, pp. 59, 71.

[27] Hubert Howe Bancroft, *History of Utah* (San Francisco, 1890), p. 495.

point of a bayonet. Determined to resist what they thought was an unjust action on the part of the United States government, the Mormons began to drill troops and eventually could have put seven thousand men into the field. Small detachments of Mormon cavalry were dispatched to harass the baggage trains of Colonel Albert Sidney Johnston; and these hindrances, plus the lateness of the season, forced the United States Army commander to go into winter quarters at Camp Scott, on the Black Fork of the Green River, two or three miles from Fort Bridger.[28]

While these developments took place in the so-called "war" between the Mormons and the United States, the little Salmon River Mission faced a growing uneasiness among the tribes of the Lemhi area. On November 30, 1857, the secretary wrote: "There is much movement amongst the Indians. They say that they are going to Beaver Head, but they will not tell what they are going for." Just before Christmas the chief of the Nez Perce arrived at the fort from a chase after Bannock who had stolen a number of horses. The rest of the Nez Perce joined their chief on December 26 and held a war dance at the fort. The following day President Smith of the mission held a council meeting with them in an attempt to settle the matter of the stolen horses, but the Indians refused to talk over peace terms until the horses were returned. The party left Fort Lemhi the following day, and the next day the Mormons learned that sixty or seventy Shoshoni horses had been taken by the Nez Perce. The Shoshoni immediately stopped their

---

[28] *Ibid.*, p. 496.

recently adopted practice of burning fences, put on their war paint, and, with the Bannock, prepared to make war on the Nez Perce. In desperation, Smith held a feast for all the Bannock and Shoshoni around the fort in an attempt to quiet them. The mission journal says: "Most of the Indians ate feast but some would not eat, saying that they were not dogs, nor were hungry enough to sit down and eat off the ground; they accordingly stood off and looked and acting quite mumpy."[29]

The excitement among the tribes had by now spread far beyond the narrow limits of Lemhi Valley. A. P. Dennison, Indian agent at The Dalles, wrote to the Superintendent of Indian Affairs for Oregon, in January of 1858, that the Mormons at Salmon River and Salt Lake City were offering guns and ammunition to any Indians who would join them.[30] Major Owen wrote to the Oregon superintendent that "the present alarming state of affairs" made his position in Bitter Root Valley more dangerous because it was the only route of escape for the Mormons on Lemhi River.[31]

An indication of impending trouble for the Lemhi Mission came on January 11, 1858, when some Bannock and Shoshoni from the Snake River area appeared at the fort with the report that the Bannock, Mattigan, recommended that the two tribes fight the Mormons before going to war against the Nez Perce.

---

[29] Moore, "Salmon River Mission Record," *op. cit.*, pp. 79-82.

[30] A. P. Dennison to J. W. Nesmith, Portland, Oregon, January 12, 1858. U.S. National Archives, Records of the Bureau of Indian Affairs, Oregon Superintendency, No. 16, Copies of Letters Received, 1858.

[31] Owen, *op. cit.*, II, 173.

About two weeks later some Shoshoni warriors came into the settlement "all painted up." They were "very saucy and wanted to fight the Mormons," but left after Smith gave them six and one-half bushels of wheat on the promise they would not appear again in war paint. Finally, the Bannock chief, Grand Coquin, appeared at the fort on February 16 and asked for flour, but accepted wheat when Smith told him that the former was very scarce. Before leaving the fort he entered and examined the horse corral thoroughly. The mission secretary, commenting on his actions, said, "This was thought queer as he had been there and seen it before."

Although the Mormons refused to be alarmed by these suspicious activities, a later report to them described the manner in which the two tribes had agreed on hostile action. When the Bannock first arrived at Lemhi River in February, they held a war dance and asked the Shoshoni to help them raid the white settlement. Most of the Shoshoni were opposed to such action, so the Bannock held another war dance and then informed the Shoshoni that, unless they took part in the projected affair, they could expect an attack from the Bannock. This threat decided the Shoshoni and, on the twenty-fourth of February, John W. Powell, a mountaineer who lived with them, came in to warn the Mormons. Powell said he had been up all the previous night trying to dissuade the Bannock from their intention of burning the hay and straw of the settlement and driving off all the horses and cattle. Smith dismissed the warning with the statement that it was just another of the man's lies.[32]

At ten o'clock on the morning of February 25, about two hundred Bannock and Shoshoni warriors were observed riding in the direction of the Mormon herd of cattle. Smith and a small group of the missionaries hurried out to attempt to bring the herd into the stockade. In the resulting skirmish two of the Mormons were killed, five were wounded, and the Indians got away with two hundred and fifty head of cattle and twenty-nine horses. At a council of war it was decided to send to Brigham Young for instructions concerning possible abandonment of the mission.[33]

After the messengers had left, the Mormons settled down inside the fort to secure themselves from further attack. One of their first acts was to hold a meeting on March 4 and "cut off from the church" all those Indians who were known to be in the hostile party. The following day, three Shoshoni came into the fort as delegates of the Shoshoni chiefs. They were seeking terms of peace and said the chiefs promised to return all the cattle now in their possession —some thirty head. According to their story the Bannock had taken the rest of the cattle and all of the horses after a quarrel during which a Shoshoni squaw was killed.[34] By March 17, many of the Shoshoni were again visiting the settlement, and the secretary wrote: "Our fort is again filled with begging natives.

---

[32] Moore, "Salmon River Mission Record," *op. cit.,* pp. 84-90.

[33] *Ibid.,* pp. 91-100.

[34] John V. Bluth, "The Salmon River Mission," *Improvement Era,* III, No. 11 (September, 1900), 911.

The feelings which their appearance causes in the minds of the brethren, cannot well be described."[35]

Messengers from Salt Lake City arrived on March 26 with orders from Brigham Young to abandon the mission. Five days later, ten men left in advance of the main company to carry a report of conditions at Fort Lemhi to the church leaders. On March 31, the Indians attacked the party on Bannock Creek and killed one man. Finally, the entire missionary group left Lemhi Valley on April 1 for Salt Lake City, thus bringing to a close the mission to the Indians of the Oregon Country.

The attack on the Salmon River settlement seemed to give additional proof to the Mormons that the troops and the mountaineers were arming the Indians and instigating them to attack Mormon outposts. Special anger was directed at John W. Powell, the trader to the Bannock and Shoshoni. A member of the relief expedition to Fort Lemhi later testified that the Indians had gone on the warpath because Powell had warned them that the Mormons intended to take their lands and drive off the game.[36] An editorial in the *Deseret News* of March 17, 1858, accused Powell of "assisting them [Indians] in the plundering, wounding and killing of peaceful and unoffending American citizens."[37] Brigham Young also believed that Powell was "most actively engaged with the Indians in the massacre and robbery. . . ."[38]

[35] Moore, "Salmon River Mission Record," *op. cit.*, p. 105.

[36] Robert L. Bybee, Dictation (MS in L.D.S. Church Historian's Office, Salt Lake City), p. 1.

[37] *Deseret News*, March 17, 1858, p. 13.

[38] "Journal History," *op. cit.*, March 31, 1858.

Before making a final report of the affair to Governor Alfred Cumming, the Secretary for Utah Territory, William H. Hooper, obtained eyewitness accounts and examined affidavits filed in Salt Lake County. His findings revealed that during the winter prior to the descent on the Salmon River settlement, many rumors existed among the Indians to the effect that they would be employed by the "soldiers" to drive off the cattle and horses of the Mormons as soon as the mountain passes were open. There had been no misunderstandings between the Bannock and Shoshoni and the white settlers until a small detachment of "soldiers" from Fort Bridger arrived at Beaver Head to buy stock. Proceeding from the camp of this party of whites, J. W. Powell had visited the Indian villages, had incited the "Bannacks and Shoshones" to drive off the stock, and had made arrangements to meet the Bannock at Soda Springs. From this spot, Powell, accompanied by the soldiers, conducted the Indians and their stolen cattle to Camp Scott.[39] A *Deseret News* editorial, agreeing with this account, said: "It is not a difficult matter, for a good arithmetician to count the toes upon a naked foot, when it is put out."[40] After reviewing the information he had received concerning Powell's activities and a current rumor that the army had offered the Indians $150 for every Mormon brought in to Colonel Johnston's camp,[41] Brigham Young concluded:

---

[39] William H. Hooper to A. Cumming, Salt Lake City, April 13, 1858. U.S. Congress, Senate, *Report of the Secretary of War*, Ex. Doc., II, No. 1, Part II, 35th Cong., 2nd Sess., Serial No. 975 (Washington, 1859), 74.

[40] *Deseret News*, April 14, 1858, p. 35.

[41] Jacob Hamblin, *Autobiography* (1st ed.; Salt Lake City, April 9, 1858).

It must be conceded that the above facts, circumstances and reports, transpiring at this particular juncture of affairs, strongly impel the conclusion that some person or persons [are] connected with the policy of several of the powers that be, "towards the 'Mormons' "; and that the mildest term in use in the army, when speaking of us, is the "damned 'Mormons.' "[42]

Although most of the Saints would have agreed with their leader in his indictment of the troops, the army could also point an accusing finger at Brigham Young. At the beginning of the "Utah War," Captain Stewart Van Vliet had been sent by the United States Army commander to Salt Lake City to purchase forage and lumber for the armed forces. In conversation with the captain, Brigham Young had said:

If the [troops] dare to force the issue, I shall not hold the Indians by the wrist any longer for white men to shoot at them; they shall go ahead and do as they please. If the issue comes, you may tell the government to stop all emigration across the continent, for the Indians will kill all who attempt it.[43]

This statement was apparently the basis for a rumor that soon spread throughout the Rocky Mountains that the Mormons were supplying the Indians with arms and ammunition to fight the "Gentiles." Almost a year after the Fort Lemhi episode, Major John Owen, visiting in Salt Lake City, asked Brigham Young about this charge:

I found myself completely swamped by a few very ingenious questions propounded in a very polite & quiet way One

---

[42] "Journal History," *op. cit.,* March 31, 1858.
[43] Bancroft, *op. cit.,* p. 507.

was—Have you heard Maj. Owen of the Emmissaries I keep employed in China for the purpose of poisning the Tea ships to the U. S., etc. I couldn't help smiling and came to the conclusion that My first conviction was correct which was that the Evidence against them as a community for furnishing Powder & Ball was to[o] slim to be Entertained.[44]

The members of the Utah Expedition did not agree with Major Owen's conclusion and, in addition to denying the charges of inciting the Bannock, made some countercharges against the citizens of Utah. The detachment of "soldiers" sent to Beaver Head by Colonel Johnston proved to be a party of ten white traders commissioned by the army to contract for the delivery of five hundred head of beef cattle by April 1, 1858. The group was also commissioned "to induce the mountaineers and Indians to bring in any horses they might wish to sell." Upon returning to the army camp, B. F. Ficklin, the leader of the party, gave Colonel Johnston a report of the incident at Fort Lemhi and concluded that, while the cause of the attack was unknown, it was common knowledge that the Bannock were engaged in stealing cattle from the emigrants in the Humboldt River area and selling the stock to the Mormons.[45]

---

[44] John Owen to J. W. Nesmith, Fort Owen, Washington Terr., February 2, 1859. U.S. National Archives, Records of the Bureau of Indian Affairs, Washington Superintendency, Flathead Agency, Letters Received, No. 22.

Brigham Young's remark about the poisoning of tea ships probably referred to an article in *Harper's Weekly* for October 31, 1857, p. 649. Under the title "How the Mormons Propose to Conquer the World," the writer not only accused the Mormons of poisoning Chinese tea imported into the United States but also insisted that the Saints poisoned liquor and tobacco manufactured for sale to "Gentiles."

[45] U.S. Congress, Senate, "Report of B. F. Ficklin," in *Report of the Secretary of War*, Ex. Doc., II, No. 1, Part II, 35th Cong., 2nd Sess., Serial No. 975 (Washington, 1859), p. 68.

The constant editorials in the *Deseret News* concerning Ficklin's part in the Salmon River incident finally led that trader to make a sworn statement denying any implication in the affair. Before the Chief Justice of the Utah Supreme Court, then residing at Camp Scott, Ficklin said:

I did not *say* or *do* anything myself, neither did any man under my command, to induce any Indians to interfere with the Mormons . . . on the contrary, I took every opportunity to tell all Indians and whites whom I met on the trip . . . that Colonel Johnston did not desire, and would not permit, any interference from Indians. . . . The attack on Salmon River Fort, by Bannocks and Snakes, was induced by the Mormons furnishing a party of Nez Perces' arms and ammunition to make war on them (the Bannocks and Snakes).[46]

In answer to the charges of the *Deseret News*, W. M. F. Magraw and James Bridger wrote to the army's adjutant general at Camp Scott defending Colonel Johnston in his dealings with the Indians. At the beginning of the Utah War, Johnston had held a meeting with Chief Washakie of the Eastern Shoshoni and, through interpreter James Bridger, had advised the chief to take his people to the buffalo country, out of the way of the trouble between the government and the Mormons. On another occasion, when a chief, Little Soldier, had complained about the wrongs done his people by the Mormons, the colonel had advised the Indian leader to have nothing to do with the existing difficulties. The letter concluded that: "Colonel Johnston's conduct on the two occasions alluded to, and his policy . . . forbids even

---

[46] U.S. Congress, Senate, "Report of B. F. Ficklin," *ibid.*, p. 79.

the supposition that he . . . could have been in any way connected with the Utahs' or Pannacks' difficulties. . . ."[47]

A final countercharge against Mormon accusations was made by John W. Powell. He filed a sworn statement in which he said that Brigham Young tried to bribe the Bannock into joining the Saints in war on the United States. The Indians refused the offer and, instead, wanted to join the government troops in the war against the Utah people. Powell dissuaded them from attacking the Salmon River settlement. The Bannock chose to take hostile action because the Mormons would not pay them for their land as promised; and, furthermore, the white settlers furnished ammunition to a war party of Nez Perce who subsequently stole some horses belonging to the Bannock and Shoshoni.[48]

Another mountaineer who had been living with the Bannock supported Powell in his explanation of their hostility to the Lemhi missionaries. This man, Craven Jackson, testified that the Bannock were angry because the Mormons refused to pay for the land acquired in Lemhi Valley. In addition, the action of the settlers in furnishing ammunition to the Nez Perce enabled that tribe to steal some Bannock horses. With the Nez Perce safe from pursuit, the Bannock decided to drive off the Mormon stock as the next best means of recouping their losses.[49]

Major John Owen conjectured that the Bannock

---

[47] U.S. Congress, Senate, W. M. F. Magraw and James Bridger to F. J. Porter, Camp Scott, Utah Terr., April 28, 1858, *ibid.*, p. 82.

[48] U.S. Congress, Senate, "Affidavit of John W. Powell," *ibid.*, p. 80.

[49] U.S. Congress, Senate, "Statement of Craven Jackson," *ibid.*, p. 81.

drove the Saints from Salmon River because of the fear that the white settlement was only the first of many that would eventually deprive the Indians of their country.[50] When Captain C. H. Miller was in the Snake River area in 1859, on his work for the Superintendent of Pacific Wagon Roads, he learned of a "celebrated prophet of the western Snake tribe" who lived near Fort Boise and wrote of him:

I consider him one of the most dangerous and desperate men now living west of the Rocky mountains, for the Indians have a superstitious reverence for him. He is extremely hostile to the Mormons. This noted partisan was the chief cause of the expedition against the Mormon settlement of Salmon river, which was attacked by the Pannacks and the Snakes on their learning that the American government had commenced war upon the Mormons of Salt Lake.[51]

After reviewing the many possible causes for the Bannock attack on Fort Lemhi, and after sifting the evidence of charges and recriminations which the Mormons and their opponents hurled at each other, the conviction becomes clear that responsibility for the hostile action lay mainly with the Bannock. Above and beyond any influence exerted by trader, soldier, or missionary, a situation existed in February of 1858 which gave the Bannock an almost unrivaled opportunity to indulge in their age-old customs of horse stealing and war. First, the Nez Perce had stolen their horses, which called for retaliation on the Nez

[50] John Owen to E. R. Geary, Salem, Oregon, May 31, 1859. U.S. National Archives, Records of the Bureau of Indian Affairs, Washington Superintendency, Flathead Agency, Letters Received, No. 22.

[51] U.S. Congress, House of Representatives, "Report of C. H. Miller," in Report of the Secretary of the Interior on Pacific Wagon Roads, op. cit., p. 70.

Perce, or any likely substitute. Second, a group of white traders in Beaver Head had advertised that they would pay high prices in money or goods for cattle and horses. Third, the war of the United States government against the Mormons seemingly assured the Indians that any hostile action against the Saints would result only in applause from the troops rather than the customary punitive expedition which usually followed an Indian raid on a white settlement. Faced with this auspicious combination of circumstances, the Bannock followed their natural inclination and went on the warpath.

The relations of the Mormons with other Indian tribes were noticeably affected by the Bannock attack on Fort Lemhi. The fact that almost no effort was made on the part of the Mormons or of the United States troops to punish the Bannock emboldened all the other tribes. As a result, Brigham Young asserted to Governor Cumming in April, 1858, that:

For seven years the people have been at peace with the Indians; they came to our houses to eat and drink with us; but they now come and draw their bows on our wives, and take blankets from our beds. They say the Mormons are squaws, they won't fight.[52]

When C. H. Miller met with the Shoshoni chief, Pocatello, in 1859, this tribal leader pretty well summed up the Indian point of view by saying that he knew:

. . . that there was a greater man than Big-um, the Great Father of the Whites, before whom Big-um was as a little finger to the whole hand; and much frightened, Big-um,

---

[52] "Journal History," *op. cit.*, April 14, 1858.

with all his warriors, had run away towards the south when
the blue-caps, or soldiers, the bands of the White Father,
came in sight. . . .[53]

The enmity of the Bannock for the Mormons, which
erupted in the attack and killings at Fort Lemhi, was
not just a temporary condition, as the same C. H.
Miller would have testified. In 1859, he and a companion, laying out a road in advance of the main
party of construction workers, met with a camp of
Bannock.

. . . it was a position of extremity with us, for a council
of war was held, in which we were not permitted to join.
The medicine pipe was smoked, and a discussion took place
as to whether we should be killed or not, the Indians believing us to be Mormons. While the Chief and the leading
men were holding council I approached them, and, taking
the pipe from the hand of the last smoker, smoked it myself,
and told them, by the language of signs, that I had come a
long way to see them, but that I could only hold a talk at
my own camp, which was three days' ride back. At this
time the women and the young men came forward, crying
with loud voices, in the Shoshonee or Pannack language,
"Shoot, shoot! they are Mormons." The nominal Chief of
this party, however, who is a temperate and quiet man, said
that we had visited them in their camp, and that he and
six of his best warriors would go with us and hear more;
that we might possibly be Americans, and that, although
his heart was very bad against the Mormons, he loved the
children of his "Great Father," and should not permit any
harm to come to them within the borders of his camp.[54]

In the years following 1859, the Mormon settlers
and the emigrants to Oregon and California con-

---

[53] U.S. Congress, House of Representatives, "Report of C. H. Miller,"
op. cit., p. 72.
    [54] Ibid., p. 70.

tinued to suffer from the raids and depredations of the Bannock. Their hostility to the whites was not effectively checked until 1863, when General Patrick E. Connor defeated them and the Shoshoni at the battle of Bear River.

The Battle of Bear River

FOR A time after the siege at Lemhi River, the Bannock apparently were on friendly terms with the United States troops at Camp Scott. Captain Jesse Gove wrote his wife in May, 1858, that a large camp of Bannock was established near the fort. The chiefs called to pay their respects to Colonel Johnston, and the soldiers returned the compliment by visiting the Indian village. Gove said, "They are fine looking Indians and said to be the best in the mountains."[1] At about the same time, Captain J. H. Simpson was encountering Bannock west of Salt Lake City and was receiving an entirely different impression, recording that they were of "a very thievish, treacherous character."[2]

During the month of May, 1858, while the Bannock were at Camp Scott, Indian Superintendent Jacob Forney of Utah held a conference and arranged peace terms between the Eastern Shoshoni and the Northern Ute. The Bannock chiefs attended the meetings but did not participate in the "talk." Forney

---

[1] Jesse A. Gove, *The Utah Expedition, 1857-1858; Letters of Capt. Jesse Augustus Gove, 10th Inf., U.S.A.*, ed. by Otis G. Hammond (Concord, N.H., 1928), p. 161.

[2] J. H. Simpson, *The Shortest Route to California, Illustrated by a History of Exploration of the Great Basin of Utah* (Philadelphia, 1869), p. 47.

discovered to his surprise that the tribe was separate
and distinct from the Shoshoni, although the two frequently combined for hunting expeditions. The leading chief and his five hundred Bannock followers accepted the presents Forney gave them and agreed
to the home assigned to them within the large area
claimed by Chief Washakie. Jim Bridger assured the
superintendent that he had been trading with the
Bannock for about thirty years, and that they had
numbered 1,200 lodges when he first met them. Probably 1,200 people would have been more accurate,
but at least Bridger was well acquainted with the
Bannock and, no doubt, gave the Indian agent a
very good idea of their status among the tribes of
the region.[3]

While the Utah superintendent was taking cognizance of the need for establishing governmental
supervision over the Bannock, other officials were
warning Washington authorities that it would be
necessary to pay the Indians for the right of way of
public roads through their lands. Superintendent F.
W. Lander of the Fort Kearney, South Pass, and
Honey Lake Wagon Road spoke of the absolute necessity of reimbursing the Bannock and Shoshoni in order to forestall possible depredations by the tribes.

---

[3] U.S. Office of Indian Affairs, *Annual Report of the Commissioner of
Indian Affairs, 1858* (Washington, 1859), p. 213; also the *Annual Report . . . 1859* (Washington, 1860), p. 363.

Hebard says, "The object of this permission [to be in Washakie's terri-
tory] was doubtless to put the Bannocks under the watchful eye of
Washakie. But it failed to bring the benefits expected, for there was
a further increase of depredations against the emigrants." This may
have been true, but probably it was merely a recognition on the part
of Forney that the Bannock and Shoshoni lived together and inhabited
the same area. Grace R. Hebard, *Washakie; an Account of Indian
Resistance to the Covered Wagon and the Union Pacific Railroad Invasion of their Territory* (Cleveland, 1930), p. 91.

He pointed out that, while the Sioux and Cheyenne had been paid annuities for many years, the Bannock and Shoshoni had never received substantial presents of any kind. A subordinate of Lander, C. H. Miller, wrote in November, 1858, that the emigrants destroyed the grass in the regions where the Indians usually wintered their horses, and that it would be unjust if the government did not pay the tribes for the use of their lands. He further pointed out that annuity payments would tend to settle the uneasiness of the Bannock who were becoming concerned about the destruction of the wild game upon which they depended for food. Most of the mountaineers with whom Miller had talked believed that the Bannock would "inevitably" attack the first emigrant trains that left Fort Hall for Oregon during the next year. Admitting that the Bannock under their chief, Le Grand Coquin, were the most dangerous of all the Indians he had met, the white man made an unusual defense of their code of ethics.

I do not think the term "treacherous," as usually applied to Indian tribes, is always just. We can hardly say that a tribe is treacherous which definitely asserts, through its chief, that it will not permit the passage of white men through their country. It has been in the most manly and direct manner that these Indians have said that if emigrants, as has usually been the case, shoot members of their tribes, they will kill them when they can.[4]

On the other hand, Miller also remarked that the Bannock often tried to frighten emigrants into giving

---

[4] U.S. Congress, House of Representatives, *Report of the Secretary of the Interior on Pacific Wagon Roads*, Ex. Doc. 108, 35th Cong., 2nd Sess., Serial No. 1008, March 1, 1859 (Washington, 1859), pp. 71, 49-73.

them food and were, as a result, sometimes killed by the alarmed travelers.

Except for Superintendent Forney's brief visit with part of the Bannock in May of 1858, no other agent of the Indian Office met them until the next spring, when John Owen of the Flathead Agency made a short stopover at Fort Hall on his way from Salt Lake City. He saw only a few of the tribe, most of them being away on the summer hunt. Upon reaching his post at Fort Owen, he discovered that only a few days earlier the Bannock had run off one hundred horses belonging to the people of Bitter Root Valley. From this time until October, 1859, the threat of Bannock depredations hung over the heads of the whites near Fort Owen. The agent wrote that the settlers were "measurably helpless" before the expected onslaughts of the Bannock, and indicated that he intended to hold a council meeting with the tribe as soon as he could get to Fort Hall.[5]

Farther to the south, Oregon Trail emigrants were also feeling the lash of Bannock and Shoshoni raiding parties. Samuel Smith of Brigham City, Utah, wrote Superintendent Forney that reports had reached him of an attack on a wagon train on the road two hundred miles north of that community. As later information revealed, the emigrant party was set upon in a canyon of the Goose Creek Mountains, about fifteen miles from Raft River. Seven people were killed and a number wounded. The Indians involved,

[5] Owen to Geary, Flathead Agency, August 16 and October 10, 1859, in John Owen, *The Journals and Letters of Major John Owen, Pioneer of the Northwest, 1850-1871*, ed. by Seymour Dunbar and with notes by Paul C. Phillips (2 vols.; New York, 1927), II, 191, 192-93.

Bannock and Shoshoni, attempted to sell their plunder to the citizens of the northern Utah settlements. In retaliation, Forney asked the military at Camp Floyd, near Salt Lake City, to send troops after the marauders. A company of dragoons under Major Isaac Lynde left in early August for Bear River Crossing where a headquarters was set up, and patrols were sent out to scour the country. A few days later, Lieutenant E. Gay, with a small force, left Camp Floyd to investigate the Goose Creek massacre and to apprehend the guilty parties, if he could catch them.[6]

Arriving at Box Elder Valley, Lieutenant Gay was told by the settlers that a band of from one hundred and fifty to two hundred Bannock and Shoshoni was encamped in Devil's Gate Canyon. From reports, the officer was convinced that these were the Indians he sought and, therefore, he made a surprise attack on them with his force of forty-two men. The troops drove the Indians up a steep mountainside, only to find the pursuit up the precipitous slopes an impossible task. Gay had only six men wounded, and estimated that his soldiers killed about twenty of the Indians. Of some twenty horses captured, one proved to be an animal taken from an emigrant party which had been attacked near Sublette's Cutoff during the preceding month. In concluding his official report, the lieutenant noted that about two hundred Bannock had just arrived in Cache Valley to join a

[6] Samuel Smith to Dr. Forney, Brigham City, Utah Terr., August 1, 1859. U.S. Congress, Senate, Ex. Doc. 42, 36th Cong., 1st Sess., Serial No. 1033 (Washington, 1860), pp. 19-22; *Deseret News*, August 17, 1859, p. 192.

Shoshoni group of three hundred. This threatened danger led the commanding officer at Camp Floyd to send another company of dragoons to strengthen the force under Gay; then the combined units headed for Major Lynde's post at the Bear River Crossing of the Oregon Trail.[7]

While en route to the crossing, Lieutenant Gay made a prisoner of Chief Pocatello, a Shoshoni leader, who came to visit the officer in his camp. Major Lynde released the Indian and explained the action to his superior on the grounds that nothing could be proved against Pocatello and that it was dangerous to antagonize all the Indians in the area.[8] The *Deseret News* criticized the army for allowing the chief to go and asked, "Why was he not securely kept? and through whose agency was he permitted to escape?"[9]

Meanwhile, reports of Indian attacks continued to come in to Lynde at Bear River. F. W. Lander reported to Superintendent Forney, on August 16, that four whites had been killed in an attack on a wagon train twenty miles east of the junction of the Fort Hall and Hedspeth roads. The Bannock and Shoshoni leaders of the hostiles were listed as Chief Sawwith ("The Steam from a Cow's Belly"), Ah-gutch ("The Salmon"), Jah-win-pooh ("The Water Goes in the Path"), Jag-en-up ("The Mist After the Rain"), and Chief Jag-e-oh ("The Man Who Carries

---

[7] E. Gay to F. J. Porter, Box Elder, Utah Terr., August 15, 1859. U.S. Congress, Senate, Ex. Doc. 42, 36th Cong., 1st Sess., Serial No. 1033 (Washington, 1860), pp. 22-25; *Deseret News*, August 24, 1859, p. 196.

[8] Lynde to Adjutant at Camp Floyd, Bear River Ford, Utah Terr., August 26, 1859. U.S. Congress, Senate, Ex. Doc. 42, 36th Cong., 1st Sess., Serial No. 1033 (Washington, 1860), p. 32.

[9] *Deseret News*, September 14, 1859, p. 220.

the Arrows"). Lander pointed out in his letter that these subchiefs were renegades from both the Bannock and Shoshoni tribes, and that the principal chiefs of the two nations wanted an end of the depredations. Apparently Lander had made some sort of payment of annuity goods to the Indians because he noted that, although forty lodges of Bannock came in to the "payment," the "Kamas Prairie and Fort Boise Pannahs" refused to do so.[10]

A band of Shoshoni attacked a company under Daniel Beal on August 20 near Marsh Creek and killed one man. Part of the survivors were cared for by army doctors at Lynde's encampment.[11] A more disastrous affair occurred about September 2 some twenty-five miles west of Fort Hall between Portneuf Bridge and Snake River, in the heart of the Bannock country, when a party of six men, three women, and ten children was attacked at sundown by a band of Indians. Eight Americans were killed, and the survivors traveled for three days on foot before meeting a detachment of troops under Lieutenant Livingston. The soldiers were escorting a party to Walla Walla, but they stopped to send nine men back to investigate the scene of the massacre. There they found evidence typical of the kind that caused soldier and citizen alike to swear vengeance on all Indians, hostile or not:

One little girl five years old had both her legs cut off at the knees; her ears were also cut off and her eyes were

[10] F. W. Lander to Forney, Raft River, Washington Terr., August 16, 1859. U.S. Congress, Senate, Ex. Doc. 42, 36th Cong., 1st Sess., Serial No. 1033 (Washington, 1860), pp. 28-29, 31.

[11] *Deseret News*, September 7, 1859, p. 212.

dug out from their sockets, and to all appearance the girl, after having her legs cut off, had been compelled to walk on the stumps—for the sole purpose of gratifying the hellish propensity of savage barbarity.[12]

The difficulty of determining which Indians were guilty of such atrocities did not bother most emigrants or settlers. Their answer in most cases was to kill all "redskins." But the Indian Office and the army attempted to ferret out the perpetrators of such massacres, at the same time endeavoring to keep the other Indians from going on the warpath. In a letter to the military authorities at Camp Floyd, Superintendent Forney ascribed most of the forays to the Bannock and to three small bands of Shoshoni located in the Box Elder region of northern Utah. The good Shoshoni had left to join Washakie's band. Later, Forney indicated: "It is quite obvious to me that the Bannock Indians of Oregon have instigated all the northern difficulties; and that the Shoshonees of this Territory are only performing a secondary part."[13] Judge Eckels of Utah Territory asserted that the Bannock and a few Shoshoni were the principal offenders, but he also was certain that the Indians were sometimes led and abetted by white renegades. He cited the example of an attack on a train commanded by Nelson Miltimore in which some of the attackers spoke English and wore long beards.[14]

---

[12] Ibid., September 21, 1859, p. 227.

[13] Forney to Commanding Officer, Camp Floyd, Utah Terr., September 22, 1859. U.S. Congress, Senate, Ex. Doc. 42, 36th Cong., 1st Sess., Serial No. 1033 (Washington, 1860), p. 34.

[14] D. R. Eckels to J. Thompson, Camp Floyd, Utah Terr., September 23, 1859, ibid., p. 111.

After maintaining his force at Bear River Crossing for almost three months, in late October Major Lynde moved his command to Camp Floyd. His formal report of the summer operations described the obvious difficulties that any force would meet in trying to run down small and elusive bands of Indian adversaries. The emigration for the year had been great —as many as three hundred wagons per day having passed his camp. Although warned of Indian raids, many of the overland travelers had kept their weapons in the wagons and laughed at the soldiers who tried to warn them of possible attack.[15] Despite the efforts of the army on Bear River, the *Deseret News* was caustic in its criticism, describing the "farce" in which companies of soldiers intended to starve out the Indians, "A novel way of conducting an Indian war. . . ." After the troops had returned to Camp Floyd, an editorial sarcastically inquired: "How many officers will be promoted for 'gallant and meritorious conduct' during the campaign?"[16]

As a result of the army's experience in attempting to protect emigrants who would not protect themselves, Colonel A. S. Johnston summed up Major Lynde's activities and then made specific recommendations to his superior: (1) instead of roving patrols, troops should be stationed at Bear River Crossing, Fort Hall, and Goose Creek Mountains; (2) Indian agents should be appointed for the Bannock and Shoshoni to watch over the tribes and keep them away

---

[15] Lynde to Commanding Officer, Camp Floyd, Utah Terr., October 24, 1859, *ibid.*, p. 38.

[16] *Deseret News*, August 31, 1859, p. 204; *ibid.*, October 19, 1859, p. 260.

from emigrant roads; (3) troops should have orders to attack all Indians found near roads, on the assumption that they were hostile groups; (4) traders should be kept out of Indian areas; and (5) the Military Department of Utah should be extended to the forty-fourth parallel so that the troops would have jurisdiction in the home areas of the Bannock and Shoshoni.[17] The military authorities of Oregon recognized this difficulty of policing the faraway Bear River country, and Captain H. D. Wallan of Oregon advised the necessity of co-operating with the Utah military to patrol the Oregon Trail. His reconnaissance along that road to Salt Lake City, in 1859, gave him some acquaintance with "the athletic. . . , well-armed, and formidable" Bannock and the necessity for a strong force to keep them in check.[18]

By 1860 the Bannock apparently were divided into two large groups—a southern one of forty-five lodges (about three hundred people) , under Chief Mopeah or "Bush of Hair in the Forehead," and a northern one of sixty lodges under Chief Le Grand Coquin. When F. W. Lander gave an annuity payment (their first) to Chief Mopeah's band in July, 1859, at Salt River, he did not think that the Bannock were "irreclaimably hostile," but admitted that their "horse-stealing proclivities" prevented friendly relations with the whites from lasting long. The main obstacle to

---

[17] Johnston to Scott, Camp Floyd, Utah Terr., November 2, 1859. U.S. Congress, Senate, Ex. Doc. 42, 36th Cong., 1st Sess., Serial No. 1033 (Washington, 1860) , pp. 25-27.

[18] H. D. Wallan to Superintendent of Indian Affairs for Oregon and Washington Territories, Fort Vancouver, December 10, 1859. U.S. Congress, House of Representatives, *Depredations and Massacres by the Snake River Indians*, Ex. Doc. 46, 36th Cong., 2nd Sess., Serial No. 1099 (Washington, 1860), p. 8.

a permanent peace, as all the chiefs pointed out, was the refusal of many of the young men to give up their quest for the honors of battle. Their activities inevitably dragged the rest of the tribe into difficulties with the whites. As Chief Pocatello put it, "there were some things that he could not manage, and among them were the bad thoughts of his young men towards the whites, on account of the deeds of the whites towards his tribe."[19] Certainly the events of 1859 had emphasized the growing friction between the two peoples, and the early 1860's continued the theme.

During the years 1860 and 1861, sporadic attempts were made by the Indian Office of the Northwest to quiet the Bannock and scattered Shoshoni tribes. Reports were circulated, in February of 1860, that the Bannock had fled to the mountains in fear of retaliation by the troops for depredations committed during the winter in the Green River area.[20] Three months later, the Indian Superintendent wrote from Portland, Oregon, to Major John Owen, placing the Snake River Indians under his "temporary supervision" and instructing him to visit the Bannock and Shoshoni at Fort Hall. After distributing presents to the tribes, he was to tell them to cease their depredations and prepare for a council to be held in July of the next year, at which time a special agent appointed by the President of the United States would visit them. This suggestion was in line with Owen's repeated requests

---

[19] F. W. Lander to Commissioner of Indian Affairs, Washington, February 10, 1860, *ibid.*, pp. 121-37.

[20] Will H. Wagner to F. W. Lander, February 29, 1860. U.S. Congress, House of Representatives, *Fort Kearney, South Pass, and Honey Lake Wagon Road*, Ex. Doc. 63, 36th Cong., 2nd Sess., Serial No. 1100 (Washington, 1860), p. 25.

for a council with the Indians. But, as had happened in the past, the supply of presents failed to arrive, and the Owen mission to Fort Hall was a failure.[21] By September, 1861, the proposed council meeting still had not taken place, and the Indian agent could only report that the Bannock and their allies justified their raids against the whites because the government officials had never "talked with them; have never given them any presents, have not even broke tobacco with them, or smoked with them, while the Blackfeet and other Indian tribes have had presents from our people for the privilege of making roads through their country."[22]

A good example of the insolence and disdain with which the Bannock regarded the whites at this time was reported by Granville Stuart, who headed a party of traders into the Big Hole country of Montana in late 1860. Under Chief Le Grand Coquin, or "Arro-ka-kee," the Bannock displayed open hostility to the whites and quite brazenly killed one of the herd of cattle belonging to the traders. Stuart's description of Le Grand Coquin might explain the reason for the term "big," as used in reference to the chief, because the Indian leader was six feet two inches in height and weighed about two hundred and seventy-five pounds.[23]

From the Big Hole River to the Humboldt River, government officials were aware of the Bannock and

[21] Geary to Owen, Portland, Oregon, May 23, 1860, Owen, *op. cit.*, II, 209; Owen to Geary, Flathead Agency, Washington Terr., September 2, 1860, *ibid.*, II, 222.

[22] *Report of the Commissioner of Indian Affairs, 1861*, p. 156.

[23] Granville Stuart, *Forty Years on the Frontier;* ed. by Paul C. Phillips (2 vols.; Cleveland, 1925), I, 155.

their depredations, and the great range of the tribe helped to explain the problem faced by the military and the Indian Office in their endeavor to keep the Bannock under control. Lieutenant Colonel Smith of Camp Floyd wrote in May, 1860, that "the Indians, Bannocks principally, intend to plunder every train that passes over the road [Humboldt] this summer. . . ."[24] Smith indicated that he would send out patrols to guard the roads, a precaution that Colonel Lander also advised in his report on the emigrant roads. Again, the problem of jurisdiction came up, this time because the creation of the new territory of Nevada left its Indian agents with only hazy notions as to whether or not the Bannock and certain Shoshoni were under their charge.[25]

While there were not as many attacks on emigrant trains during 1860 and 1861 as there had been in 1859, scattered reports indicated that the Bannock and a few Shoshoni bands still had to be watched. In Cache Valley, Utah, a party of citizens arrested an Indian for stealing a horse. Ten more Indians rode up and demanded the release of their comrade. Although the whites warned the arrested man that he would be shot if he tried to escape, he made the attempt anyway and was killed. After a short engagement with the citizens, the rest of the Indians withdrew and, coming upon an unsuspecting group of white men, killed two and wounded three of their number.[26] A month later, in September of 1860, a

---

[24] U.S. Congress, Senate, *Report of the Secretary of War*, Ex. Doc., 36th Cong., 2nd Sess., Serial No. 1079 (Washington, 1860), p. 70.

[25] *Report of the Commissioner of Indian Affairs, 1861*, p. 109.

[26] *Deseret News*, August 1, 1860, p. 173; *ibid.*, October 3, 1860, p. 248.

wagon train near the City of Rocks, west of Fort Hall, was attacked by a band of sixty Indians, but the timely arrival of a patrol of soldiers prevented any loss of life. The emigrants lost all their equipment and were left in a destitute condition.[27]

During this two-year period, 1860-61, the incident which apparently aroused the most excitement among settlers and government officials was the infamous "Otter Massacre." The forty-four members of this emigrant party fought for their lives in August, 1860, when a band of Snakes or Bannock set upon them as they were traveling along Snake River about twenty miles below Shoshone Falls. Eighteen were killed in the engagement, five died of wounds and were eaten by the starving survivors, four children were taken prisoner, two children were lost in the mountains, and only fifteen escaped. The captive children caused great concern, and every effort was made to find them. Major John Owen was instructed to search for them in his district and, while consenting to do so, could not refrain from pointing out that a share of the burden for such affairs as the Otter massacre rested on the shoulders of the whites:

. . . These Indians [Bannock and Shoshoni] twelve years ago were the avowed friends of the White Man I have had their Young Men in My Employment as Hunters Horse Guards Guides &c &c I have traversed the length & breadth of their Entire Country with large bands of Stock unmolested. Their present hostile attitude can in a great Measure be attributed

---

[27] U.S. Congress, House of Representatives, *Indian Depredations in Oregon and Washington*, Ex. Doc. 29, 36th Cong., 2nd Sess., Serial No. 1097 (Washington, 1860), pp. 79, 85; U.S. Congress, Senate, *Report of the Secretary of War*, Ex. Doc., 36th Cong., 2nd Sess., Serial No. 1079 (Washington, 1860), p. 143.

to the treatment they have recd from unprincipled White Men passing through their Country. They have been robd Murdered their women outraged &c &c and in fact outrages have been committed by White Men that the heart would Shudder to record.[28]

Owen instructed his agent, L. L. Blake, to choose two competent Bannock and Shoshoni interpreters and then to visit the two tribes in an endeavor to discover the whereabouts of the lost children. In addition, Blake was to procure all the information possible for transmission to the Military Department of Oregon which intended to send a military expedition against the Fort Hall Indians during 1861.

As usual, the movement against the tribes was not made. In fact, Owen found it impossible to visit them in late 1861 because the annuity goods did not arrive at Fort Owen. In a council held during the spring of the year, the few Bannock and Shoshoni who attended denied any complicity in the Otter massacre and ascribed it to the Indians of the Humboldt Sink area.[29] On the other hand, Chief San Pitch, of a Utah Shoshoni band, reported to Utah Agent Benjamin Davies that the Bannock were holding the four captive children in the Goose Creek Mountains. San Pitch offered to aid in locating the children, and also promised to "commit no more murders or robberies on emigrants." Despite Davies' belief that this leader would "faithfully observe" his pledge, the Sho-

---

[28] Owen to Geary, Flathead Agency, Washington Terr., February 13, 1861, Owen, *op. cit.*, II, 243.

[29] Owen to L. L. Blake, Flathead Agency, Washington Terr., February 18, 1861, *ibid.*, II, 247-48; Owen to B. F. Kendall, Portland, Oregon, September 12, 1861, *ibid.*, II, 262-63.

shoni's offer of eternal friendship was evidently only
following the Indian pattern of promising anything
and of throwing the blame for depredations onto
another group.[30]

A good barometer of the mounting tempo of Indian
opposition was the overland mail. The various concerns engaged in the cross-country postal business
noted a definite rise in the number of attacks by
Indians on the mail carriers. Beginning in 1851, the
troubles had increased until, by 1862, they had become chronic. They continued until the Indian Peace
Commission of 1867 succeeded in quieting most of
the tribes.[31] Indeed, the year 1862 provided the newspapers and Indian agents with so many stories of
depredations that the accounts tended to become almost repetitious.

The Bannock started the year early by attacking
their old friends, the Flathead, in the Hell Gate Defile in Montana country. Besides killing two of the
defenders, the Bannock destroyed the equipment of
the Flathead and ran off their horses. Major Owen
could not understand the changed attitude and wrote
that the two tribes had been on friendly terms for
many years.[32] Later in the spring, several small white
companies that left Salt Lake City for the new Salmon
River mines found the Indians so hostile that they
were forced to fortify themselves in a good defensive
position, and were afraid to leave until reinforcements

---

[30] *Report of the Commissioner of Indian Affairs, 1861*, p. 133.

[31] LeRoy R. Hafen, *The Overland Mail* (Cleveland, 1926), pp. 64, 67, 242.

[32] Owen, *op. cit.*, I, 254.

arrived. A pack train, traveling in the other direction from Salmon River, was raided by a band of Indians and lost eight men in the fight.[33]

As early as the first part of August, which traditionally marked the beginning of intensive Indian depredations, the *Deseret News* remarked that "The immigration for the last fifteen years, has hardly ever been freed from their [Indian] attentions; but for the last few months the Red Skins, especially the Snakes and Bannocks, appear to have unreservedly seceded from 'the rest of mankind.' "[34] The editor seemed to think that the mining operation on Salmon River was the chief cause of the unrest.[35] But James D. Doty of the Utah Indian Superintendency became convinced that the two tribes were determined to wage "war" on the United States. Chief Little Soldier of the Utah Diggers was his informant and, according to the story, the Bannock and Shoshoni had formed an alliance for the purpose of annihilating all settlers and emigrants in their country. To achieve this end they had set aside the great "peace" chief, Washakie, and had elected Pash-e-go, a Bannock chief and "man of blood," as his successor. Anticipating a general uprising against the whites in late fall, the warriors were then taking their families to the Salmon River Mountains to remove them from danger. All these movements and preparations were instigated by War-i-gika,

[33] *Deseret News,* May 28, 1862, p. 381; *Sacramento Union,* July 7, 1862, p. 1.

[34] *Deseret News,* August 13, 1862, p. 30.

[35] *Ibid.,* August 6, 1862, p. 45.

the great Bannock prophet in whom the Bannock and Shoshoni had unbounded confidence.[36]

Conditions had become so bad in the general Snake River area by August and September that it was necessary for public notices to be posted, warning emigrants. On Blackfoot River, the heart of the Bannock homeland, one traveler found a notice advising all small parties to combine into large wagon trains before proceeding any farther.[37] The situation was so serious that Indian Commissioner Charles E. Mix published the following proclamation:

TO THE PUBLIC: From information received at this department, deemed sufficiently reliable to warrant me in so doing, I consider it my duty to warn all persons contemplating the crossing of the plains this fall, to Utah or the Pacific Coast, that there is good reason to apprehend hostilities on the part of the Bannock and Shoshone or Snake Indians, as well as the Indians upon the plains and along the Platte river.

The Indians referred to have, during the past summer, committed several robberies and murders; they are numerous, powerful, and warlike, and should they generally assume a hostile attitude are capable of rendering the emigrant routes across the plains extremely perilous; hence this warning.[38]

Superintendent Doty of Utah was able to underscore these warnings by compiling a long list of depredations that had been reported to him. In June

---

[36] *Report of the Commissioner of Indian Affairs, 1862*, p. 213. The prophet, War-i-gika, was no doubt the same prophet referred to by C. H. Miller in 1859. Both accounts spoke of him as residing in the Walla Walla country.

[37] R. H. Hewitt, *Notes By the Way; Journey Across the Plains* (Olympia, 1863), p. 26.

[38] *Report of Commissioner of Indian Affairs, 1862*, p. 215.

a group of Californians headed toward the States was attacked by "Eastern Bannocks," and all but two killed. Three emigrant trains were plundered near Soda Springs and all the people killed. During the following month, several trains were attacked; and, as Doty suggested, there were many depredations which were never reported. Another party of Californians was attacked in September while on its way east, six men being killed. The Indians involved in this affair had American horses and carried a new American flag.[39]

Fort Bridger felt the wrath of the Indians when two hundred horses were stolen from the post. A long chase by sixty-two volunteers resulted in the recapture of only about forty of the animals. A company bound for Salmon River had five men killed and two badly wounded. Six or seven members of an Iowa company were killed when they were attacked on Sublette's Cutoff. The survivors lost all their equipment and supplies and were forced to spend the winter in the northern Utah settlements. The *Deseret News* reported that "emigrants, ferrymen and mountaineers were abandoning the route entirely, afraid to continue longer in the country."[40]

No longer was the raiding being done by small bands of renegades, but as many as three hundred warriors gathered to harass and destroy the emigrant trains. This fact was emphasized in the incident that

---

[39] *Ibid.*, pp. 210-11; *Sacramento Union*, October 2, 1862, p. 2; *Deseret News*, September 24, 1862, p. 100.

[40] *Deseret News*, September 17, 1862, p. 92; *ibid.*, August 13, 1862, p. 52; *ibid.*, August 27, 1862, p. 69; *Sacramento Union*, September 22, 1862, p. 5.

came to be known as "Massacre Rocks." West of the American Falls of Snake River, a small party of eleven wagons was attacked by about one hundred Indians and, by the time a larger wagon train appeared, most of the men in the small group had been killed. The next morning a force of forty well-armed whites took the trail of the Indians to recover the stolen stock; but when three hundred mounted warriors descended upon them, the travelers retreated immediately, three more men having been killed. Fearing to proceed to California until reinforcements came along, the whites waited until they numbered almost seven hundred people, with two hundred wagons, before heading west. The group was harassed by Indians all the way to the Humboldt and had constantly to be on guard.[41]

Also suffering from the general Indian disturbance were the Mormon settlements of northern Utah. The Utah Shoshoni bands and their Bannock friends stole horses at every opportunity, and they became so bold and insistent that, in many instances, the Mormon policy of "it is easier to feed than to fight them" was fast becoming outright blackmail as the settlers' supplies of beef and flour disappeared into the hands of the Indians.[42]

It is little wonder that the citizens of Utah looked with expectancy upon the coming of Colonel Patrick E. Connor and his California Volunteers on September 10 as an assurance at last that the government intend-

---

[41] *Deseret News*, November 26, 1862, p. 173; Byron Defenbach, *Idaho, the Place and Its People* (3 vols.; Chicago and New York, 1933), I, 405-6.

[42] *Deseret News*, September 10, 1862, p. 85; *ibid.*, October 8, 1862, p. 116.

ed to stop the Indian assaults in the territory.[43] Connor's military force was sent to Salt Lake City to afford protection to the mail routes and, as some people suspected, also to keep an eye on the Mormons while the Civil War was in progress. Opportunity soon came for the troops to display their ability as Indian fighters. Major Edward McGarry, with two companies of soldiers, was instructed to rescue a white boy who had been captured by Chief Bear Hunter of a Shoshoni band. In a dawn attack upon Bear Hunter and about forty of his people in Cache Valley, the troops surrounded the Indian village but captured only two squaws and one brave, the other warriors having escaped to a near-by hill. After a short battle the Indians asked for a parley, and the whites held Bear Hunter and four others as hostages until the boy was brought in. Three Indians had been killed during the engagement.[44]

A second expedition under Major McGarry left Salt Lake City on December 4 to attempt to recover some of the stock taken from emigrants during the preceding fall, and "to give them [Indians] a little taste of the fighting qualities of the Volunteers, should opportunity present."[45]   Near Bear River the troops captured four Indians and then sent an Indian boy to the encampment of the Shoshoni and Bannock with the message that the four prisoners would be exe-

[43] *Ibid.*, September 10, 1862, p. 85.

[44] McGarry to Adjutant General, Camp Douglas, Utah Terr., November 28, 1862, in *The War of the Rebellion, a Compilation of the Official Records of the Union and Confederate Armies* (Washington, 1897), Series I, Vol. L, Part I, p. 182.

[45] *Deseret News*, December 10, 1862, p. 188.

cuted unless the stolen stock was brought into the army camp by the next day at noon. Upon receipt of the information, the Indians packed up and started into Bear River Canyon, making no attempt to return the cattle and horses. Living up to his promise, the major had the four prisoners shot the next day. The *Deseret News* believed that the execution would make the Indians more hostile than ever, and reports soon came in substantiating this belief. The Indians held several councils in the vicinity of Bear River and determined to avenge the killing of their four men, being "mad, and determined to do as much injury as possible to the white race. . . ."[46]

The animosity of the Indians along Bear River soon became evident. George Clayton and Henry Bean, dispatch carriers from Bannock City, were killed shortly after McGarry's meeting with the Shoshoni bands, and friendly Indians reported that the hostile bands were determined to kill every white man they should meet north of Bear River until the deaths of their comrades had been avenged.[47] On January 3 a group of ten men, en route from the mines to Salt Lake City, was annihilated by the Indians. Only three days later, a party of eight men coming in from the Salmon River mines was attacked at Bear River and one, John Smith, was killed.[48]

As a result of the death of John Smith, William Bevins, one of the survivors of the party, filed an affidavit before Chief Justice John F. Kinney of Utah Ter-

---

[46] *Ibid.*, December 17, 1862, p. 197; *ibid.*, December 31, 1862, p. 212.
[47] *Ibid.*, January 14, 1863, p. 232.
[48] *Ibid.*, January 21, 1863, p. 237; *ibid.*, January 28, 1863, p. 244.

ritory concerning the death of his partner. The justice issued a warrant for the arrest of Bear Hunter, San Pitch, and Sagwitch, the Shoshoni chiefs accused of the crime, and assigned service of the warrant to Marshal Isaac L. Gibbs. The marshal, under Kinney's direction, requested military assistance from Colonel Patrick E. Connor and his California Volunteers. But Connor reported: "I informed the marshal that my arrangements for our expedition against the Indians were made, and that it was not my intention to take any prisoners, but that he could accompany me."[49] Thus, the colonel had already decided upon a full-scale punitive expedition against the whole group of Northern Utah Indians "to chastize them if possible" for their depredations upon travelers.

To forestall the possibility that the Indians might run for the mountains if they saw a large body of troops approaching, Connor determined upon the greatest possible secrecy and started his infantry on the march from Salt Lake City on the night of January 22, 1863. The cavalry left two days later, both detachments traveling by night and resting by day. News of the approach of the troops soon reached Franklin, Idaho, however. Chief Bear Hunter and some of his braves came into the settlement and did a war dance around the house of Preston Thomas, the Mormon bishop, demanding more gifts of wheat. Bear Hunter returned the next day and was informed by the Mormons that the soldiers were only a short distance away and that he might be killed; whereupon he rejoined, "May-be-so soldiers get killed too." But

---

[49] *The War of the Rebellion, op. cit.,* pp. 185, 187.

the chief immediately left for camp to warn his people.[50]

Early on the morning of January 29, Colonel Connor moved his cavalry in advance of the infantry in order to ensure that the Indians would not get away. At daybreak the encampment was sighted on the north side of Bear River, and the troops swam their horses across the ice-laden stream to begin the attack. The Indian position was well selected, being in a deep ravine about one mile from the river. A treeless plain in front gave them a clear field of fire on the troops. To the right, the mouth of the ravine on Bear River, and to the left, the head of the ravine near some low hills afforded them two avenues of escape. They had intertwined the thick willows in the gulch to form a chain of natural fortifications, and they had dug holes in the side of the ravine to afford firing positions. The women and children were in the tipis at the bottom of the defile.[51]

As soon as the troops had crossed Bear River and approached the mile-long plain leading to the Indian position, one of the chiefs came out from the ravine and rode up and down in front of his men dangling a spear on which hung a scalp. The warriors, meanwhile, shouted to the approaching troops, "Fours right, fours left; come on you California sons of b——!" The Indians began to shoot as soon as the soldiers were in range, and the effectiveness of their fire

---

[50] *Ibid.*, p. 186; Franklin County (Idaho) Historical Society, *The Passing of the Redman* (Preston, Idaho, 1917) ; Fred B. Rogers, *Soldiers of the Overland* (San Francisco, 1938) , p. 70.

[51] *War of the Rebellion, op. cit.*, p. 186; Rogers, *op. cit.*, p. 71; *Deseret News*, February 11, 1863, p. 260.

A chief rode in front of his men dangling a spear on which hung a scalp

soon forced the army men to dismount and take up positions as skirmishers. In fact, the principal white casualties of the fight occurred during this first exchange. As soon as the infantry arrived, Colonel Connor sent a detachment of cavalry to aid them in crossing the river, so that finally over two hundred men were in combat with the Indians. After the first frontal attack, the commanding officer sent detachments to either flank of the ravine. Their enfilading fire soon converted the Indian avenues of escape into death traps. The battle lasted over four hours, and the Indians fought courageously, as indeed they must, with no possible means of escape in sight. Toward the end of the engagement, the affair became almost a massacre as the Indians broke from the ravine and attempted to escape.[52]

The list of casualties suffered by both sides depicted graphically the intensity of the struggle. The most careful account of casualties placed the soldier losses at twenty-three dead, forty-four wounded, and seventy-nine disabled by freezing. Estimates of the number of Indians killed ranged from the Connor report of two hundred and twenty-four known dead to nearly four hundred, as noted by Corporal Tuttle of the attacking force. The Indian casualties were at least three hundred. In his official report, Connor mentioned that he left a small quantity of wheat for the "160 captive squaws and children" that survived the battle, but did not say how many of these noncombatants were killed. The correspondent of the

---

[52] *War of the Rebellion, op. cit.,* pp. 186-87; Rogers, *op. cit.,* pp. 71-73; *Deseret News,* February 11, 1863, p. 261; *Sacramento Union,* February 17, 1863, p. 1.

Sacramento Union wrote that "In the melee among the willows, several women and children were wounded, which was unavoidable under the circumstances."[53]

William Hull, one of three Mormons sent by Bishop Thomas the next day to search for Indian survivors, has left a graphic description of the battleground:

> Never will I forget the scene, dead bodies were everywhere. I counted eight deep in one place and in several places they were three to five deep; all in all we counted nearly four hundred; two-thirds of this number being women and children.
>
> We found two Indian women alive whose thighs had been broken by the bullets. Two little boys and one little girl about three years of age were still living. The little girl was badly wounded having eight flesh wounds in her body. They were very willing to go with us. We took them on our horses to the sleigh, and made them as comfortable as possible.[54]

Various reports indicated that perhaps as many as one hundred warriors escaped by swimming the river or by means of the hills to the left of the ravine. The chiefs Pocatello and Sagwitch missed the battle, having left the day before. Chief Bear Hunter was killed while making bullets at a campfire. After the fight Connor's forces destroyed the seventy tipis found hidden in the willows and captured one hundred and seventy-five horses, over one thousand bushels of

---

[53] *Sacramento Union*, February 12, 1863, p. 3.
[54] Daughters of Idaho Pioneers, *History of the Development of Southeastern Idaho* (1930), p. 13.

wheat, and much plunder that undoubtedly had been taken from emigrant trains.[55]

Although some criticisms were made of Connor's ruthless tactics of taking no prisoners, and of his near-massacre methods in the final stages of the battle, most Westerners would have agreed with the members of the Mormon Church branch at Logan that the action of Colonel Connor was the "intervention of the Almighty, in subduing the Indians of the Bear River area.[56]

The battle did have far-reaching significance as far as the Bannock were concerned. From 1863 to the present, most accounts of the engagement list the Indians who took part as "Bannock and Shoshone." It should be pointed out, however, that all the chiefs involved were Shoshoni, the leaders of Northern Utah Shoshoni bands. Undoubtedly some Bannock warriors did participate in the fight, but the affair was mainly directed and fought by the Shoshoni of the Bear River country. The significance to the Bannock of the battle of Bear River did not lie in the number of their warriors who may have been slain there, but in the effective and merciless manner in which the troops of the United States could and did check the resistance of a hostile tribe. The lesson struck home to the Bannock and to many of the other Indians along the western reaches of the Oregon and

---

[55] *War of the Rebellion, op. cit.,* pp. 186-87; Rogers, *op. cit.,* pp. 74-76; *Deseret News,* February 11, 1863, p. 261.

[56] Edward W. Tullidge, *History of Salt Lake City* (Salt Lake City, 1886), p. 76.

California trails.[57] Superintendent Doty summed it up in his report for 1863:

The battle with the Shoshones . . . on Bear River was the severest and most bloody of any which has ever occurred with the Indians west of the Mississippi. . . . It struck terror into the hearts of the savages hundreds of miles away from the battle field.[58]

---

[57] Hebard marveled at the "recuperative powers" of the Bannock as a result of the battle of Bear River, assuming, as have many writers, that the major portion of the Indians involved were Bannock: "On the word of James P. Beckwourth they were 'annihilated' by the trappers in 1826, and on the word of Joseph L. Meek again in 1836. The latter event . . . was not, however, an annihilation, though it was a defeat sufficiently decisive to keep them fairly peaceful for many years. But it was again necessary to chastise them during the Civil War and Colonel . . . Patrick E. Connor did the job with great thoroughness in the famous Bear River fight of January 29, 1863." Hebard, *op. cit.*, p. 357.

[58] U.S. Congress, House of Representatives, Ex. Doc. 381, 38th Cong., 1st Sess., Serial No. 1182 (Washington, 1863), p. 539.

Treaty Period, 1863-1869

THE salutary effects of the battle at Bear River permeated the entire Snake River area and lasted until well into the 1870's. From 1863 to 1869, newspaper accounts and letters of Indian agents carried fewer reports of depredations. In March of 1863, a correspondent of the *San Francisco Bulletin* suggested that the whites might expect more trouble from the "meanest Indians out" (the Bannock) when spring came.[1] Despite these expectations, the *Deseret News,* a month later, could record only that the Indians were far from friendly and desired vengeance for their defeat at Bear River.[2] Near Brigham City, a band of Indians did mistreat a boy herding cattle and, although prevented from driving off the herd, they succeeded in killing one white during their flight from the scene.[3] Emigrants to Oregon reported seeing Indians on Camas Prairie, but indicated that the natives were quite peaceful. The travelers passed on a rumor that a wagon train had been attacked about forty miles west of Fort Hall.[4]

---

[1] *San Francisco Bulletin*, May 5, 1863, p. 3.

[2] *Deseret News,* April 22, 1863, p. 341.

[3] *Ibid.,* May 13, 1863, p. 364.

[4] Maury to Adjutant General, Oregon District, Boise River, Idaho Terr., July 13, 1863, in *The War of the Rebellion, a Compilation of the Official Records of the Union and Confederate Armies* (Washington, 1897), Series I, Vol. L, Part I, p 216.

Not only had Bannock and Shoshoni forays almost ceased, but these Indians became the objects of attack themselves. Superintendent James D. Doty visited the Indians of Camas Prairie during the summer of 1863 and learned that Chief Snag and two others of his band had been murdered in Bannock City by a group of miners. Proceeding to the Montana town to investigate, Doty discovered that the report was true. The chief and his two men had come in at the demand of the whites of the settlement to surrender an alleged white child which they held. The child turned out to be a half-breed and a member of the tribe; but while the three Indians were sitting peacefully in the street, a group of miners shot them down. Doty revealed his helplessness to do anything about arresting the murderers as "there were no civil officers there, and no laws but such as have been adopted by the miners."[5]

The attitude of the whites of the Snake River area toward the Indians was well summarized in an editorial of the Boise *Idaho Statesman* for October 6, 1867:

We are of that class of philanthropists who do not believe in waging a war of extermination against the Indian. We rather incline to the more Christian-like mode of making treaties for the establishment of peaceful relations with them. This would be our plan of establishing friendship upon an eternal basis with our Indians: Let all the hostile bands of Idaho Territory be called in (they will not be caught in any other manner) to attend a grand treaty; plenty of blankets and nice little trinkets distributed among them; plenty of

[5] U.S. Office of Indian Affairs, *Annual Report of the Commissioner of Indian Affairs, 1863* (Washington, 1864), p. 539.

grub on hand; have a real jolly time with them; then just
before the big feast put strychnine in their meat and poison
to death the last mother's son of them.[6]

With such an attitude on the part of the whites,
and with their ability to back up their promises of
avenging depredations by calling on United States
troops, it was little wonder that, after the Bear River
battle, the Indians preferred to spend their time in
the buffalo country away from the danger of troubles
with the other race.

Except for certain intertribal difficulties, the Bannock and Shoshoni were inclined to be quiet and
peaceful during the later 1860's. One overland traveler noted that he expected little trouble from the two
tribes and, upon meeting with a group of Bannock
hunters, found them to be friendly and also talkative
as far as he could understand their " 'chinook,' a
sort of gibberish made up of French, English, and
Indian."[7] In a defense of their previous warlike attitude, the Commissioner of Indian Affairs argued that
the scarcity of game and the settlement of the whites
in their country had reduced these Indians to extreme destitution and had compelled them to resort
to plundering activities in order to get the necessaries
of life. Said he, "It is not to be expected that a wild
and warlike people will tamely submit to the occupation of their country by another race, and to starvation as a consequence thereof. . . ."[8] Agent John

---

[6] *Idaho Statesman*, October 6, 1867, p. 2.

[7] Lewis F. Crawford (ed.), *Rekindling Camp Fires, The Exploits of
Ben Arnold (Connor)* [Cedar Rapids, 1926], pp. 66, 79.

[8] *Report of the Commissioner of Indian Affairs, 1864*, p. 155.

Burche of Nevada reported that the tendency of all the tribes, after the battle of Bear River, was to keep away from the emigrant roads during the summer in order to lessen the chance of trouble with the whites. Chief Winnemucca of the Nevada Paiute met Burche in council in May, 1863, and promised to persuade Chief Pas-se-quah (Pas-ego) of the "Pannakes of Nevada and Idaho" to come in to a conference. At Humboldt River the agent met the two chiefs, and Pasego promised that no depredations would be committed by the Bannock if the whites refrained from aggressive acts. To ensure peace, the chief said he intended to keep his people away from the Humboldt Road and away from the courses of overland travel. The promise was kept, and no accounts of murders or robberies reached the ears of the Nevada Indian agent. He characterized the Bannock as the "most powerful and warlike tribe that dwell between the Rocky Mountains and the Pacific," and described in detail their magnificent horses and large stores of rifles and ammunition.[9]

In great part, as far as the regions traversed by the Oregon and California trails were concerned, the conditions of peace after the battle of Bear River came as a result of the various treaties which were negotiated by representatives of the Indian Office with the different bands of Shoshoni and the Bannock during 1863. General Connor's victory, and his later demonstrations of force in the Snake River Valley, convinced the Indians of the necessity of coming to terms with

---

[9] *Ibid.*, pp. 289-92.

the government if they wished to escape the wrath of the troops.

Rumors came in to the army at Camp Douglas, during April of 1863, that the Shoshoni chief, Pocatello, who had escaped the Bear River slaughter, was eager for a fight with General Connor. Although the Bannock had left for the vicinity of the Wind River Mountains, Connor determined to visit the Fort Hall area anyway, in the hope that he could complete the job of subduing all the Shoshoni bands.[10] Another purpose of his northern expedition was to establish a military post at Soda Springs for the protection of the overland emigration to Oregon and California. In early June Connor left Salt Lake City with a large force of cavalry, proceeding at night and resting by day, in the hope of surprising the "bloodthirsty redskins." The command was disappointed in its attempt to "scare up a few hundred wild Shoshones or Bannocks," and presently began to march by day.[11] At Snake River Ferry, General Connor came upon seventeen lodges of Shoshoni, whose male occupants left at the approach of the "Black Coats." The warriors came back into camp when they learned that the general merely wished to talk to them. Eventually, about three hundred Shoshoni gathered for a "pow wow," and Connor and Superintendent Doty attempted to impress on them that their attacks must cease or they would be given the same treatment that their friends had received in the previous January. Presents were then distributed to them. The chiefs Pocatello,

---

[10] *Deseret News*, April 22, 1863, p. 341.
[11] *San Francisco Bulletin*, June 20, 1863, p. 1.

Sagwitch, and San Pitch were never found, having left for safer areas.[12]

Agent Doty left the military force at Snake River Ferry and traveled on to Camas Prairie. En route, and at the prairie, he met only scattered bands of Indians, all of whom professed the greatest friendliness toward the whites and the United States government.[13] The council meeting at Snake River and the show of force by the troups accomplished immediate results—evidenced by Jacob Meeks' appearance at Salt Lake City early in August with twelve or fifteen stolen horses which the Indians had given up at the suggestion of General Connor. Four Bannock chiefs accompanied Meeks and had an interview with Doty. They indicated that their people were in a destitute condition and that they desired peace with the whites and aid from the government. The Superintendent of Indian Affairs supplied them with three thousand pounds of flour and six or eight beef cattle, with the understanding that he and General Connor would meet them in five or six weeks at Snake River for the purpose of signing a treaty of peace.[14]

The visit of the four Indian leaders to Salt Lake City was, no doubt, motivated by the fact that two treaties had already been signed between the government and two of the Shoshoni tribes. Doty and Agent Mann had negotiated a treaty with Chief Washakie and the Eastern Shoshoni at Fort Bridger on July 2, and Doty and Connor had signed a treaty with the

[12] *War of the Rebellion, op. cit.,* pp. 226, 227.

[13] *Report of the Commissioner of Indian Affairs, 1863,* p. 515.

[14] *Deseret News,* August 5, 1863, p. 29.

Northwestern Shoshoni under Chief Pocatello at Box Elder on July 30. The agreements provided for terms of amity and peace, the government agreeing to supply a certain amount of annuity goods each year in recognition of the fact that the white settlers and emigrants had destroyed the grass and the wild game which had formerly provided the living for these Indians. On October 1 the Western Shoshoni at Ruby Valley, Nevada, assented to a similar pact, and the Gosiute Shoshoni of "Tuilla Valley," west of Salt Lake City, signed a treaty on October 12.[15]

Two days later, Superintendent Doty, accompanied by General Connor, kept his promise to the Bannock by coming to terms with them at the Treaty of Soda Springs. These "mixed bands of Bannocks and Shoshones," one hundred and fifty men with their families, were under the principal Bannock chief, "Tosokwauberaht" (Le Grand Coquin) , and two sub-chiefs, "Taghee" and "Matigund." Doty estimated the total population of the tribe to be about one thousand.

After terms of friendship had been agreed upon, Doty, in behalf of the government, agreed to pay the Bannock five thousand dollars a year in annuity goods to compensate them for damages done to their pasture lands and hunting grounds and to aid in their subsistence. The peculiar thing about this financial settle-

---

[15] *Report of the Commissioner of Indian Affairs, 1864*, p. 155; Charles J. Kappler (ed.) , *Indian Affairs, Laws and Treaties* (2 vols.; Washington, 1903) , II, 649-52.

A correspondent of the *Sacramento Union* reported that, during the "talk" preceding the treaty at Fort Bridger, the Shoshoni were forced to acknowledge Washakie as their chief again, and they claimed that "they had been induced to act badly by the Bannocks" but would be good in the future. *Sacramento Union*, July 19, 1863, p. 1.

ment was that the five thousand dollars was to come from the ten-thousand-dollar annuity which had been promised to Chief Washakie and his Eastern Shoshoni under the treaty of July 2, signed at Fort Bridger. This sharing of annuities resulted in mutual dissatisfaction. In effect, it was a violation of the Fort Bridger agreement, because the annuity of the Eastern Shoshoni was thus reduced to five thousand dollars without their consent.

In addition to the annuity settlement, Article II of the agreement also adopted all of the provisions of the treaties concluded with the Eastern Shoshoni and the Northwestern bands of Shoshoni earlier in July. Article III exacted a promise from the Bannock that they would not molest travelers along the Oregon and California trails and along the new roads between Salt Lake City and the mines near Boise City and Beaver Head; and, in return, the assembled Indians received three thousand dollars' worth of provisions and goods distributed by Agent Doty as a representative of the government. The final article, IV, defined the country claimed by the Bannock as extending from the lower part of Humboldt River and Shoshone Falls on Snake River eastward to the Wind River Mountains.[16]

The five treaties negotiated by Doty, in 1863, with the various Shoshoni tribes and the Bannock were confirmed with minor amendments by the Senate of

[16] *Report of the Commissioner of Indian Affairs, 1864*, pp. 317-19; *Report . . . 1865*, p. 143; *Report . . . 1867*, p. 188; U.S. National Archives, Records of the Bureau of Indian Affairs, "Unratified Treaty of October 14, 1863, between the United States and the Mixed Bands of Shoshone and Bannack," Record Group 75.

the United States. It was then necessary to hold conferences with the five groups to get their consent to
the revised treaties. During 1864 the Shoshoni of
Ruby Valley, Box Elder County, and Tooele Valley
were met and gave consent to the new agreements.
But the Eastern Shoshoni and Bannock had left for
their fall buffalo hunt before Doty could get them
together in another council. Eventually, the Eastern
Shoshoni assented to their treaty, and along with those
for the other Shoshoni groups, it was ratified. The
Soda Springs Treaty was ratified by the United States
Senate "upon condition that a section be added, de-
fining the character of the Indian title to the land,
recognized by the Government." The treaty was
never formally proclaimed, perhaps because the Bannock refused their acquiescence to the added section
or because the agreement abrogated the terms of the
Fort Bridger Treaty of 1863. At any rate, it remained as a *de facto* agreement during the next five
years, until the Great Treaty of 1868 replaced it.[17]

The establishment of Idaho Territory in 1863 led
to more direct control of the Indians of Snake River
by the government. By the summer of 1865 the initial
steps of government had been accomplished; and
Governor Caleb Lyon of Lyonsdale, as *ex officio*
Superintendent of Indian Affairs, was ready to turn
his attention to this urgent problem. He and other
Idaho officials had been constantly reminded of the
necessity for action by the petty depredations of a few

---

[17] *Report of the Commissioner of Indian Affairs, 1864,* p. 160; F. H.
Head to N. G. Taylor, Washington, D.C., February 15, 1868, U.S.
National Archives, Records of the Bureau of Indian Affairs, Utah
Superintendency, Letters Received, 1868, Record Group 75.

loose bands of Shoshoni near the capital city of Boise.
The *Idaho Statesman* day after day reiterated its demands that something be done about the situation,
and the editor expressed the prevailing sentiment in
July of 1865:

> Now what we want is more cavalry. Not for protection,
> but for chastisement of the Indians. We have had protection
> enough. It is now time that protection were made superfluous
> by at once removing the necessity for protection. We must
> either whip those Indians into peaceful behavior or kill them
> off.[18]

In September, therefore, Governor Lyon held councils with the Boise Shoshoni and the Shoshoni and
Bannock at Camas Prairie. His investigations, as a
result of the conferences, led him to propose to the
Indian Commissioner that an agency be located at
Camas Prairie for the winter, and that a reservation
be established on Snake River to care for the Indians
of "southern Idaho" during the summer months. He
suggested that the reserve include about forty thousand acres and he emphasized the necessity of a permanent home for the Indians. Following this suggestion,
the Indian Commissioner directed Lyon to appoint
agents where needed and to conclude a treaty with
"the great Kammas Indians and the Indians of southern Idaho" providing for a reservation on Snake River
which would include the fishing grounds.[19]

Meanwhile, the government was failing to keep its
promises to the Bannock under the treaty of 1863 and,

---

[18] *Idaho Statesman*, July 15, 1865, p. 1.
[19] *Report of the Commissioner of Indian Affairs, 1865*, p. 234.

in November of 1865, head Chief Taghee asked M. A. Carter of Soda Springs to write the Idaho executive. Carter explained that the tribe had not received any supplies for over a year, and that Taghee would have his people back at Fort Hall the next spring to learn the intentions of the government toward the Bannock.[20]

Under the prompting of government official and Indian leader alike, Governor Lyon called a council meeting with "certain bands of *Bannocks* and *Snake* Indians" of southeastern Idaho in the early spring of 1866 and signed a treaty with them in which they agreed to go on a reservation provided for them by the government. Shortly after, Lyon left the governorship, and the Indian Commissioner withheld action on the treaty until Lyon's successor had had an opportunity to acquire further information concerning the Indian situation in Idaho.[21]

The new executive, D. W. Ballard, received the assistance of a special Indian agent sent from Washington, D.C. This man, George C. Hough, left Washington in the early summer of 1866 and reached San Francisco via New York City and Nicaragua. Intending to travel to Boise by way of Portland, he changed his route through Chico, California, to investigate rumors that "Bannocks and other Indians . . . were committing depredations along the stage road." He became convinced that Nevada Paiutes were responsible for the attacks, and finally affirmed: "I feel assured

---

[20] M. A. Carter to Caleb Lyon of Lyonsdale, Soda Springs, Idaho, November 14, 1865, Idaho State Historical Museum, Indian Affairs.

[21] *Report of the Commissioner of Indian Affairs, 1866,* p. 13.

that if the Bannocks & Shoshones in this section of
Idaho were provided with a reservation and some food
& clothing that they would be peaceable & cease stealing from the settlers."[22]

From this August, 1866, report of Agent Hough,
Governor Ballard learned that the Bruneau Shoshoni,
numbering four hundred people, and the Boise and
Camas bands of Shoshoni were quite willing to move
to a reservation. Hough favored the establishment
of a single reserve at Fort Hall large enough to accommodate all the Indians of southern Idaho, instead of
several smaller reservations scattered along Snake
River.[23] Governor Ballard thereupon reported to the
Indian Commissioner that although the Boise and
Bruneau Shoshoni were so loosely organized that it
would be almost impossible to negotiate a formal
treaty with them, he was in favor of placing them
upon a reservation because, first of all, they desired
such a course; and secondly, they were at the mercy
of white volunteers who habitually went on scalp-
hunting expeditions, "under the stimulus of rewards
offered at public meetings of $25 to $100 per scalp."[24]

Acting upon the advice of Governor Ballard, the
Indian Commissioner instructed him on October 1,
1866, to set aside two reservations in Idaho, one for
the Boise and Bruneau Shoshoni in southern Idaho,
and one for the Coeur d'Alene and other Indians in
northern Idaho. Ballard chose a reservation in the

[22] George C. Hough to D. W. Ballard, Boise City, August 3, 1866, U.S.
National Archives, Records of the Bureau of Indian Affairs, Idaho
Superintendency, Letters Received, 1866-1880, Record Group 75.

[23] *Report of the Commissioner of Indian Affairs, 1866*, p. 189.

[24] *Ibid.*, p. 38.

Fort Hall region for the Shoshoni bands. He pointed out that its location as a permanent home for these Indians was dependent upon the acquiescence of Washakie's Eastern Shoshoni in the proposed arrangements because the government, in the treaty at Fort Bridger, had included the Fort Hall area within the hunting range of the Eastern Shoshoni. The governor was evidently convinced that these Indians would not protest the loss of the Fort Hall area, which was on the extreme western limits of their home country.[25]

The boundaries of the proposed "Boise and Bruneau bands of Shoshones and Bannock Reservation" were defined by the Idaho agents as follows:

Commencing on the south bank of Snake River at the junction of the Port Neuf River with said Snake River; then south 25 miles to the summit of the mountains dividing the waters of Bear River from those of Snake River, thence easterly along the summit of said range of mountains 70 miles to a point where Sublette road crosses said divide; thence north about 50 miles to Blackfoot River; thence down said stream to its junction with Snake River; thence down Snake River to the place of beginning.[26]

The total area amounted to approximately 1,800,000 acres and included Fort Hall within its limits. At the time, the nearest white settlement was on the Malad River about seventy miles distant, although "6 or 8" people had located within the reservation limits.

---

[25] N. G. Taylor to O. H. Browning, Washington, D.C., May 23, 1867, in Kappler, *op. cit.*, II, 835-36.

[26] D. W. Ballard to D. N. Cooley, Boise City, November 18, 1866, U.S. National Archives, Records of the Bureau of Indian Affairs, Idaho Superintendency, Letters Received, 1866-1880, Record Group 75.

A telegraph line ran through the new reserve from Salt Lake City to Montana, along the road to the mines. These evidences of encroaching civilization led Governor Ballard to urge prompt action on the part of the Commissioner of Indian Affairs to legalize the new home for the Indians of southern Idaho. By executive order of June 14, 1867, President Andrew Johnson finally established Fort Hall as defined above.

While the governmental machinery in Washington slowly ground out the legislation establishing a reservation, Governor Ballard and his agents were faced with the problem of providing some kind of home for the Indians of southern Idaho, so that they and their white neighbors would not become involved in a war. Agent Charles F. Powell was instructed in July, 1866, to take charge of the Boise and Bruneau Shoshoni and a band of Bannock, all of whom were encamped near the city of Boise. Powell chose a spot at the forks of the Boise River, thirty miles from the city, and moved the Indians there. He characterized the Shoshoni as indolent beings who exerted themselves only when hungry. The Bannock, he noted,

. . . are more enterprising and restless, given to athletic exercises and to the chase. They seem very anxious to get away from the present restraint, and indulge the wild freedom they have hereto enjoyed; they are given to martial displays, dancing, beating drums, etc.[27]

Their chief, Bannock John, had good control over his people, although Powell reported many "bad, vicious young men" among them. According to a census

---

[27] *Report of the Commissioner of Indian Affairs, 1867*, p. 252.

taken by the agent, he had under his charge 283 Boise Shoshoni, 300 Bruneau Shoshoni, and 100 Bannock.

At the request of the leaders of this portion of the Bannock tribe, a military escort was provided to conduct them to Boise for an interview with Governor Ballard in June of 1867. The chief executive reported that the head men, Bannock John and his brother Bannock Jim, were both married to sisters of "Tar-gee, the Head Chief of the Bannock tribe." Ballard's conversation with these two gave Idaho authorities first-hand information about the tribe:

Q. Who is the Head Chief of all the Bannacks?
A. "Tar-gee" (Hard sound of "g").
Q. What other Chiefs have the Bannacks?
A. "Koo-ser-gun" is second chief—no more—
Q. How many of Bannack Indians are there?
A. I do not know—from sixty to one hundred lodges.
Q. How many will a lodge average?
A. From eight to eleven.
Q. Did you ever hear of General Connor?
A. Yes.
Q. Did "Tar-gee" and "Koo-ser-gun" have a talk with General Connor?
A. Yes, four years ago.
Q. What was their understanding at this talk?
A. That the Bannacks were to hunt Buffalo, and go into the Boise country whenever they choose as long as they remain friendly.
Q. Are the Boise Bruneaus and Bannacks friendly?
A. Yes and have always been.
Q. Could they live together in peace?
A. Yes.
Q. Would [you] like to live on a reservation? provided we build you houses, teach you to farm etc.?
A. We want to hunt Buffalo and fish.
Q. But if allowed to hunt Buffalo and to fish at proper times?

A. That would suit us.

Q. Would all the Bannacks like this arrangement?

A. I think so but Tar-gee would want to talk first.

Q. What time in the year would [you] like to hunt Buffalo?

A. Latter part of summer.[28]

As the fall of 1867 approached, this small Bannock group became restless and demanded to be allowed to go on their annual buffalo hunt, if the government did not take some action to subsist them for the winter. They were finally allowed to go, but returned to the charge of Agent Powell at Boise River, even though he had reported to his superiors that the area was not suited as a wintering ground for the Indians. In August of 1868, these three bands were still being administered by Powell in the Boise region.[29] The action of Governor Ballard in setting up this temporary reservation met with the approval of most citizens of the territory, and the *Idaho Statesman* summed up the general attitude:

Governor Ballard, without waiting for the red tape at Washington to confirm his recommendations in regard to the Fort Hall reservation, where all the Indians in this portion of the Territory could be sustained, has instituted a temporary reservation, and all the Indians disposed to be friendly are gathering there, while General Crook is after the rest. When he gets near enough to them to talk, the reservation will be proposed to their chiefs, and if they refuse they will be killed or put on the reservation by force, and certainly shot if they don't stay there.[30]

---

[28] D. W. Ballard to Charles E. Mix, Boise City, August 3, 1866, U.S. National Archives, Records of the Bureau of Indian Affairs, Idaho Superintendency, Letters Received, 1866-1880, Record Group 75.

[29] *Report of Commissioner of Indian Affairs, 1867,* p. 253; *Report . . . 1868,* p. 662.

[30] *Idaho Statesman,* July 20, 1867, p. 2.

During the long and slow process involved in establishing the Fort Hall Reservation, the principal tribe of the Bannock, numbering some eight hundred people, was still being nominally supervised by the Indian Office under the Treaty of Soda Springs of 1863. The Bannock showed up at the Fort Bridger agency in the summer of 1864 to receive the presents promised them under the agreement. Unfortunately, some of the goods were burned en route to the agency and the remainder arrived so late that the tribe was not at hand to receive them, having gone after a winter's supply of buffalo meat. Again, in 1865, the presents were so delayed that the majority of the able Indians left for the buffalo country, afraid that they would again be disappointed and so suffer from lack of food supplies.[31] The following year, Agent Mann met the Bannock when they appeared at the agency in company with the Eastern Shoshoni. The latter received ten thousand dollars in annuity goods in which the Bannock were not allowed to share. Mann, however, was so moved by the Bannock report that they had never received any presents from the government that he supplied enough food for their immediate wants, paying for it himself. The tribe was at this time under the competent leadership of Chief Taghee, who had taken control at the death of Le Grand Coquin. Mann described the new chief as a leader in whom "I fully repose confidence."[32]

Fully realizing the inequality of distributing ten thousand dollars' worth of annuity goods to the East-

[31] *Report of the Commissioner of Indian Affairs, 1865*, p. 143.
[32] *Report of the Commissioner of Indian Affairs, 1866*, pp. 126-27.

ern Shoshoni while their neighbors received nothing, Agent Mann wrote his superiors, in 1867, recommending that a like sum be assigned for annuity goods to the Bannock. The Indian Commissioner followed the suggestion and asked the Secretary of the Interior for an increased appropriation ($5,000) to take care of a Bannock annuity, explaining that while it was unjust to expect the Eastern Shoshoni to give up half of the annuity guaranteed them under their treaty, it was likewise unjust to abrogate the agreement with the Bannock.[33] Mann had attempted to get the Eastern Shoshoni to share their presents with the Bannock, but Chief Washakie peremptorily refused to do so. Chief Taghee informed the agent that his people felt very much hurt because the government distributed goods to all the Indians around them, while they received none. Taghee emphasized that the tribe was friendly and peaceable and entitled to some compensation for the losses sustained from white encroachments on their hunting lands. They were being forced to travel farther each year in pursuit of the buffalo and suffered constant raids and battles with hostile tribes in the plains area.[34]

In addition to the efforts of Agent Mann in behalf of the Bannock, the Idaho Indian Superintendent was also doing everything in his power to get them settled in a permanent home. Word came to the Bannock in August of 1867 that Superintendent Ballard wished to meet them in council. Although the agent had not called such a conference nor even authorized any-

---

[33] *Report of the Commissioner of Indian Affairs, 1867,* pp. 11, 174, 183.
[34] *Ibid.,* p. 189.

one else to hold one, he thought it best to meet with the Indians, now that they had gathered together. On August 21 the meeting began with an address by Ballard in which he went over the familiar arguments for the settlement of the Indians on a reservation. He informed the Bannock that during the previous year he had selected a tract of country at Fort Hall for them and other tribes and that through unofficial channels he had heard of the approval of the reservation.

Now, [said Ballard,] are you willing to relinquish your title to all the country you have ever claimed . . . provided the government of the United States secures to you and your children, and to such other friendly Indians as may be induced to go thereon, the sole ownership of said reservation *forever*, supply you with subsistence til you can raise sufficient for yourselves and furnish you an agent, teachers, books, implements of husbandry, etc.

Chief Taghee answered:

I thought when the white people came to Soda Springs and built houses and put soldiers in them, it was to protect my people, but now they are all gone, and I do not know where to go nor what to do.

The white people have come into my country, and have not asked my consent. Why is this? And why have no persons talked to me before? I have never known what the white people wanted me to do. I have never killed white people who were passing into my country. What you say to me I shall never forget. All the Bannock Indians will obey me and be good, but the Sheep-eaters are not my people . . . and I cannot be responsible for them. I will answer for the Bannocks. The Boise and Bruneaus are poor; they cannot travel far; they have no horses to hunt the buffalo, but they are good Indians, and are my friends. The buffalo do not come so far south now as formerly, so we must go further to the

Chief Taghee answered for his tribesmen

north to hunt them. The white people have scared them away.

I am willing to go upon a reservation, but I want the privilege of hunting the buffalo for a few years. When they are all gone far away we hunt no more; perhaps one year, perhaps two or three years; then we stay on the reservation all the time. I want a reservation large enough for all my people, and no white man on it, except the agent and other officers and employes of the government. I want the right of way for my people to travel when going to or coming from the buffalo country, and when going to sell our furs and skins. I want the right to camp and dig roots on Cañon prairie when coming to Boise City to trade. Some of my people have no horses. They can remain at Camas prairie and dig roots while others go on. Our hunting is not so good as it used to be, nor my people so numerous.

I will go from here to the buffalo country, where I will meet all my tribe, and will tell them of this talk and of the arrangements we may make.

I am willing to go on to a reservation as you propose, but when will you want me to go? We can go next spring.[35]

For the first time since the Treaty of Soda Springs in 1863, the Bannock thus had an opportunity to present to official ears their hopes and desires, and Chief Taghee made the most of the occasion. Ballard replied that he could not be certain when the Bannock would be allowed to move onto the Fort Hall Reservation, but he hoped that such an event could take place by the spring of 1868. In the formal agreement that followed, both parties agreed that the Bannock would move to the reservation by June 1, 1868. The other provisions of the agreement signed at Long Tom Creek on August 26, 1867, were as outlined by Superintendent Ballard in his opening remarks to

---

[35] *Report of the Commissioner of Indian Affairs, 1868*, pp. 657-58.

the Indians. The Bannock chiefs signing the pact were: "Tygse, Peter, To-so-copy-notey, Pah Vissigin, McKay, and Jim." The agreement never became effective and, on June 1, 1868, the Bannock were still in search of a home.

During the spring and summer, Ballard and other officials continued to receive letters from the white settlers in the Fort Hall region, and one from Taghee himself, all inquiring about how long it would be before the Indians could settle on the reservation.[36] M. A. Carter of Soda Springs expressed the consensus of the group:

> They [Bannock] have been and are now on the most friendly terms with the whites, and have manifested this disposition notwithstanding there were many circumstances which would have aggravated Indians of less kind feeling to open hostility. Namely the neglect of the Gov't. to provide them an agent and to thereby establish trading posts where they could dispose of their furs and skins and provide themselves in return with blankets provisions and ammunition.
>
> At a treaty over two years ago between Gen'l Connor and the Bannack Indians many obligations were undertaken, which have never in any degree been carried into effect leaving the Indians much cause to be dissatisfied. For if we bind ourselves in certain treatys [sic], and then wilfully neglect to perform the functions of each treaty, we can expect but little better from the untutored red man, who have only discrimination sufficient to know that they have not received what has been so solemnly promised to them.[37]

The constant requests of the agents at Boise and Fort Bridger for a formal treaty with the Bannock,

---

[36] *Ibid.*, pp. 658-59.

[37] M. A. Carter to J. M. Ashley, Soda Springs, July 19, 1868, U.S. National Archives, Records of the Bureau of Indian Affairs, Idaho Superintendency, Letters Received, 1866-1880, Record Group 75.

and their assignment to a reservation, finally brought results when the Indian Peace Commission of 1867 sent representatives to treat with the tribe and the Eastern Shoshoni. Agent Luther Mann was directed on the first of May, 1868, to gather the two peoples at Fort Bridger in preparation for a council meeting with the commissioners, who expected to arrive June 4. Chief Taghee displayed his control over the Bannock by having eight hundred members of the tribe assembled at the agency by May 15. Mann had been authorized to provide subsistence for the Indians until the arrival of the Commission, but the poor condition of the roads delayed the wagon trains. In disgust, about half of the Bannock left for their summer fishing resorts. The Shoshoni under Washakie gathered more slowly, but stayed when they were finally assembled. General C. C. Augur, heading the representatives of the government, arrived June 15 and held informal conferences with Taghee and Washakie and the other leading men until the supplies came. In this initial period Augur learned what lands were claimed by the two peoples. Taghee wanted the country around Soda Springs, Portneuf River, and Camas Prairie. Augur expressed his desire that the Bannock should agree to settle with the Shoshoni for the time being. Finally, the supply wagons having arrived, the great council got underway.[38]

General Augur opened the meeting by telling the Indians that the government wished them to be at

[38] *Report of the Commissioner of Indian Affairs, 1868*, p. 617; Grace R. Hebard, *Washakie; an Account of Indian Resistance to the Covered Wagon and the Union Pacific Railroad Invasion of their Territory* (Cleveland, 1930), pp. 119, 120.

peace with the whites and so wanted them to go on
a reservation where they would have a permanent
home and could receive subsistence aid from the Indian Office. He said:

In a few years the game will become scarce and you will
not find sufficient to support your people. You will then
have to live in some other way than by hunting and fishing.
[The government] . . . wishes you, therefore, to go to this
reservation now and commence to grow wheat and corn and
raise cattle and horses, so that when the game is gone, you
will be prepared to live independently of it. . . . Your Great
Father desires . . . that you should remain at peace, not only
with white men but with all other Indian tribes. . . . He
wishes the Shoshones and Bannocks to be together where
you can have one agent to attend to you.[39]

Chief Washakie then addressed the council and said
he would be satisfied with the Wind River country
for the Shoshoni reservation. When Chief Taghee was
questioned concerning the territory he claimed, he
answered, "As far away as Virginia City our tribe has
roamed. But I want the Port-Neuf country and Kamas
plains."

General Augur asked Chief Taghee why the Bannock could not live in peaceful relations with the
Shoshoni on the same reserve. The Indian leader said:
"We are friends with the Shoshones, and like to hunt
with them; but we want a home for ourselves."

The commissioner then asked, "If you have a separate home, can you and the Shoshones get along with
one agency and come to the Shoshone reservation for
your annuities, etc.?"

---

[39] Hebard, *op. cit.*, p. 120.

"We want," replied Taghee, "to receive anything that is for us on our own ground."

Augur said he did not know the country well enough to locate a reservation for the Bannock but, when they were ready to go on a reserve, someone would be sent to survey it for them.[40]

As a result of the meeting, Augur was able to report to the president of the Peace Commission that there was no such thing as the "mixed bands of Bannock and Shoshones." The Bannock were a distinct and separate tribe and, from this time on, the Indian Office treated them as such.

After the conferences had been completed, General Augur assembled the Indian leaders on July 3 and had the terms of the treaty explained to them so that all understood. After the reading of the treaty, the chiefs assented to it and signed their marks in the presence of the commissioners. Presents were then given out, the Bannock receiving a particularly valuable lot because of their having been overlooked for so many years.

The significant portions of the Treaty of Fort Bridger relating to the Bannock may be summarized as follows: Article 1 provided for the arrest and arraignment of Shoshoni and Bannock accused of crimes. Article 2 agreed that, when the Bannock desired a reservation or when the President of the United States thought it best that they be put on a reservation, a tract should be selected for them "in their present country, which shall embrace reasonable portions of the 'Port Neuf' and 'Kansas Prairie'

[40] *Ibid.*, pp. 123-24.

countries." Article 3 provided for the construction of certain buildings (including a school) on the reservations proposed for the Eastern Shoshoni and the Bannock, and also listed the employees which the government would hire to maintain the agencies. Article 4 stated that the Indians would make their homes on the reservation but that they would still have the right to hunt on the unoccupied lands of the United States. Article 5 provided that the agent for the Indians would make his home on the Eastern Shoshoni reservation "but shall direct and supervise affairs on the Bannock reservation." Article 6 outlined the procedure whereby a head of a family could be allotted not over 320 acres of farming land on the reservation, and a person over eighteen years of age but not the head of a family could receive at least 80 acres of land; the individual was to choose his own land which was to be guaranteed to him. Article 7 established compulsory education for all Indian children between the ages of six and sixteen. Article 8 provided that an individual who had taken up an allotment of land was to receive $100 worth of seeds and agricultural implements the first year and $25.00 worth of seeds and implements for the next three years. Article 9 listed the annuity goods which the government promised to deliver to the Indians by September 1 of each year, for a period of thirty years; in addition to clothing, each "Indian roaming" was to receive ten dollars a year, and each "Indian engaged in agriculture" was to have twenty dollars a year. Article 10 provided for the employment of certain agency employees, including a physician. Article

11 stipulated that all treaties for the cessions of reservation lands had to be signed by a majority of the adult male Indians on the reserve. Article 12 provided prizes in money to the best Indian farmers during the initial three years of farming operations. Article 13 provided that annuity goods should be paid to the Bannock and Shoshoni each year at Fort Bridger until the Wind River Agency was established.[41]

Six Bannock chiefs signed the treaty: Taghee, Tay-to-ba, We-rat-ze-won-a-gen, Coo-sha-gan, Pan-sook-a-motse, and A-wite-etse. The United States Senate finally confirmed the Treaty of Fort Bridger, and it was proclaimed February 24, 1869.[42]

Contrary to expectations, many of the citizens of Idaho looked upon the treaty with some disapproval. Their chief grievance was that the fifteen thousand dollars' worth of presents and the twenty dollars apiece in money which was distributed to the Bannock by General Augur aroused the envy and anger of the Boise and Bruneau Shoshoni. Governor Ballard and Agent Powell had to hold a special council to quiet these peoples. The *Boise Democrat,* commenting on this turn of affairs, said, "We do not want any child's play in regard to Indian affairs." The newspaper pointed out that Agent Powell, rather than Augur, should have negotiated with the Bannock.[43]

---

[41] Kappler, *op. cit.,* II, 786-89. For full text of Treaty of Fort Bridger, see Appendix II.

[42] U.S. Congress, *Statutes at Large, Treaties and Proclamations of the United States of America from December, 1867, to March, 1869;* ed. by George P. Sanger (Boston, 1869), XV, 673, 677.

[43] *Boise Semi-Weekly Democrat,* August 1, 1868, p. 3.

With the exception of other Indians who were jealous of presents given to the Bannock, the treaty was well received. On April 13, 1869, Agent Powell arrived at Fort Hall Reservation and took charge of the agency. His journey from Boise had turned into quite a trek for, in addition to the 300 Boise Shoshoni, 850 Bruneau Shoshoni, and 150 Bannock whom he chaperoned to the new station, he picked up a great number of Indians on the way. He immediately began to erect buildings to care for the supplies which he expected would arrive shortly.[44]

Meanwhile, the Bannock were on a buffalo hunt with the Eastern Shoshoni in the region of the Wind River Mountains. On their way back to the Fort Hall area they stopped at Fort Bridger and there received from Agent Mann the four thousand dollars in presents which the Peace Commission had authorized for distribution to them. Mann paid tribute to Chief Taghee as a "most reliable and excellent Indian, and to his prudent counsels the moderation and patient endurance of broken faith by this tribe is due."[45] Governor J. A. Campbell of the new Wyoming Territory also noted that "during the entire period, from the fall of 1863 up to the present, the Bannocks have observed the treaty stipulations strictly."[46]

When the Bannock reached Fort Hall, Chief Taghee met with Powell and told the agent that he and his people wanted the Fort Hall Reservation for their home. Governor Ballard endorsed Powell's recom-

———
[44] *Report of the Commissioner of Indian Affairs, 1869*, p. 728.
[45] *Ibid.*, p. 716.
[46] *Ibid.*, p. 713

mendation that the Bannock be allowed to make their home on the new reserve and passed it on to the Indian Commissioner. As explained by the commissioner, the Fort Hall Reservation embraced a portion of the "Port Neuf and Kansas prairie" country which Article 2 of the Treaty of Fort Bridger had assigned to the Bannock. Therefore, by executive order of President U. S. Grant, on July 30, 1869, the Bannock were granted a home on the Fort Hall reservation.[47]

It was during the treaty period, also, that reports began to reach officials of the Office of Indian Affairs concerning another tribe of "Bannock" that inhabited the headwaters of the Yellowstone, Gallatin, Madison, and Snake rivers, often wintering in the Salmon River Mountains near Lemhi River. At the Treaty of Soda Springs in 1863, Chief "Tindooh" (Tendoy) sent word to Superintendent Doty that he was unable to attend the council but assented to the terms of the treaty.[48] This is the same chief that C. H. Miller had praised so highly in 1859. The white man had at that time presented Tendoy with a fine rifle in token of governmental appreciation for his service and friendship to the Americans.[49] Tendoy was leader of a mixed band of Shoshoni and a few Bannock who ranged in the Beaverhead country of Montana and west, across the mountains, into Idaho.

Governor Thomas F. Meagher of Montana Territory reported in April, 1866, that a tribe made up

[47] *Ibid.*, p. 728; Kappler, *op. cit.*, II, 838-39.

[48] *Report of the Commissioner of Indian Affairs, 1864*, p. 320.

[49] U.S. Congress, House of Representatives, *Pacific Wagon Roads*, Ex. Doc. 108, 35th Cong., 2nd Sess., Serial No. 1008, March 1, 1859 (Washington, 1859), p. 71.

of "Shoshones (or Snake) and Bannocks" lived in
the area along the southwestern boundary of the
territory. According to him the misery, filth, and
dire want revealed by their lodges were "exceeded
only by the huts of the Terra del Fuegans."[50] He
listed them as numbering 110 Shoshoni and 500 Bannock, an estimate much too high. As a result of this
report, the Indian Commissioner instructed Agent
Mann of Fort Bridger to investigate the status and
numbers of the tribe. Mann's information indicated
that there were one hundred lodges of Bannock, plus
a few lodges of Shoshoni, in the group which lived
in the same area occupied by a tribe of Too-ree-reka,
or Sheepeaters.[51] The Sheepeaters were later mentioned by Agent Powell in August, 1868, as among
those Indians which were jealous of the presents given
the Bannock at the Fort Bridger Treaty.[52]

The inaccuracies and lack of information about
this northern tribe were somewhat dispelled by Agent
Alfred Sully of Montana Territory in September,
1869. Although he still called them by the general
name of "Bannocks," he correctly estimated their
numbers as being "not . . . over five hundred souls."
His description of their poverty and of the country
through which they ranged stamped them as the Indian tribe that was shortly to be known as the Lemhi
tribe, from their home on Lemhi River. As later
information revealed, Chief Tendoy had gradually
been able to amalgamate into one tribe the Sheep-

---

[50] *Report of the Commissioner of Indian Affairs, 1866*, pp. 199-200.
[51] *Report of the Commissioner of Indian Affairs, 1867*, p. 189.
[52] *Report of the Commissioner of Indian Affairs, 1868*, p. 663.

eaters and other scattered Shoshoni and a small number of Bannock. The Bannock members of the Lemhi rarely numbered over one hundred and came originally from the main Bannock tribe at Fort Hall. Agent Sully was one of the first to record that the Lemhi boasted that not one of them had ever shed the blood of a white man. This characteristic became almost traditional with the tribe and was due, for the most part, to the firm control exercised by Tendoy. For the first time, also, Sully learned that these Indians did not want to go on the reservation at Fort Hall; "they expressed the greatest aversion to that place; for what reason I could not learn."[53] From this time until the early 1900's, the Lemhi obstinately refused to move to Fort Hall and were successful for a time in gaining a reservation of their own.

---

[53] *Report of the Commissioner of Indian Affairs, 1869*, pp. 731-32.

The similarity of language of the Northern Paiute and the Bannock often led observers to confuse the two peoples. In 1866, Agents H. G. Parker and Franklin Campbell of Nevada recited certain troubles they were having with the "Bannock," but an investigation of their reports indicates that the people they called Bannock ranged in the southeastern corner of Oregon and southwestern Idaho, the home of the Northern Paiute. It is entirely possible that a few Bannock may have been involved in the troubles listed by the agents, but these "fifteen hundred . . . Bannocks" were not the true Bannock tribe which made its home around the Fort Hall area. *Report of the Commissioner of Indian Affairs, 1866*, pp. 114-20.

Hunting for Subsistence, 1870-1877

WITH the movement of Agent Powell and the Boise and Bruneau Shoshoni to Fort Hall in 1869, the reservation began its active life as an agency. At this time President Ulysses S. Grant was interested in improving the Indian Office and in reducing the number of unscrupulous agents who had become entrenched in the service. For this reason he delegated the nomination of the agents to the religious organizations interested in Indian welfare. The Quakers, therefore, were given the selection of agents in the Plains areas. The other agencies, except those in Oregon, were manned by army officers. In Idaho Territory, Colonel L. DeFloyd Jones became the Superintendent of Indian Affairs, and First Lieutenant W. H. Danilson was appointed to command the Fort Hall Agency. Their tenure was short-lived, however, because the Army Appropriation Act of July 15, 1870, provided that any officer on the active list who accepted a civil appointment must first give up his commission. The nomination of agents for those posts so vacated was then divided among the several religious bodies. The agent at Fort Hall was nominated by the Methodist missionary organization but, by the early 1880's, the policy of nomination by religious bodies was abandoned.[1]

The establishment of Fort Hall Reservation and the official assignment of the Bannock to it should have settled all questions concerning a permanent home for them but, under the Treaty of Fort Bridger of 1868, their annuity goods were sent to the Eastern Shoshoni Wind River Reservation. The first distribution of the supplies took place at the Wyoming reserve in the fall of 1869 and necessitated that the Bannock make the long trip there to get their annual presents. Chief Washakie was very anxious that the Bannock settle on his reservation. But Chief Taghee, disturbed by Washakie's proposal and by the fact that the annuity goods were being sent to Wind River, requested the agent at Fort Hall to ask for a representative of the government to hold a council with the Bannock in which the tribe could be definitely assured that they would not be removed from Fort Hall. In September, 1872, the agent at Wind River protested that the Bannock annuity goods had again been sent to him and warned that if the Bannock came to get their presents, it would be impossible for him to subsist them for the winter. A number of the less independent Bannock continued to live near Wind River Agency, knowing that they would receive their annuity supplies there. The complaints of the Wind River and Fort Hall agents finally reached

---

[1] Laurence F. Schmeckebier, *The Office of Indian Affairs* ("Institute for Government Research, Service Monographs of the United States Government," No. 48 [Baltimore, 1927]), p. 54; U.S. Office of Indian Affairs, *Annual Report of the Commissioner of Indian Affairs, 1869* (Washington, 1870), pp. 721, 730.

Washington, and the Indian Commissioner directed that, beginning in 1873, all the Bannock goods would be sent to Fort Hall.[2]

Not only did the Bannock have difficulty in obtaining their annuity goods, but they also found that the promise of the government to subsist them on the reservation was consistently not kept. During the previous summer, Superintendent DeFloyd Jones had requested an appropriation of $75,000 for food supplies for the Indians at Fort Hall, pointing out that even this amount would give them only half rations daily of flour and beef. In addition, he asked for money with which to buy clothing and other provisions, as provided for under the Treaty of Fort Bridger.[3]

Chief Taghee came in to Fort Hall in August, 1869, and drew a few rations in preparation for leaving on the fall buffalo hunt. He told Agent Danilson that he hoped this hunt would be the last for his people. The chief wanted them to settle down on the reservation, to pursue a civilized life, and to become farmers. In December, most of the tribe returned to Fort Hall, well equipped with wigwams and ponies, but in need of food and clothing. Danilson reported that it would be impossible for him to feed the Bannock on the meager food supplies he had been able to get for the Shoshoni on the reservation.

Throughout the period from 1869 to 1877, the

---

[2] *Report of the Commissioner of Indian Affairs, 1869*, p. 730; *Report . . . 1870*, pp. 32, 175; *Report . . . 1872*, p. 270.

[3] *Report of the Commissioner of Indian Affairs, 1869*, pp. 721, 739; Danilson to Jones, Fort Hall Agency, Idaho Territory, December 3, 1869, in Fort Hall Agency Letter Book, Copies of Letters Sent, 1869-1875 (MS at Fort Hall Agency, Fort Hall, Idaho), p. 19.

agents at Fort Hall could never secure enough food and clothing from the government to subsist all the Indians on the reservation. Of the two tribes, the Shoshoni were the more docile but also the more dependent on the Indian Office for subsistence. During 1869 there were six hundred Bannock and five hundred Shoshoni assigned to the agency; but the next several years saw the numbers of Shoshoni increasing as isolated bands chose to come, or were forced to come, in to the reservation. The Shoshoni early made attempts at farming and settled down to live at Fort Hall. Therefore, when there were not enough provisions available to subsist the entire group of Indians, it was the Bannock who left to hunt buffalo and a meat supply. Being more independent and less inclined to a farming life, their reaction to promises not kept was to revert to their old ways of gaining a livelihood. It was seldom that any Shoshoni groups left the reservation on hunting expeditions, and then it was usually because of pressure exerted by the agent, who realized that his meager supplies would not feed them.

From the first the government failed to live up to Article 2 of the Fort Bridger Treaty. In September, 1869, Agent Danilson sent in a requisition for clothing supplies for the Bannock but, by December, the goods had not arrived and the Indians were "very much disappointed." When Taghee and his people returned from the buffalo country in June of 1870, their ponies were "jaded," their families had few robes, and the entire lot was desperately in need of clothing. Taghee had a "talk" with Danilson and, upon discovering that the supply of blankets promised by the treaty had not been sent to the agency, he said "he would not stand it," and the agent reported, "I think he meant just what he said." Taghee demanded a council with the Idaho superintendent so that he could get definite word about the blankets. In transmitting this request to Superintendent DeFloyd Jones, Danilson said the Bannock were in such an excited state that prompt action would be necessary to avoid an outbreak. Earlier in the year the agent had written his superior, "It seems as though the government has failed in almost every particular in complying with the terms of the treaty made at Fort Bridger in July 1868."[4]

To avoid a possible war with the Bannock, Jones supplied three thousand dollars from the Idaho Territorial incidental fund for the purpose of buying blankets promised the Bannock. About one fourth of the blankets were distributed to the tribe in August, and the Indians stayed on the reservation impatiently awaiting the remainder which were finally given to them a few weeks later. Danilson distributed, to the 520 Bannock and 256 Shoshoni present at the time, 292 pairs of blankets, 2,360 yards of calico, 250 pounds of lead, 50 pounds of powder, 10,000 percussion caps, 100 pounds of tobacco, and 4 dozen butcher knives. The Bannock were pleased with the articles given them but they still felt that they had not received everything that had been promised by their treaty.[5]

---

[4] Danilson to Jones, Fort Hall Agency, Idaho Terr., January 12, 1870, *ibid.*, p. 25.

[5] Danilson to Jones, Fort Hall Agency, Idaho Terr., December 3, 1869, June 2, July 9, and August 9, 1870, *ibid.*, pp. 40, 43, 44, 47; *Report of the Commissioner of Indian Affairs, 1870,* pp. 183, 187-88.

Shortly after receiving their supplies, the tribe left for the buffalo country. Superintendent Jones was of the opinion that the Bannock did not intend to settle down on the reservation but came in only two or three months of the year to collect their annuity goods before reverting to their old life again. Recognition of this natural migratory tendency had to be tempered with the fact that the Bannock knew there was not enough food on the reservation to subsist them if they should choose to winter there. The new agent, J. N. High, reported in January, 1871, that Taghee and the Bannock were still in the plains area and acknowledged that it was perhaps as well, because he would not be able to subsist them on the reservation with the limited appropriation which had been given him. It might be noted here that High addressed his letter to the Commissioner of Indian Affairs in Washington, D.C., because the office of Superintendent of Idaho Territory had just been abolished. From this time on, the Fort Hall agents were under the direct supervision of the Indian Commissioner.[6]

The return of the Bannock tribe from the buffalo country early in 1871 brought the news that their great chief, Taghee, had died during the winter. His death had profound repercussions that lasted until the Bannock went to war in 1878. In fact, the inability of any other chief to control the Bannock as had Taghee was one of the indirect causes of the war. The war chief, Pan-sook-a-motse, or Otter Beard,

---

[6] *Report of the Commissioner of Indian Affairs, 1870*, p. 183; High to Parker, Fort Hall Agency, Idaho Terr., January 3, 1871, in Fort Hall Agency Letter Book, *op. cit.*, p. 65.

The Bannock on a buffalo hunt

took nominal control of the tribe and directed that the warriors meet at Fort Hall in August to choose a new leader. At the council, it was agreed that Taghee's son, a boy of sixteen also named Taghee, should be the next chief. But immediately there began a struggle to determine who should act as regent until the boy reached his maturity. The conflict was never satisfactorily settled, and the tribe split into two groups. A small faction of about one hundred Bannock accepted the leadership of Pagwhite, or Bannock Jim, while most of the tribe remained under Otter Beard. When Otter Beard died in early 1874, the chieftainship descended upon another subchief, Tyhee, who at first was not happy with the assignment because he feared that the position would shortly cause his death, too. Throughout the later years of the nineteenth century, Chief Tyhee was the acknowledged headman on the reservation and soon assumed a position of leadership as strong as that formerly held by Taghee. After the death of Tyhee, the son of Taghee became the prominent Bannock leader until his death in December of 1924.

The junior Taghee later became known as Pat Largy or Pat Tyhee on the reservation. This second Chief Tyhee was a man of magnificent aspect—standing six feet four inches in height and weighing well over two hundred pounds, with a mental ability equally remarkable.[7]

---

[7] Berry to Parker, Fort Hall Agency, July 8 and August 10, 1871, in Fort Hall Agency Letter Book, *op. cit.*, pp. 382, 392; Berry to Walker, Fort Hall Agency, August 20, 1872, *ibid.*, p. 113; Reed to Smith, Fort Hall Agency, March 1, 1874, *ibid.*, p. 172.

Dr. Sven Liljeblad, of Idaho State College, who has spent several years studying the Bannock language, explains the meaning of the

The lack of a strong leader, for the first few years after Taghee, aroused grave fears on the part of the whites and increased the demands of the agents and others for appropriations large enough to keep the Bannock on the reservation where they could be under surveillance. Judge Clitus Barbour met the tribe at Camas Prairie in the summer of 1872 and reported that the lack of a responsible head had left the tribal organization in "a very demoralized state."[8] Barbour advised all the "good friendly" Bannock to attach themselves to Chief Tendoy of the Lemhi so as to forestall implication in probable difficulties with the whites. This suggestion became more formal when government commissioners met the Bannock in council, in the fall of 1873, to limit the reservation boundaries and to decide upon other measures. The United States agents emphasized the value to the Fort Hall agent of a responsible leader who could "mold these Indians to the wishes of the Government." For such a position, the commission recommended Chief Tendoy, whom they characterized as "one of the noblest Indians in America." They pointed out that the chief's father was a Shoshoni and his mother a Bannock, which fitted him to be the leader of the two tribes. Recognizing that Tendoy did not want the position, the commission suggested that if all the Lemhi were removed to the Fort Hall Reservation, the chief would probably change his views and then

---

name "Taghee" as follows: ". . . Taghee, by the Bannock Indians pronounced *tàgî*, [is] a word related to the verb *tàki* 'to burst.' Pat Tyhee's Bannock name was Puhigwatsi . . . which means 'wagging the green,' i.e. 'wagging a green branch.' " Letter from Sven Liljeblad to author, Pocatello, Idaho, March 25, 1955.

[8] *Idaho Statesman*, July 2, 1872, p. 2.

accept the leadership of all Indians on the reservation. In terms of highest praise for Tendoy's business ability and integrity, the commission thus submitted him as their solution to the problem of controlling the leaderless Bannock.[9] But Tendoy never accepted the position; his Lemhi did not move to Fort Hall, and the headship of the Bannock remained with Tyhee, except for the short interval during 1877-78 when Chief Buffalo Horn took control of the warlike element of the tribe.

As long as the Bannock continued their yearly wanderings in search of buffalo, they were sure to meet other tribes; and sometimes these contacts led to time-honored horse-stealing activities which resulted, occasionally, in scalpings and battles. During their hunt in the Wind River country in 1870, the Bannock combined with the Eastern Shoshoni to engage the Arapaho in several encounters, and the "discipline was wholesome for the Arrapahoes," according to one white trader who witnessed the battles.[10] Bannock and Shoshoni meetings with the Sioux were, similarly, engagements of some magnitude. In 1868 that powerful Plains tribe drove them out of the Yellowstone country and, in the following summer, a fight with the Sioux resulted in the deaths of twenty-nine Bannock and Shoshoni warriors, with an unknown number of Sioux being slain.[11]

[9] U.S. Congress, House of Representatives, *Bannock and Other Indians in Southern Idaho*, Ex. Doc. 129, 43rd Cong., 1st Sess., Serial No. 1608 (Washington, 1873), pp. 1-3.

[10] E. S. Topping, *The Chronicles of the Yellowstone* (St. Paul, 1883), p. 79.

[11] Thomas Barker to I. B. Sinclair, Fort Boise, June 26, 1868, U.S. National Archives, Records of the Bureau of Indian Affairs, Idaho Superintendency, Letters Received, 1866-1880, Record Group 75; Charles F. Powell to D. W. Ballard, Fort Hall, June 30, 1869, *ibid*.

In the spring of 1872, two white men were authorized by the Crow agent in Montana to arrest two Bannock accused of stealing some Crow horses. The whites captured the two Indians and shot one down when they allowed him to try to escape. In revenge, other Bannock warriors shot a defenseless white trapper a few days later. In the same year, Chief Little Iron, a subordinate leader of the Crow, killed a Flathead. In retaliation, some Crow friends of the Flathead threatened to kill two Bannock friends of Little Iron. The chief and his allies swore to kill the white trader at the Crow Agency if the two Bannock were hurt. So the final victim of this intertribal row was thus forced to open his stores and supply all concerned with presents to placate them and save his own life.[12]

The winter of 1872 also found the Bannock at war with the Nez Perce, a portion of whom attacked the Bannock camp at Fleishman Creek in Montana. Forewarned of the assault, the Bannock hid themselves in tunnels in the snow; and when the Nez Perce rushed the empty lodges, the Bannock warriors opened fire, killing one enemy and wounding another.[13]

Many of the intertribal difficulties involving the Bannock could have been prevented if the government had lived up to its promise to subsist the Indians on the reservation. When Chief Otter Beard showed up at Fort Hall in July, 1871, he became the spokesman for the tribe in place of Taghee, and demanded a

---

[12] Topping, *op. cit.*, pp. 91-93.

[13] Thomas H. Leforge, *Memoirs of a White Crow Indian*, as told by Thomas B. Marquis (New York: D. Appleton-Century Company, Inc., 1928), pp. 75-76.

council with the agent, M. P. Berry. After a powwow lasting ten days, the Indian council again pledged its loyalty to the government, and one subchief said that "bad words had been whispered into his ears for a long time, but now his ears were closed and his eyes open."[14] These favorable results were obtained by Berry only after a prolonged description of the great power of the United States and the certain destruction of every Indian who opposed the wishes of the government. The principal grievance of the Indians was the bad faith of the government in not providing them with houses, food, and clothing as had been pledged. The food situation had been so bad throughout 1871 that Agent Berry had been forced to send the Shoshoni on a hunting expedition to the Teton country during the summer. As winter approached, he reported that, because of crop failures on the reservation, it would be necessary for the government to provide subsistence for all the Indians on the reservation, except the Bannock. That tribe refused to starve on the reservation and left for the buffalo plains again in the fall, even as Berry wrote to his superior that "the Bannock tribe . . . could have been induced to remain here permanently and give up hunting as a business, had this agency been prepared to subsist them. . . ."[15]

The summer of 1871 also saw the start of the difficulties over Camas Prairie which finally culminated in the outbreak there of the Bannock War in 1878.

---

[14] *Report of the Commissioner of Indian Affairs, 1871* (Washington, 1872), pp. 540-43.

[15] *Ibid.*, p. 540

The Bannock visited the prairie in June of 1871, as was their usual custom, to gather the camas root before leaving for the buffalo hunt. They discovered that much of the great plain was being used by white men as feeding grounds for large herds of hogs. The Bannock were highly indignant because the animals destroyed the camas plant. Furthermore, as their agent pointed out after talking to the chiefs, the Fort Bridger Treaty guaranteed the prairie to them as part of their home country. Article 2 designated that "portions of the . . . 'Kansas Prairie' countries" were to be retained by the tribe for its use. Berry further explained that, as there were no areas by that name within the limits of the treaty land, it was obvious that the spelling of the name was a clerical error. White men were merely using the mistake as a subterfuge for claiming the Camas Prairie as open for settlement and use by the whites.[16]

When Agent Berry gave the Bannock "permission" to go on the annual buffalo hunt in the fall of 1871, he also authorized them to return to the reservation by way of Camas Prairie, so that they could harvest a supply of camas. Part of the tribe, under Chief Otter Beard, accomplished the mission and returned to Fort Hall without having any difficulties with the whites. But some other Bannock, under Pagwhite, became involved in an attack on three white men at Wood River. The band killed one of the whites, wounded another, and took the seven horses belonging to the party. Two days later, the Bannock braves

---

[16] *Ibid.*, pp. 542-43; Berry to Walker, Fort Hall Agency, January 1, 1872, in Fort Hall Agency Letter Book, *op. cit.*, p. 102.

attacked a mule train of forty-seven animals and captured the whole lot.[17]

At the time, Chief Tendoy and his Lemhi were encamped only seven miles away and were engaged in trading with the Nez Perce. When Tendoy learned of the incidents, he went in search of the wounded white man and his companion and placed them under his protection. Then, gathering his warriors about him, he rode to the Bannock camp and demanded the return of the stolen horses and mules. The Bannock denounced the chief as a traitor and threatened to fight him. Tendoy thereupon called upon all Bannock who were friendly to the whites to join him. As a consequence, a large group under the subchief, Major Jim, joined with the Lemhi and forcibly retook the stolen animals. Tendoy returned the stock and the white men to Boise where the governor of Idaho presented him with a flag and some supplies as a reward for his faithfulness to the cause of peace.[18]

When Pagwhite's band reached Camas Prairie, Judge Clitus Barbour headed a delegation of citizens sent to investigate the murder on Wood River. The judge met with Tendoy and some of the members of Pagwhite's band; Pagwhite himself was not present,

---

[17] It should be pointed out that the Bannock were not the only ones guilty of such attacks. In June, 1868, a detachment of soldiers had to be sent to Camas Prairie to protect a group of Bannock from some white marauders. Reporting the incident, Lieutenant Thomas Barker said: "I learned on the road that a party of white men had been in search of these Indians for the avowed purpose of chastening them for horse stealing. But in my opinion their real object was to kill the Indians, and get possession of their horses." Thomas Barker to I. B. Sinclair, Fort Boise, June 26, 1868, U.S. National Archives, Records of the Bureau of Indian Affairs, Idaho Superintendency, *op. cit.*

[18] Berry to Walker, Fort Hall Agency, August 20, 1872, in Fort Hall Agency Letter Book, *op. cit.*, p. 113; *Report of the Commissioner of Indian Affairs, 1872,* p. 292.

Courtesy Arden M. Hansen, Fort Hall Agency

PROBABLE SIGHT OF OLD FORT HALL ON SNAKE RIVER

CHIEF PAT TYHEE

BANNOCK WOMAN AND CHILD

Courtesy A. Lillibridge

POCATELLO JUNCTION, JUNE 1886. LOOKING SOUTH FROM HARRISON AVENUE

having gone to Boise to return four stolen horses. The Bannock admitted four other killings of white men in the Montana area during the previous year and blamed their young warriors for the deeds. The Bannock prophet, Pe-te-go, was the principal spokesman and revealed that Pagwhite had directed the raid on the mule train. The assault on the three whites had been made by four young braves. Upon hearing of it, Pagwhite had gone after the warriors and brought them back. So the four had started out a second time; but, when the news reached Pagwhite, he had crawled into his tipi and let them go. Barbour also learned that Chief Winnemucca of the Nevada Paiute was sending runners to the Bannock with "superstitions" designed to arouse the Indians to war. One story being circulated was that "on a certain day, not far distant, all the dead Indians will rise from their graves and collect in some plain, making a great and powerful army, strong enough to overpower and wipe out all the white men."[19] The Barbour investigation had been prompted in part by a report from some Umatilla that the Bannock claimed the three whites attacked at Wood River were bad men who had robbed and terrorized travelers and had killed two Bannock men.[20]

After the investigation by Judge Barbour, rumors reached Boise that the 1,000 to 1,200 Bannock and Shoshoni at Camas Prairie intended to travel to the Weiser River to trade with the Umatilla and other Indians. The Idaho citizens and the newspaper edi-

[19] *Idaho Statesman,* July 2, 1872, p. 2.
[20] *Ibid.,* June 27, 1872, p. 2.

tors became so apprehensive that Governor T. W. Bennett and Major Downey visited the Indian camp and exacted a promise that the Indians would not go to the Weiser, but would return to Fort Hall. Contrary to their promise, the whole encampment moved to the Weiser because the Umatillas refused to come to Camas Prairie for fear of possible trouble with the whites. The *Idaho Statesman* thereupon attacked Agent High as the instigator of all the trouble because he had sent the Indians to Weiser River, "so as to keep them away from the reservation in order to get rid of feeding them."[21] The editor added later, "Whether he has anything to feed the Indians or not, we don't know. We know he ought to have, and he or his predecessor is to blame if he has no food for them...."[22] The excitement over a possible Indian outbreak grew so intense that a petition signed by "Many Citizens" of Weiser River was published by the *Statesman* on August 9, 1872:

Once more our fair country is overrun with Indians from all parts of Idaho. . . . Women and children are terrified, families have left their own homes, and moved in with their neighbors for better protection. . . . We have begged, prayed, and petitioned Governors and Indian Agents for the removal of our Indians. . . . Our prayer was answered by sending a very young gentlemanly officer through here to inform the good people of Weiser, that the poor Indian must live somewhere. The authorities could have sent a bottle of Mrs. Winslow's Soothing Syrup through here with much less expense, and with just as good an effect. . . .
These Indians will never traverse the Upper Weiser another season. Forbearance with us has ceased to be a virtue,

---

[21] *Ibid.*, July 20, 1872, p. 2.
[22] *Ibid.*, July 27, 1872, p. 2.

and as we find that we need look for no assistance from authorities, we will with our own strong arms, protect ourselves. If they attempt another raid through here we will give some of them passes that will do them for all time and insure their safe transit to their happy hunting ground.[23]

Despite all the excitement engendered by the Indians, bent only on doing some peaceful trading, no other troubles occurred, and the Bannock and Shoshoni returned to the reservation in late August.

The question of what should be done about the murderers of the white man on Wood River puzzled the Fort Hall agent because the Fort Bridger Treaty made no provision for such an affair. Directed by the Indian Commissioner to arrest the culprits, the agent made arrangements with the civil authorities at Boise. The Bannock, however, refused to give up the braves and, "saucy and impudent," returned to the reservation. The agent, with a force of soldiers, surrounded the Bannock camp at night, secured two of the murderers, and arrested Pagwhite, releasing him only when he promised to bring in the remaining criminals. Pagwhite subsequently brought in two more and turned them over to the agent. After the four were put under charge of the military, a long delay ensued while the civil authorities determined the procedure for conducting a trial. The agent considered the prompt arrest of the four Indians to be a salutary lesson for the Bannock.[24] It was, indeed, a sure sign of the gradual subordination of the Ban-

---

[23] *Ibid.*, August 17, 1872, p. 3.
[24] High to Walker, Fort Hall Agency, September 14, 1872, in Fort Hall Agency Letter Book, *op. cit.*, p. 119; *ibid.*, November 4, 1872, p. 131; *ibid.*, December 5, 1872, p. 133.

nock to the authorities of the United States, because
here, for the first time, Bannock warriors were arrested and imprisoned for a deed which would have
brought only honor to them in days past.

The return of most of the Bannock to Fort Hall
for the winter of 1872 placed the agency in a serious
predicament. As Agent High explained to the Indian
Commissioner, the "unusual and unexpected" action
of the Bannock would exhaust the supply of beef by
February of the next year, and the dead of winter
would find the Indians without means of subsistence.
The annuity goods were again sent to Wind River
agency by mistake, but High was able to get them
transferred to Fort Hall by January for distribution
to the Bannock. High joined most of his predecessors
in censuring the government for failing to live up to
the Fort Bridger Treaty stipulations and said the
Bannock were compelled to lead a "vagabond life"
in search of food and clothing. He spoke of them
as "as fine material for the Christian philanthropist
as can be found among the Indian tribes." The lesson of the winter of 1872 was not lost upon the Bannock and the following year they went after buffalo,
determined to depend upon themselves as providers,
for they could no longer trust the Great Father in
Washington.[25]

Some of the agents outlined from time to time the
exact amount of beef and flour required to subsist
the Indian population of Fort Hall Reservation. The
Fort Bridger Treaty entitled the Bannock to $6,937
for the clothing annuity and $16,000 for rations and

---

[25] *Ibid.; Report of the Commissioner of Indian Affairs, 1872,* p. 656.

other necessaries of life. The nontreaty Shoshoni on the reservation were to receive $20,000 a year in food, clothing, and farm implements. The population of the agency, in the early 1870's, ranged from 1,200 to 1,500. In 1875 Agent Danilson estimated that it required 547,500 pounds of flour and a like amount of beef to feed 1,500 Indians during one year. For that year the allowance for them was 125,000 pounds of flour and the same amount of beef. As he explained, the subsistence allowed the Indians would give each about two pounds of flour and two pounds of beef a week, or enough for one meal per day for two days out of seven. Faced with such realism, the Bannock chose to go on the annual hunt, even though it required a journey of six hundred miles or more. As a consequence of the absence of the Bannock nearly every year, the Shoshoni on the reservation were able to get along on the subsistence provided, and they became more accustomed to reservation life than did their neighbors who were away nine months of every year.[26]

By 1873, affairs at Fort Hall had become as routine as limited appropriations would allow, but many problems besides subsistence arose to plague the agents. According to the *Idaho Statesman* of April 26, 1873, there were really no limits to the reservation which supposedly contained about 1,568,000 acres of land.[27] The year before, Agent High reported that white

---

[26] Danilson to Smith, Fort Hall Agency, July 31, 1875, in Fort Hall Agency Letter Book, *op. cit.*, p. 290; *Report of the Commissioner of Indian Affairs, 1872*, p. 539; *Report . . . , 1875*, p. 258.

[27] *Report of the Commissioner of Indian Affairs, 1872*, p. 539; *Idaho Statesman*, April 26, 1873, p. 2.

settlers were encroaching on reservation property along the southern and eastern borders, and so he requested that the line be surveyed.

The vaguely defined boundaries resulted, in part, from the manner in which the reservation was surveyed in the first place. After the ratification of the Fort Bridger Treaty and after the order which gave the Bannock a home at Fort Hall, the governor of Idaho was instructed to have the reservation surveyed. According to the common talk of the time, the Idaho executive went to the Portneuf country with a surveying party, "looked around a little and then with a wave of his hand said, 'Boys, survey out a good sized reservation around here for these Indians.'" The governor then returned to Boise; and the surveyor, who was to be paid by the mile, proceeded to his work. In consequence, a reservation much larger than intended was set apart for the Bannock and Shoshoni.[28]

Such factors as the reservation boundary and the annual hunting expeditions of the Bannock were only a few of the problems which finally led the Office of Indian Affairs, in 1873, to send a commission to treat with the Bannock and Shoshoni to arrange an amicable settlement. General John P. C. Shanks, Governor T. W. Bennett of Idaho, and Henry W. Reed, as the commission, arranged to meet the Indians at Camas Prairie on August 25, 1873; but, as anyone familiar with the customs of the tribe could have foretold, only a few were there. At the second meeting, arranged for November 5, 6, and 7 at Fort

---

[28] John Hailey, *The History of Idaho* (Boise, Idaho 1910), pp. 225-26.

Hall, both tribes were fully represented. As outlined by General Shanks, the principal reason for the new agreement was to abrogate Article 4 of the Treaty of Fort Bridger of 1868, which secured to the Bannock the right to "hunt on the unoccupied lands of the United States." The increase of white population and the scarcity of game for Indian subsistence were advanced as reasons for the change in the treaty, and this amendment was made Article 1 of the new pact. Seven other articles were included, designed chiefly to halt encroachments on the reservation by white men who continually placed the Indian Department in embarrassing, troublesome situations. Article 2 placed the building and operation of public roads through the reservation under the Secretary of the Interior so that the practice of charging exorbitant tolls could be controlled. To prevent private traders and stage companies from pasturing large herds of horses and cattle on reservation grasslands, Article 3 was included in the agreement. Article 4 was designed to prevent the cutting of hay and timber on the reservation by whites. The fifth article provided for changes in the reservation boundaries; the southern line of the reserve included some fifty-two families who had been well established there before the reservation was set up, and the line was moved north to ensure them their homes. As compensation to the Indians, the opposite boundary was moved farther north and, incidentally, included seventeen improvements which were chiefly stock ranches and liquor establishments. In the words of the agreement, the new boundaries of the reservation were as follows:

Beginning at a point on the south line of said reservation due west of a point five miles south of a point where the stage-road from Corinne, Utah, to Helena, Montana, now crosses the main branch of the Port Neuf, (near the toll-gate); thence due east past said point until it intersects the south or east line of said reservation; thence following the line of the present survey, and continuing the east line of said reservation due north to the center of Snake River; thence down the center of Snake River to the mouth of the Port Neuf; thence with the line of said survey to the place of beginning.

Article 6 merely recorded that all provisions of the Treaty of Fort Bridger remained valid except for the change in Article 4. To remove the troublesome and unlicensed traders and whites from the reservation, Article 7 explicitly stated that such persons could live at Fort Hall only by permission of the Indian Department. Article 8 provided that when any Indian family had begun farming (as outlined under Articles 6 and 8 of the Fort Bridger Treaty), it should be entitled to a house built by the government and should also be given one milch cow.[29]

The agreement was signed on November 7, 1873, by 230 men of the two tribes headed by the Bannock chiefs Otter Beard, Tyhee, and Pagwhite, and by the Shoshoni chiefs Captain Jim, Gibson Jack, and Pocatello. The chiefs fully expected the agreement to go into effect soon; but, by September, 1874, Agent Reed was still regretting the inaction of Congress in not ratifying it, and remarked that the Indians "seem to think that such treaties amount to nothing."[30] By

---

[29] U.S. Congress, House of Representatives, *Bannock and Other Indians in Southern Idaho, op. cit.,* pp. 1-6.

[30] *Report of the Commissioner of Indian Affairs, 1874,* p. 284.

1879, the agreement was still unratified. The *Idaho Statesman* explained the failure of Congress to act on the agreement: Congressman Shanks had proposed a bill embodying the provisions as drawn up by his commission, but John Hailey, Idaho delegate to Congress, insisted that the bill be amended to provide for payment of the property of fifteen of the seventeen settlers included within the new reservation boundary on the north. The amendment was finally made, but Shanks refused to present the new bill for ratification, believing that the so-called settlers were not entitled to compensation. The reasons for congressional inaction were not as important to the Bannock as was the fact that the Great Father in Washington had repudiated his word. The Indians were to meet with more examples of governmental infidelity in the future.[31]

The Commission of 1873 also took cognizance of the loose bands of Shoshoni wandering around the country, held councils with some, and finally recommended to the Indian Department that all of them be placed on the Fort Hall Reservation. In July, 1869, Chief Pocatello and his band of two hundred Shoshoni were at Fort Hall, and the agent recommended at that time that they be assigned to the reservation.[32] Nothing further came of the suggestion and, in July, 1871, Agent High requested the military to arrest Pocatello and his group of twelve "outlaws" for depredations committed on travelers be-

---

[31] *Idaho Statesman*, February 8, 1879, p. 2.
[32] *Report of the Commissioner of Indian Affairs, 1869*, p. 728.

tween Salt Lake City and Montana.[33]   Again in December of 1872, the Fort Hall agent recommended that Pocatello's band be put on the reservation to get them away from the Mormon settlers in northern Utah.[34] In an attempt to bring Pocatello and other Shoshoni chiefs under the control of the Office of Indian Affairs, Agent Berry in October, 1871, made a trip through Cache Valley and succeeded in persuading a number of the wandering Shoshoni to settle at Fort Hall.[35]

As a result of the negotiations conducted by the commissioners, the Northwestern Shoshoni who had originally signed the Treaty of Box Elder in July, 1863, agreed to move to Fort Hall. Of the 400 Indians involved, Pocatello and the 101 people under him were already at Fort Hall. Chief San Pitch, with 124 people, and Chief Sagwitch, with 158 people, decided to settle on Bannock Creek. Only Chief Tav-i-wun-shear and his group of seventeen failed to move to Fort Hall, preferring Wind River Reservation instead. The commission also recommended that the 1,945 Western Shoshoni of Nevada and the 500 Lemhi Indians be sent to Fort Hall; but this suggestion was not followed, because the two groups refused to go.[36]

Except for the recognition that the Lemhi existed, the Indian Department failed to provide a home for these people until J. A. Viall took over the Superintendency of Indian Affairs for Montana in 1871.

---

[33] Fort Hall Agency Letter Book, *op. cit.*, p. 73.

[34] *Ibid.*, p. 133.

[35] *Ibid.*, p. 93.

[36] U.S. Congress, Senate, Ex. Doc., 42, 43rd Cong., 1st Sess., Serial No. 1580 (Washington, 1873), pp. 12-34.

At first, arrangements were made to move the Lemhi to the Crow Reservation. The Indians were agreed, until hostilities broke out between the Crow and the main Bannock tribe over some stolen horses. The Bannock element of the Lemhi, therefore, concluded to ask for a home in the Idaho country. Agent A. J. Simmons finally located the Lemhi on Lemhi River about twenty miles above the mouth of the stream. Simmons reported the interest of the Indians in farming, and his superintendent requested an annual appropriation of $5,000 for agricultural implements and seeds so that the Lemhi could make a start at becoming self-sufficient.[37]

By 1872, an annual gift of $25,000 was being given to the Lemhi, and the Indian Commissioner recommended that, inasmuch as they did not have a reservation, it would be best to move them to Fort Hall. The Indian agents were unanimous in their praise of Chief Tendoy, the principal accolade being given him by the Commission of 1873, which, as already noted, wished to make him the titular head of all the Bannock and Shoshoni in eastern Idaho. Despite the belief of the Indian Commission that the Lemhi would be willing to go to Fort Hall, the Indians continued to ask for a reservation of their own. In May, 1874, the Indian Commissioner ordered Agent Harrison Fuller to move the Lemhi to Fort Hall. Fuller obediently called a council, read the commissioner's instructions to Tendoy and his people, but soon learned that they "positively refused to go." The agent re-

---

[37] *Report of the Commissioner of Indian Affairs, 1870,* p. 193; *Report . . . 1871,* p. 415.

solved his embarrassment over his inability to carry out departmental orders by writing to the commissioner for further instructions. Agent High, at Fort Hall, made all preparations to receive Tendoy's band and, when they did not appear, attributed their refusal to the influence of "evilminded or interested men."[38]

The determination of Chief Tendoy and his people to secure a reservation of their own ultimately received the reluctant approval of the Office of Indian Affairs. The tribe had signed a treaty with the United States at Virginia City on September 24, 1868; but the agreement had never been ratified, and the tract of land assigned to them had never been set aside for their use. By a presidential executive order of February 12, 1875, the Lemhi Valley Indian Reservation of about one hundred square miles was established on Lemhi River for the "mixed tribes of Shoshone, Bannock, and Sheepeater Indians."[39] The tribe, at the time, numbered about seven hundred people, of whom over one hundred were Bannock. The Lemhi Reservation became a sort of crossroads for the Nez Perce, Flathead, Shoshoni, and Bannock on their way to and from the buffalo country or en route to trade horses and robes. Most of the tribes stopped off for rations at the agency, and this constant drain on supplies often forced the agents to send the Lemhi out on hunting expeditions.[40]

Similar problems of limited appropriations and gov-

---

[38] *Report of the Commissioner of Indian Affairs, 1872*, p. 49; *Report . . . 1874*, pp. 264-65, 284.

[39] *Report of the Commissioner of Indian Affairs, 1877*, p. 241.

[40] *Report of the Commissioner of Indian Affairs, 1876*, p. 44.

ernmental failure to live up to treaty stipulations
made the position of the agents at Fort Hall anything
but a pleasant one. When the Bannock came in from
the winter's hunt, in the spring of 1874, expecting
or at least hoping for some aid in subsistence, the
agent was obliged to show them an empty larder and
send them back on a summer hunt. After thus having
spent almost a year away from the agency in search
of food, many of the Bannock decided to live at the
reservation and depend on the government for subsistence during the winter of 1874-75. The supply
of beef gave out about the first of January, and the
Bannock and Shoshoni were barely able to live on
the reduced rations for the remainder of the winter.
The Bannock, as a result, "became thoroughly disgusted" with the reservation and left for their old
hunting grounds early in the summer. Agent Danilson was convinced that they would have remained
at the agency permanently if the Indian Department
had been able to subsist them.[41]

While 250 of the Bannock spent the winter of
1876 in the buffalo country, the remaining 400 chose
again to stay on the reservation. Food supplies proved
to be even less abundant this year than in the previous year. Although only half rations were distributed, all the flour and most of the beef had been
consumed by March 1, 1876; and, by April 20, the
issue of general rations ceased completely. More than
one thousand Indians were thus thrown upon their
own resources at a time when the snow still lay on

---

[41] *Report of the Commissioner of Indian Affairs, 1875*, p. 258.

the ground and hunting was very difficult. Danilson described his desperate situation as follows:

Large numbers came to the office begging most piteously
for food, stating that their children were crying for bread,
which I well knew was the truth. It is not an easy matter
to describe how an agent with any feeling of humanity is
affected under these circumstances, or to convince the Indians
it is not his fault that more food is not furnished. They
behaved most admirably under the circumstances and left
the agency with sad and sorrowful hearts.[42]

While many observers would have agreed with
Superintendent DeFloyd Jones, in 1870, that the Bannock used the reservation only as a rendezvous where
they gathered to collect their annuity goods, by 1875
it was quite unjust of the Indian Commissioner to
describe the tribe as having "scarcely taken the first
step toward civilization," and ascribing the reason to
the fact that they spent "more than half the time in
hunting outside the reserve."[43]

Despite the firm conviction of most of the agents
that the Bannock would have been eager and happy
to settle down on the reservation for twelve months
of the year, most white settlers were convinced that
no such desire existed with the Indians. The Legislative Assembly of Wyoming Territory expressed this
conviction in a memorial addressed to the Congress of
the United States on February 23, 1876. The resolution stated that the annual trips of the Indians
(Bannock, Eastern Shoshoni, etc.) were "ostensibly

---

[42] *Report of the Commissioner of Indian Affairs, 1876*, pp. 42-43.
[43] *Report of the Commissioner of Indian Affairs, 1870*, p. 183; *Report
. . . 1875*, p. 45.

made for the purpose of hunting, but really made for the purpose of plunder, murder, and all crimes of which the Indians are capable (and their names are legion)," and then continued:

> While all the power of the Government has been threatened, and in a measure used, to prevent white men from trespassing on their lands, so uselessly held by them to the exclusion of those who would mine for precious metals, (which it is well known exist there) and who would cultivate the soil and make valuable territory thereof, these lawless pets have been allowed to leave their reservations (so called) whenever they would, to prey upon and devastate the property, lives, and peaceful occupations of these frontier settlers, with the virtual consent of their guardians, the agents of the Government. While the blood-seeking brave (God save the word!) and his filthy squaw have fed at public expense in those hatch-holes of fraud known as agencies, the widow and children of the white man slain by the treacherous Indian have been obliged to depend on their own energies or the bounty of neighbors for the necessaries of life.[44]

While the citizens of Wyoming expressed their grievances to their representatives in Washington, the Bannock also sought redress for wrongs by selecting the governor of Idaho to represent them before the national authorities. Chiefs Pagwhite of the Bannock and Captain Jim and Gibson Jack of the Shoshoni, with other leaders, sought a conference with Governor D. P. Thompson in July of 1876. A correspondent of the *Idaho Statesman* interviewed them and learned that they feared the government intended to drive them out of their country and move them to

---

[44] U.S. Congress, House of Representatives, Misc. Doc. 123, 44th Cong., 1st Sess., Serial No. 1702 (Washington, 1875), p. 1.

the Indian Territory in the Oklahoma region. The
Utah Indians had been spreading such a rumor, and
the Bannock and Shoshoni were afraid it was true.
Furthermore, the Indian leaders indicated that they
had asked former Governor T. W. Bennett for a
change of administration at the agency, but the Great
Father at Washington had had no ear for their
troubles. They eventually met Governor Thompson
and asked him to lay their grievances before the authorities in Washington.[45]

After the conference, the chiefs returned to the
reservation where the Shoshoni spent the next winter.
Four hundred and fifty of the Bannock, determined
to fend for themselves after their experience of the
previous winter, traveled to the plains area in search
of subsistence. The 212 Bannock and 845 Shoshoni
remaining at the agency fared well on the ample food
stocks made available by the departure of the main
Bannock group.[46]

The pattern of life on the reservation during the
1870's was dependent on the amount of food that
could be provided by the government. The Indians
had not yet learned to farm for a livelihood and,
indeed, could not have done so in large numbers
anyway, because they were not furnished with the
necessary tools and seeds. The Shoshoni, more docile
and "civilized," chose to remain on the reservation
as wards of the government. The Bannock, more independent and self-sufficient, refused to remain at the
agency when they could not be assured of the sub-

---

[45] *Idaho Statesman*, July 22, 1876, p. 2.
[46] *Report of the Commissioner of Indian Affairs, 1877*, p. 78.

sistence promised them by treaty. Thus, during a period when they should have been learning to adjust themselves to the new economy of individual farms, the Bannock were forced by the neglect of a careless and indifferent government to continue their nomadic wanderings to obtain camas and buffalo.

The Bannock War of 1878

WHEN the Bannock returned from the winter hunt, early in 1877, an event outside their realm forced a change in their routine of subsistence activities. Chief Joseph and his Nez Perce, aggrieved and harassed, took to the warpath in the summer of that year. To prevent sympathetic allies from joining the hostiles, the Office of Indian Affairs took steps to keep all neighboring Indians within the shelter of their reservations. Throughout the year, therefore, the Bannock were forced to remain at Fort Hall under government protection and to accept the scant rations given them. The war hysteria started by the Nez Perce spread to the Bannock at Fort Hall and built up in intensity under the close and unaccustomed restraint of enforced reservation life.[1]

About August 1, a rumor came to the agency that United States troops were being sent to fight the Bannock. Before the ensuing excitement had subsided, a tramp appeared at Fort Hall declaring that he had been driven there by a band of Nez Perce. Hurried preparations were made by the Bannock to go in pursuit of this group. While the hysteria was

---

[1] U.S. Office of Indian Affairs, *Annual Report of the Commissioner of Indian Affairs, 1878* (Washington, 1879), p. xii.

at its height, a Bannock warrior, armed with a Winchester rifle and a revolver and fortified by some whisky, left the camp and seriously wounded Robert Boyd and Orson James, two white teamsters who were passing the agency. Apparently there was no provocation for the attack, unless a story related by Sarah Winnemucca was true. This daughter of Chief Winnemucca of the Nevada Paiute recorded later that a certain "Bannock Jack," with fifteen Bannock families, appeared at the Malheur Reservation in Oregon in May or June, 1878. Bannock Jack said that two of the Bannock

. . . got drunk and went and shot two white men. One of the Indians had a sister out digging some roots, and these white men went to the women who were digging, and caught this poor girl and used her shamefully. The other women ran away and left this girl to the mercy of those white men, and it was on her account that her brother went and shot them.[2]

While it is doubtful that Boyd and James were guilty of the crime charged, the incident could have been perpetrated by two other whites, and the Bannock might have been merely using the Indian method of avenging a wrong by attacking any white man. The chiefs of both Bannock and Shoshoni denounced the shooting and promised that the murderer would be turned over to United States authorities.

After considerable delay, the guilty man was arrested on November 23, 1877, by authority of Agent Danilson. A number of Bannock gathered around

---

[2] Sarah Winnemucca Hopkins, *Life Among the Paiutes; Their Wrongs and Claims;* ed. by Mrs. Horace Mann (Boston, 1883), p. 138.

the trading post at the time of the arrest and, in the excitement, a friend of the prisoner shot and killed Alexander Rhoden, a white man employed in delivering cattle to the reservation. Danilson, convinced that the Bannock were seeking trouble, telegraphed the military post at Fort Hall. The next morning Captain A. H. Bainbridge, commander at the post, arrived at the agency with fifteen soldiers and joined with the agent in demanding that the Bannock bring in the guilty man, Tambiago. They replied that he, with his father and two brothers, had crossed Snake River and could not be found. After repeated warnings by Danilson and Bainbridge, the Bannock made other attempts to bring in Tambiago but were never successful.[3] The obvious hostility of the tribe finally led the agent to ask for more troops to hold the Bannock in check. On the fifth of December, therefore, three companies of infantry arrived at the reservation, and their commander, Major Bryant, immediately held a council with the Indians and gave them ten days in which to deliver the culprit to him. Again they declared that Tambiago could not be found.[4]

General John E. Smith visited the agency December 26 and demanded that the Bannock bring in the guilty man, but to no avail. On January 9, Captain Bainbridge arrested a suspicious-looking Indian seen loitering in the vicinity of Taylor's Bridge, and the man was soon identified as Tambiago. The prisoner was sent to Malad City to await investigation and trial.

---

[3] *Report of the Commissioner of Indian Affairs, 1877,* p. 78.
[4] *Report of the Commissioner of Indian Affairs, 1878,* pp. 49-50.

The Bannock became thoroughly aroused over the arrest of Tambiago. Even earlier, about fifty Shoshoni had moved from the reservation to Marsh Valley because of threats made against them by the Bannock. The white settlers near the reservation were similarly alarmed and had either built stockades for protection or were in the process of building them.[5] On January 15, three companies of cavalry reached the agency and, the following morning, General Smith directed the troops to surround two of the Bannock villages of about thirty-two lodges. The soldiers captured 53 warriors, 32 guns, and about 300 horses. The prisoners were marched to the agency; the father and two brothers of Tambiago were sent to the military post at Fort Hall and, after an address by Smith, the remaining Bannock were returned to their camps.[6] Throughout the entire affair the Bannock displayed no fear, and "they were in no way backward in using threats and insults toward the soldiers performing this duty."[7]

The problems of the disposition of the three hundred ponies became a matter of much correspondence between the agency and the military. Danilson at first recommended that the horses be sold and the proceeds invested in farming implements. After much correspondence, he finally suggested that the horses be returned because they were needed for farming operations and "the number captured does not cripple them [Bannock] for offensive operations, and tends

---

[5] *Idaho Statesman*, January 22, 1878, p. 2.
[6] *Report of the Commissioner of Indian Affairs, 1878*, p. 50.
[7] *Idaho Statesman*, June 11, 1878, p. 3.

to make disaffected ones more troublesome."[8] The weapons captured were kept by the army on the grounds that the Bannock were well supplied with arms anyway, and the retention of the few ancient firearms would make little difference. This, of course, only added fuel to the flames of discontent which were rapidly spreading among the Bannock.

When the army commander prepared to transfer the troops from Fort Hall to Camp Douglas, Agent Danilson objected that such a course would be dangerous in the extreme, and it would then be necessary for him to abandon the agency. In April, General George Crook inspected affairs at the reservation and concluded that the "disarming and dismounting of the tribe. . . appears to have been unnecessary . . . and its remembrance will only survive as an irritant."[9] Despite the protestations of Danilson, the main body of soldiers left Fort Hall on May 5, 1878, and the agent elected to remain at the agency. After the outbreak of the Bannock War, the Office of Indian Affairs accused the military of deprecating the just fears of Agent Danilson and suggested that if troops had been left at Fort Hall the Bannock would never have gone on the warpath.

The obvious restlessness of the Bannock came to the attention of Lieutenant Colonel W. B. Royall, acting inspector general of the army, when he visited Fort Hall in March, but he was of the opinion that army officers and civilians alike regarded the Bannock "as friendly and peaceable toward the whites."

---

[8] *Report of the Commissioner of Indian Affairs, 1878,* p. xvii.
[9] *Ibid.,* p. xix.

He attributed much of the unrest to the opposition of the Bannock toward Agent Danilson who, he said, "has lost all influence, and, therefore, control of these Indians."[10]

A more direct threat of war was reported by Agent W. V. Rinehart of Malheur Agency. Two Bannock visited Malheur in March and reported that there would soon be trouble at Fort Hall. They said that the capture of their horses had determined the Bannock upon war and that as soon as the "grass came" they intended to take their women and children to Camas Prairie and then go to the buffalo country to fight the soldiers.[11]

As evidences of the warlike intent of the Bannock increased, it seemed almost incredible to most of Idaho's citizens that Agent Danilson should allow the Indians to leave the reservation as he did, in the early spring of 1878. When questioned later concerning his action, he said that he could not keep the "roaming" Bannock at the agency "when the amount of supplies was scarcely enough to feed Indians engaged in farming."[12] By the first of May, about two hundred of the most rebellious Bannock were gathered near Payne's Ferry on the Snake River, and their leader, Chief Buffalo Horn, was having difficulty controlling them.[13]

The sudden rise of Buffalo Horn to the chieftainship of the warlike element of the Bannock was due,

[10] W. B. Royall to Adjutant General, Dept. of Platte, March 19, 1878. Copy, U.S.D.I., O.I.A., Gen. Files, Idaho, W1028/1878.

[11] *Report of the Commissioner of Indian Affairs, 1878,* p. 119.

[12] *Ibid.,* p. 49.

[13] *Idaho Statesman,* May 11, 1878, p. 1.

in great part, to his proven worth as a warrior and as a leader of scouts under various United States army commanders. While serving with General George Crook in 1876, the Bannock scout volunteered to take a message from Powder River, through enemy country, to General Nelson A. Miles on Yellowstone River. In company with a Crow scout, Leforge, and "Buffalo Bill" Cody, he successfully completed the dangerous journey. Later in the same year, a lone Bannock among a group of Crow scouts, he participated in a number of battles between the forces under General Miles and the Cheyenne.[14]

With the opening of the Nez Perce War in 1877, he again volunteered for service and joined General O. O. Howard's forces on July 29. This time he was the leader of twenty Bannock scouts. The following day Howard recorded, "We had . . . our first trouble with the Bannock scouts." They refused to travel further until they had rested, but Buffalo Horn, "a young Indian, very handsomely decked off with skins and plumage," induced all but three to continue with the troops.[15] General Howard several times mentioned the "good conduct" of "this trusted Indian," but he also had to note evidences of independence on the part of the scout. After the battle at the Big Hole with the Nez Perce, the Bannock scouts and their leader disinterred the bodies of the Nez Perce women who had been slain in order to get the scalps for trophies.

---

[14] Thomas H. Leforge, *Memoirs of a White Crow Indian,* as told by Thomas B. Marquis (New York: D. Appleton-Century Company, Inc., 1928), pp. 261, 267, 273-74.

[15] O. O. Howard, *Nez Perce Joseph* (Boston, 1881), p. 175.

On August 23, while at the headwaters of Henrys Fork of the Snake River, Buffalo Horn appeared at the general's tent and asked if he and his men might hold a war dance with one hundred and fifty other Bannock scouts who had just ridden in from Fort Hall to join the troops. Permission was given and the warriors held the ceremony. About midnight, Buffalo Horn and a half-breed, Rainé, came to the general for permission to kill the three Nez Perce herders who were accompanying the military force. The three herders were brought before Howard and asked if it were true, as charged by the Bannock, that they had betrayed information to Chief Joseph's people. All three denied the charges, and the general refused to let Buffalo Horn kill them. The Bannock "was very angry in consequence, and never quite forgave me for this refusal."[16]

The esteem of the army for Buffalo Horn was also shared by many of the leading citizens of Idaho. As late as May 17, 1878, when the chief and a few of his men visited Boise, the *Idaho Statesman* commented on his worth as a scout under General Howard in the Nez Perce War: "Whatever were the shortcomings of the other Indian scouts, Buffalo Horn always stood bravely and faithfully to his duty and never failed to give perfect satisfaction."[17] What the editor failed to point out was that the long experience of Buffalo Horn in fighting under different army commanders could make him a dangerous opponent. As

---

[16] *Ibid.*, p. 232; Chester Anders Fee, *Chief Joseph, the Biography of a Great Indian* (New York, 1936), p. 211.

[17] *Idaho Statesman*, May 18, 1878, p. 1.

the leader of a hostile Bannock tribe, he would have opportunity to demonstrate his knowledge of white military tactics.

As already noted, Buffalo Horn and two hundred of his followers were at Payne's Ferry on May 1. Shortly afterward, they left to join other Bannock and the Lemhi at Camas Prairie. During almost a month spent on the plain, the Bannock refused to trade or converse with the whites as they had customarily done in the past. As they had done for several years prior to 1878, white men were herding hogs and cattle and horses on the prairie. There were about 2,500 head of cattle and 80 head of "American horses" feeding there at the time. On May 22, Buffalo Horn told some of the white herders that the prairie was his country and he wanted the cattle removed immediately. The white men in charge of the animals decided to leave before trouble began, and started to make preparations for moving away from the area.[18]

Before they could get away, an incident occurred that was to start Buffalo Horn and his people on the warpath and was to involve many hundreds of other Indians. On May 28, as later information showed, Joe, a wild son of Chief Bannock John, started on a drinking and gambling spree. After a day and night of wagering, he had lost most of his possessions and, being "mad and desperate," persuaded a companion to go with him to the cattlemen's camp.[19] At sunrise on May 30, the two Indians reached the camp of William Silvey, Lew Kensler, and George

---

[18] *Ibid.*, June 1, 1878, p. 3.
[19] *Ibid.*, June 13, 1878, p. 3.

Nesby and offered to sell a buffalo robe. While the men were examining the robe, the two Bannock shot and seriously wounded Kensler and Nesby. Silvey made his escape. The two wounded men also managed to get away, and news of the attack soon reached Boise.[20]

That night, a courier reached the city with a message to Governor Mason Brayman from a mountain man, James Dempsey. He warned that war was emminent and that the Bannock were acting "in concert" with the Umatilla and Malheur Indians. He indicated that war might still be avoided if the governor would come, with a few men, to talk to Buffalo Horn and the Bannock. The Idaho executive did not go. He later became the subject of vitriolic attacks by the *Idaho Statesman* because he had granted Buffalo Horn permission to purchase some ammunition about two weeks before the outbreak at Camas Prairie. In his own defense, Brayman replied that the Bannock chief had promised he would return to Fort Hall after digging camas, and he had been given only one hundred cartridges and a small amount of powder for hunting purposes.[21]

Meanwhile, the Bannock were engaged in a council of war that eventually resulted in their killing of Dempsey and in the decision of about two hundred Bannock warriors to engage in a general war. The excitement caused by the shooting of Kensler and Nesby almost caused fighting among the Bannock themselves. A part of the tribe was for peace and

---

[20] *Ibid.*, June 1, 1878, p. 3.
[21] *Ibid.*

soon packed up and departed for Fort Hall Reservation to escape any involvement in the activities of those favoring war. Chief Tendoy and his Lemhi also left immediately for their reservation, to get out of harm's way.[22] Chief Buffalo Horn, as leader of the dissidents, referred to the warning of one of the officials at Fort Hall that the whole tribe would be held responsible for any depredations committed by its members. Therefore, he reasoned, since all would be blamed for the shooting and would no doubt be severely punished anyway, why not go on the warpath and get some horses and supplies before having to face the wrath of the government? This argument won over about one hundred and fifty braves, and the group sacked the camp of the white herders and then headed for the Snake River, which they intended to cross for safety.[23]

During this prelude to war, Tambiago, the slayer of Alexander Rhoden, and one of the causes of Bannock resolution to fight, was still in prison. After he had been sentenced to be hanged, his father and two brothers were ordered taken from the Fort Hall stockade and sent to Omaha Barracks. Before his execution on June 28, Tambiago was asked the reasons for the Bannock decision to strike. He declared that the discontent of his tribesmen with the agent and the missionary at Fort Hall, the counseling of Dempsey for two years past that war was inevitable, and the despoiling of Camas Prairie by the whites drove

---

[22] General I. McDowell to General W. T. Sherman, June 7, 1878. Copy, A.G.O., to U.S.D.I., O.I.A., General Files, Idaho, W1004/1878.

[23] *Idaho Statesman*, June 13, 1878, p. 3.

Tambiago, his father and two brothers were sent to Omaha Barracks

his people to rebel.[24] Before going to his death, Tambiago also informed white officials that the intent of the hostiles under Buffalo Horn was to rendezvous in the Juniper Mountains, where they hoped to get the Northern Paiute to join them, and then to "proceed northward to Salmon River."[25]

Proof that some of the Bannock had begun to plan for war as early as April was indicated by the experience of Levi A. Gheen. As agent of the Western Shoshoni Reservation near Elko, Nevada, he was called to meet with a large group of Shoshoni who had assembled at the agency upon hearing that Bannock emissaries were coming to interview them and their agent. The Bannock informed Gheen that they intended to make an alliance with the Shoshoni in preparation for a general war with the whites and warned him that, if he tried to prevent the union, he would be killed. A Western Shoshoni chief, Captain Sam, joined with the agent in denouncing the Bannock scheme and declared his adherence to the cause of peace and to the defense of the whites. The Bannock from Camas Prairie told Gheen also that, if he would use his influence to have the weapons returned to the Bannock which the Fort Hall troops had taken, they would consider letting him go unharmed. Before leaving, they repeated their threats against him.[26] The same Captain Sam later reported to another Nevada agent, A. J. Barnes: "One promise made by the Bannocks was that when they had de-

---

[24] *Ibid.*, June 27, 1878, p. 3.
[25] *Salt Lake Tribune*, June 16, 1878, p. 1.
[26] *Report of the Commissioner of Indian Affairs, 1878*, p. 105.

stroyed the railways and killed the whites, they would divide both sides of the world among their friends, and kill all Indians who had not united with them."[27]

As noted above, Agent W. V. Rinehart of Malheur Reservation, in March, had already heard rumors of war from Bannock representatives, and he wrote his superior at that time that "an outbreak at Fort Hall would cause excitement and enlist sympathy among these Indians [Paiute]." At the June 1 issue of rations, forty Bannock were present and asked Rinehart for rations, which he refused them. Chief Egan, war chief of the Paiute, asked the agent to give the Bannock some rations, as visitors, but the agent was obdurate. Egan then divided his own supplies with the Bannock, and both groups left immediately afterwards. Then, on June 5, all the working Indians at the Malheur Agency quit and left without telling the agent. He learned that the Bannock and Paiute were congregating at the fish traps on Malheur River, twenty miles from the agency.[28]

The Northern Paiute of Malheur Agency were in a receptive mood when the Bannock invitation to war came to them. Their principal grievance was against Agent Rinehart, whose integrity and effectiveness as a representative of the Indian Department was certainly open to question. When the Paiute failed to come to the agency on June 7 to get their rations, Rinehart concluded that war was imminent and abandoned the agency and removed its occupants to the safety of one of the settlements.[29]

---

[27] *Ibid.*, p. 103.

[28] *Ibid.*, p. 119.

[29] *Ibid.*, pp. 119-20.

While the Paiute were gathering forces with every intent to join the Bannock, Buffalo Horn and his men were ravaging the country. They raided King Hill Station on the Overland Road and then descended on Glenns Ferry, five miles below King Hill. After crossing Snake River, the hostiles killed five white men in quick succession and entered Bruneau Valley. On June 2, some settlers sighted the one hundred and fifty Bannock warriors who were driving six hundred horses before them and were apparently headed south for the Juniper Mountains and the Duck Valley country.[30]

Meanwhile, the military had not been inactive. Captain R. F. Bernard, with over sixty men, left Fort Boise on the night of May 30 for Camas Prairie, and other units followed within the next few days. The various army troops in the field were soon joined by several bodies of militia, hastily organized by prominent citizens of Idaho Territory. The soldiers kept close on the trail of the enemy, crossing the Snake River on June 5 and heading for Bruneau Valley where the hostiles had been seen. The Bannock were not eager to stop and engage in a battle at this stage of their planned war, but preferred to continue across country toward a possible union with the Paiute. They, therefore, kept to the rougher parts of the terrain, abandoning camps hurriedly and eluding their pursuers.[31]

---

[30] For details of troop movements and military engagements, and for an over-all picture of the Bannock War of 1878, reference should be made to the excellent monograph on the subject by George F. Brimlow, *The Bannock Indian War of 1878* (Caldwell, Idaho, 1938).

[31] *Ibid.*, pp. 80-89.

Bernard's force located the bivouac of the enemy on June 8; but, before the troops could engage the Indians, a volunteer force of twenty-six men from Silver City, led by Captain J. B. Harper, met about sixty of the Bannock some six or seven miles from the small mining town of South Mountain. In this first engagement of the war, the fighting was "sharp and furious," and two whites and several Indians were killed. Among the Bannock dead was Chief Buffalo Horn, who lost his life leading the fighting. One of the Paiute scouts with the white force later claimed the credit for killing the Indian leader. This man, Pi-Ute Joe, said that during the engagement the other Paiute scouts fled, leaving him to be killed:

> I saw that I could not get away when they [Bannock] were all mustered on me, so I jumped off my horse and placed my horse between me and them, and laid my gun over the saddle, and fired at Buffalo Horn as he came galloping up, ahead of his men. He fell from his horse, so his men turned and fled when they saw their chief fall to the ground, and I jumped on my horse again and came to Silver City as fast as I could.[32]

The chief lived four days before succumbing to his wound, and his followers swore vengeance as they left to rendezvous with the Paiute.

The Paiute, meanwhile, had met the Bannock near Juniper Lake, west of Stein's Mountain. Here were gathered almost seven hundred Indians, including four hundred and fifty warriors. Chief Winnemucca, being a man of peace, refused to listen to the threats of the Bannock as they attempted to coerce their

---

[32] Hopkins, *op. cit.*, p. 146.

friends into joining in the hostilities. The subchief, Oytes, a prophet-dreamer, was eager for war, while the war chief, Egan, counselled against it. But the grievances of the Paiute, the desire for war glory, and the encouragement of Oytes finally decided the majority of the tribe in favor of the Bannock cause. Chief Winnemucca remained adamant and was held a virtual prisoner until he and his family were rescued by his daughter, Sarah. Chief Egan, convinced that his people wanted war, took over the leadership from Oytes and united with the Bannock to become the principal leader of the combined Indian forces.[33] In an interview with J. W. Scott of Camp Harney, Oregon, shortly after June 9, Egan gave his reasons for the war decisions. He said he

. . . knew they [Indians] would be subdued—that there were not enough Indians to whip all the whites—but he would fight as long as he could, and then he thought the Great Father at Washington would give him more supplies, like he did when they quit fighting before, and not try to make his people work.[34]

The hostiles, under new leadership, started north into Oregon with the hope that they would be able to enlist the Umatilla and other tribes in the Indian cause. General Oliver O. Howard, in personal command of the field troops, directed several units in pursuit of the Indians. Captain Bernard engaged the warriors on Silver Creek, forty-five miles west of Camp Harney, on June 23. Of the four companies of cavalry

---

[33] *Ibid.*, pp. 182-90; Brimlow, *op. cit.*, pp. 101-4.
[34] *Report of the Commissioner of Indian Affairs, 1878*, p. 120.

in the battle, three soldiers were killed, three wounded, and an undetermined number of Indians was slain. A number of volunteers met the vanguard of the hostiles in John Day Valley, Oregon, on June 29, and a running fight ensued in which several of the whites were killed. The Indians burned and pillaged along their entire route of march, and settlers gathered together in mining tunnels and in hastily erected stockades until the arrival of troops saved them.[35]

The Indians continued to push northward, expecting discontented Cayuse to join their ranks. To prevent any of the renegades from crossing the Columbia River, two steamers were equipped as gunboats to patrol the course of the stream between Wallula and Celilo. General Howard formed a junction with the troops under Colonel Frank Wheaton on July 7 and soon located the camp of the Indians near the Columbia River. The following day General Howard commanded his men in an attack on the hostiles at Birch Creek. After a stiff fight, the Indians were driven from their position and fled after the squaws and children, who had moved off in the direction of the Wallowa country. One soldier was killed and several wounded in the engagement, but again the Indian casualties were not known. Captain Evan Miles was ordered to take up the pursuit along the Grande Ronde River.[36]

Hoping now for reinforcements, the hostiles headed directly for the Umatilla Reservation. Agent N. A. Connoyer soon learned of their approach and sent

[35] Brimlow, *op. cit.*, pp. 125-34.
[36] *Ibid.*, pp. 135-44.

a messenger to warn Captain Miles. During his reconnaissance of the Indian force, Connoyer was cut off
from the agency and joined Miles's unit. At daybreak
on June 12, the command approached the agency
and was met by some friendly Umatilla. These Indians reported that, during the previous night, eleven
reservation Indians and about fifty of the Columbia
River Indians had joined the rebels. The main body
of the Umatilla remained at the agency, determined
to defend themselves and to aid the whites.[37]

As Miles's troops were at breakfast, about four
hundred of the hostiles came down from the hills.
Surprised at first at sight of the soldiers, the Indians
soon began long-range firing, and an engagement was
started which lasted all day. By nightfall the Indians
retreated from the field of battle, leaving the bodies
of five of their warriors. The army force escaped any
losses, suffering only two wounded men.

During the night some of the Umatilla offered their
services to Miles, who accepted the proffered aid but
apparently did not define exactly what the duties were
to be. At any rate, the Umatilla took affairs into
their own hands and decided to kill or capture Chief
Egan. Forty of them visited his camp on July 15,
giving Egan the impression they had come to join
the war group. The chief, with seven of his followers, went outside the camp to talk over the terms
of the union with the Umatilla. When a safe distance
had been reached, the Umatilla seized the Paiutes
and informed them they were to be taken to the
army camp. Egan and three of his men attempted

---

[37] *Ibid.*, pp. 145-49.

to escape and were shot down and scalped.[38] According to an account later related by Sarah Winnemucca, the Umatilla secretly aided the hostiles until they learned that the whites were offering a thousand-dollar reward for the capture of Egan. Chief U-ma-pine of the Umatilla thereupon led some of his people to get Egan and win the reward.[39]

The loss of their leader proved the turning point in the war and, after several minor engagements, the hostiles began to break up and seek refuge on reservations or among friendly tribes. Lieutenant Colonel James W. Forsyth took up the trail of the Bannock warriors and attacked them on July 20. After a sharp fight, the Bannock escaped, having killed one volunteer and wounded two soldiers. The chase was now to the east, and the Bannock were again cornered by a force under Captain Harry E. Egbert at Bennett's Creek, a Snake River tributary, on August 9. After a skirmish of four hours, the Indians escaped into the rough country lying between the Big Camas and Snake River.

By July 27, General Howard was convinced that he no longer had a united hostile group to face, and he made plans to pursue the various disorganized bands as they fled in many directions. Howard believed that the Paiute and Weiser Indians would head for the Malheur country, while the Bannock "would endeavor to get to Lemhi and Fort Hall, or perhaps carry out their insane project of going to the buffalo

[38] *Ibid.*, pp. 150-53.
[39] Hopkins, *op. cit.*, p. 190.

country and thence to Sitting Bull."[40] The various
army units in the Idaho area did much aimless wandering in their efforts to pick up the trails of the
numerous groups into which the Bannock had now
divided. Several prospectors in the Salmon River area
were murdered by the Bannock as the bands moved
though the mountains toward Lemhi. Major John
Green was assigned the task of surveying eastern Idaho
in search of the hostiles; but, by the last of September, he had concluded that most of the Bannock
had either left the territory or were safely hidden
within the ranks of friendly Indians.[41]

Throughout the Bannock War, the Lemhi Indians
had remained peaceful and friendly to the whites.
The citizens of Idaho had Chief Tendoy to thank
for this situation, because only his control prevented
many of the Bannock members of his tribe from joining their warring kin. As it was, a few of the Bannock began to break down the fences of the settlers
and to turn ponies to graze on the crops. The whites
became so alarmed that they abandoned their homes
for the safety of two stockades which they had erected at either end of Lemhi Valley. As the Bannock
warriors approached Lemhi Reservation in August,

---

[40] Howard to McDowell, October, 1878. U.S. Congress, House of Representatives, Ex. Doc. 1, 45th Cong., 3rd Sess., Serial No. 1843 (Washington, 1878) , Part 2, p. 226.

The *Idaho Statesman* indicated that difficulties arose between the
Paiute malcontents and the Bannock at the time they split up: ". . . from
information gleaned from prisoners it seems that upon parting from
the Bannock a quarrel arose about the division of accumulated plunder,
the Bannocks gaining the victory and carrying off all the valuable
firearms and horses. The surrendered Indians [Paiutes] say the Bannocks
did all the murdering and the Snakes the stealing." *Idaho Statesman*,
August 22, 1878, p. 2.

[41] Brimlow, *op. cit.*, pp. 168-77.

Agent John A. Wright left the agency and moved into Salmon City until the hostiles had passed. Wright assigned all the troubles he encountered in 1878 to the "warlike, disagreeable, exacting, and selfish" Bannock of the Lemhi tribe. He said further:

To the Shoshones and Sheepeaters I am indebted for all the labor that has been performed during the past year [1879] as farmers, laborers, or policemen, but the Bannocks, though comparatively few in number, are responsible for the immense loss of crops to the settlers in 1878 in consequence of being obliged to abandon their homes to insure their personal safety, and for retarding the work of other Indians by throwing down fences, turning their horses into fields under cultivation, and other similar conduct.[42]

Some of the hostiles were, no doubt, able to mix among the Lemhi or among the friendly Indians at Fort Hall and thus escape capture.

Many of the Bannock warriors, however, pursued their "insane project" of attempting to join the forces of Sitting Bull. By August 25, a band of the renegades was in the area of Henrys Lake, Wyoming Territory. They attacked part of a United States surveying expedition under A. D. Wilson, and were successful in running off all the pack animals. They also stole a band of horses from Mr. Raymond, a rancher of the area. Two days after the raid on the surveying party, Captain James Egan of the Military Division of Missouri, came upon the Bannock camp near Henrys Lake and captured some of the Indian stock.[43]

---

[42] *Report of the Commissioner of Indian Affairs, 1879,* p. 54.
[43] Brimlow, *op. cit.,* pp. 179-81; E. S. Topping, *The Chronicles of the Yellowstone* (St. Paul, 1883), p. 232.

As early as the fifteenth of August, Colonel Nelson A. Miles of the Yellowstone District had been alerted to watch for Bannock war parties. On August 29 he reached the Crow Agency, enlisted about seventy-five Crow scouts, and then split his force, sending one group under First Lieutenant William F. Clark to watch a pass through the mountains near the Rose-bud River, and taking the other unit up Clarks Fork of the Yellowstone River. Near Heart Mountain on Clarks Fork, Miles surprised a Bannock camp of about twenty lodges. He recorded the killing of eleven of the outlaws, although a group of Bannock picked up later reported that twenty-eight had fallen in the battle. About forty were taken prisoner, including the Bannock subchief, Ploqua.[44] The troops used a cannon in the engagement and, when the frontiersman, Finn Burnett, came upon the battleground the next day, he noted:

The thickets had been blown to bits by cannon shots, and the dead bodies of squaws and papooses lay with the remains of Bannock warriors amid the wreckage. . . . The path along which the Bannock had fled, was still slippery with blood, proving that they had transported many corpses and wounded soldiers.[45]

The American casualties were two Crow warriors and Captain Andrew S. Bennett of the army force. Miles wrote that "before the affair was over there was scarce-

---

[44] Brimlow, op. cit., pp. 183-86; Topping, op. cit., pp. 232-34; Luther S. Kelly, "Yellowstone Kelly"; the Memoirs of Luther S. Kelly, ed. by Milo M. Quaife (New Haven, Conn., 1926), p. 223; Report of the Commissioner of Indian Affairs, 1878, p. xxi.

[45] Robert Beebe David, Finn Burnett, Frontiersman (Glendale, Calif., 1937), pp. 354-55.

ly a Crow Indian, and not a single Bannock horse, to be seen in the valley."[46] The Crow warriors succeeded in capturing two hundred and fifty Bannock ponies.

A week later, Second Lieutenant Hoel S. Bishop captured part of the Bannock who escaped in the Miles fight. The remaining survivors of the battle were encountered by Lieutenant Bishop at Dry Fork, a tributary of the Snake River in Wyoming, on September 12. According to the army report, one Indian was killed; and five women, one boy, one girl, eleven horses, and three mules were captured.[47] Thomas H. Leforge apparently observed this engagement:

> The Bannock decided to surrender to the troops, and they moved in a peaceful manner to do so. Nevertheless, volleys of gun-fire were poured into them and several of them were killed. I remember that one woman had a thigh broken by a bullet. She hid out with her baby, but she was discovered, brought in to the agency, and cared for until her recovery. It seemed to me the killing of these Indians when it was plainly evident they were trying to surrender was a violation of the humanities. They did not respond to the fire.[48]

This account emphasized the nature of the Indian fighting—the Bannock women and children suffering the same hardships and undergoing the same risks as their husbands and fathers.

The activities of Colonel Nelson A. Miles and his command, in August and September, accounted for

---

[46] Nelson A. Miles, *Personal Recollections and Observations of General Nelson A. Miles* (Chicago, 1896), pp. 294-99.

[47] Brimlow, *op. cit.*, pp. 184-87.

[48] Leforge, *op. cit.*, pp. 130-31.

most of the hostiles who were bent on reaching the buffalo country. The others drifted back to the Fort Hall Reservation or joined friendly bands out on hunting expeditions. By October the last of the hostiles in the Northwest either had been captured or had become "friendly" Indians, and the Bannock War had come to an end.

During the winter of 1878-79, the Bannock prisoners were held by the army at Fort Keogh, Montana Territory; Fort Washakie, Wyoming Territory; Omaha Barracks, Nebraska; and Fort Hall. Captain A. H. Bainbridge of Fort Hall recommended that none of the captives be allowed to return to the reservation for at least two years. In December, the census taken at Fort Hall revealed that of 1,033 Shoshoni, 850 were at the agency, 148 were absent by permit on hunting expeditions, and 35 were held as prisoners. Of the 672 Bannock, 160 were present on the reservation, 75 were with Chief Tendoy in the buffalo country, 3 were held as prisoners at Fort Hall, 35 were prisoners at Camp Brown, Wyoming, 50 had been killed or captured by Colonel Nelson A. Miles, and 349 were unaccounted for. General George Crook reported in February, 1879, that the 131 Bannock prisoners in his department were located as follows: 64 at Fort Keogh, 47 at Fort Hall, 17 at Fort Washakie, and 3 at Fort Omaha. By the end of the year, the prisoners either had been returned to their original reservations or had been sent to other designated "allotments" within the territories.[49]

The Army Adjutant General's Report for 1880 list-

---

[49] Brimlow, op. cit., pp. 189-91.

ed the cost of the war. Nine soldiers and 31 citizens were killed; 15 soldiers and 3 citizens were seriously wounded. Seventy-eight Indians were reported killed and 66 wounded. There were probably three times that number of Indians killed and wounded; the army reports merely listed the known casualties. Expenditures of the United States government in fighting the war amounted to $556,636.19.[50]

There is little doubt that the Bannock Indian War has been rightly named. The Bannock took the initial steps toward an all-out campaign and deliberately fomented and aroused neighboring tribes to unite with them, according to a prearranged plan of action. The exact motives which led the Bannock to consider war with the United States cannot be so readily listed. But first and foremost, the long-standing grievance of insufficient rations played a prominent role in the decision of the Bannock to go on the warpath. Throughout the 1870's, while these Indians were endeavoring to adjust themselves to the new economy of reservation life, they were annually forced to go hunting for subsistence, even though they often desired to remain on the reservation. Some of them wished to get started in farming but had no means of securing food while going through the initial steps of preparing a crop. General George Crook visited them during 1877 and said later that he did not blame them for going to war; "starvation is staring them in the face, and if they wait much longer, they will not be able to fight. They understand the situ-

---

[50] *Ibid.*, pp. 197-99.

ation, and fully appreciate what is before them."[51]
The *Salt Lake Tribune* similarly noted that the agent
did not have "sufficient supplies to feed his Indians,
and there is enough of human nature in these un-
tutored savages to refuse to become good if they have
to undergo a process of starvation the while."[52] Although the Bannock were kept by force on the reservation during the Nez Perce War, the appropriation
for their subsistence was entirely inadequate, and this
enforced hunger only sharpened their appetite for
war when the opportunity came.[53]

Second, white encroachment on the reservation
proper and white settlements in hunting areas offered
many opportunities for the growth of ill feeling between the two races. The disappearance of game at
a time when the tribe could not get sufficient subsistence from the government was an added irritant.

Third, although the United States had agreed to
set aside reasonable portions of the "Port Neuf and
Kansas prairie" country for a Bannock reservation
under the Treaty of Fort Bridger, that action had
not been taken. The Bannock had been given the
Portneuf area; but, as the *Idaho Statesman* pointed
out, "the Camas Prairie has been surveyed and thrown
open to settlement the same as other public land" instead of having been reserved for the Bannock.[54] W.
J. McConnell, governor and later United States Senator from Idaho, confessed that he was one of the first

[51] *Army and Navy Journal*, XV, No. 47 (June 29, 1878), 758.
[52] *Salt Lake Tribune*, June 13, 1878, p. 2.
[53] *Report of the Commissioner of Indian Affairs, 1878,* p. xxii.
[54] *Idaho Statesman*, February 13, 1879, p. 2.

trespassers on Camas Prairie and admitted that "the Indians under their code of morals and government, had ample justification for the methods they pursued."[55] The practice of the whites in herding hogs on the prairie was slowly destroying the camas root, one of the principal foods of the Bannock. Although the *Idaho Statesman* was of the opinion that it was not the pasturing of stock on Camas Prairie, but "pure cussedness" on the part of the Bannock that caused them to fight, General Crook declared that the camas root was "their main source of food supply" and he did not wonder that they went to war.[56]

Fourth, the constant bickering between the Office of Indian Affairs and the Department of War alarmed the Bannock and so unsettled them that they did not know which agency was authorized to supervise them. As already noted, the Bannock disliked Agent Danilson and wanted him removed. One reason for their opposition to him was that he seemed to favor the more docile Shoshoni in his distribution of presents and goods.

Fifth, the Bannock claimed that the Shoshoni were living on the reservation only at the sufferance of the Bannock. The number of Shoshoni continued to increase each year, and the supplies promised the Bannock under the Treaty of Fort Bridger were being unjustly divided with the Shoshoni newcomers.[57]

Sixth, the excitement of the Nez Perce War pene-

---

[55] W. J. McConnell, *Early History of Idaho* (Caldwell, 1913), p. 364.

[56] *Idaho Statesman*, July 4, 1878, p. 2; *Army and Navy Journal, op. cit.*, p. 758.

[57] *Report of the Commissioner of Indian Affairs, 1878*, p. 49.

trated to the Fort Hall Reservation where the enforced idleness of the Bannock allowed opportunity for the growth of a war fever. Another contributing factor may have been that claimed by the *Idaho Statesman:*

Some of them [Bannock] were with the United States troops during the campaign against the Nez Perces last year and witnessed the light punishment inflicted upon those Indians during the campaign, and they all know how *magnanimously* the Government acted toward Joseph and the portion of his band which surrendered.[58]

Seventh, the action of the army in capturing the arms and ponies of the Bannock, following the murder of Alexander Rhoden, added to the irritation of the tribe. The killing of the cattlemen on Camas Prairie, and the leadership of Buffalo Horn in deciding upon war as a result of the incident, were the final determining factors.

It is impossible to ascribe the Bannock War to any one cause. A community of grievances had been built up among the Bannock by May of 1878 and, when the opportunity came to make a foray for scalps and glory, the Bannock warriors chose to follow Chief Buffalo Horn in a last great show of resentment against the whites who had deprived them of their country.

---

[58] *Idaho Statesman*, July 18, 1878, p. 2.

The Utah Northern Railroad
Right of Way

WHILE Bannock warriors were engaging United States troops on the field of battle, an arm of the civilization they were fighting was reaching out to provide means for bringing still more white people into their homeland. General George Crook, on July 27, 1878, wrote that the terminus of the new Utah Northern Railroad was then at Oneida, Idaho, 127 miles north of Ogden, Utah, and only 42 miles from Ross Fork Agency on the reservation.[1] This road was being projected from Ogden northward to connect Salt Lake City and the Utah settlements with the Montana mining area and the northern transcontinental lines. Under an act of Congress, March 3, 1873, the Utah Northern Railroad Company, a firm composed mostly of Utah promoters, had been granted a right of way through the public lands of the United States. The route was to be by way of Bear River Valley, Soda Springs, the Snake River Valley, and thence through Montana Territory to a connection with the Northern Pacific Railroad. In addition to the right of way, the Utah Northern was allowed "all necessary ground, not to exceed 20 acres for each

---

[1] Crook to Adjutant General, Missouri Div., July 27, 1878, U.S.D.W., A.G.O. Exec. Div., Old Files, 5759/1878 as quoted in George F. Brimlow, *The Bannock Indian War of 1878* (Caldwell, Idaho, 1938), p. 72.

ten miles in length of the main line" for station build-
ings, machine shops, switches, side tracks, et cetera.
This projected route did not affect the Fort Hall
Reservation.[2]

A later act of Congress, June 20, 1878, however,
did affect the reservation because it provided that the
railroad company could build its line "by the way
of Marsh Valley, Port Neuf River, and Snake River
Valley" instead of by way of Soda Springs and Snake
River Valley.[3] As already indicated, the terminus of
the line was in Marsh Valley by July of 1878, and the
Indian Commissioner was perturbed because whisky
was "sold by the wholesale" at Oneida, and he was
concerned lest unscrupulous whites should cause
trouble on the near-by reservation.[4]

Furthermore, the commissioner doubted that the
railway company had any legal right to build a road
through the reservation. Article 10 of the Fort Bridger
Treaty of 1868 provided that no treaty for a cession
of reservation lands would be valid until a majority
of the adult male Indians had agreed formally to
such a change. When the Fort Hall agent notified
the Indian Department in 1878 that the Utah Northern had started construction on reservation lands, the
commissioner informed the Secretary of the Interior
that, in the opinion of the Indian officials, the lands
inside the bounds of Fort Hall Reservation were not

---

[2] U.S. Congress, Senate, *Report of the Commissioner of Indian Affairs
Relative to the Failure of the Utah and Northern Railroad Company
to Compensate Certain Indians for Right of Way*, Ex. Doc. 6, 48th
Cong., 2nd Sess., Serial No. 2261 (Washington, 1885), p. 2.

[3] *Ibid.*

[4] U.S. Office of Indian Affairs, *Annual Report of the Commissioner of
Indian Affairs, 1878* (Washington, 1879), p. 51.

"public lands within the meaning of the said Acts of
Congress of 1873 and 1878, the same having been
withdrawn from the public domain and set apart as
a reservation. . . ."[5] Thus, the action of the railway
company in building through the Fort Hall Reservation was illegal on two counts: first, the Indians
had not assented to a cession of their lands; and
second, reservation property was not "public land"
and could not be so construed under the act of Congress of June 20, 1878.

To assure legality on the part of the railroad company and to protect the rights of the Indians, the
commissioner recommended that a council be held
with the Bannock and Shoshoni to gain their consent to the right of way across the reservation and
to agree upon the terms of just compensation for
their sale of the land to the Utah Northern. Following this suggestion, the Secretary of the Interior directed Agent Danilson at Fort Hall to convene the
Indians and get their consent to the right of way,
but added: "The construction of the road will be
a public benefit, and we should put no obstacle in
the way of its completion. The consent of the Indians is deemed very desirable. Take no further steps
to stop the work."[6] Danilson immediately telegraphed
the Secretary of the Interior asking if the railroad
company were to be allowed to cut timber on the
reservation and if the town at the terminus of the
road could be moved onto the reservation. The Sec-

---

[5] U.S. Congress, Senate. *Report . . . Relative to the Failure of the
Utah and Northern . . . to Compensate . . . for Right of Way. op. cit.,*
p. 3.

[6] *Ibid.*

retary wired back: "The Secretary hopes that the
railroad company will not attempt to cut wood or
build a town upon the reservation, and that the terminus will be removed beyond the reservation as speedily as possible.[7]

Agent Danilson then called the Indians together,
and they agreed to yield a right of way to the Utah
Northern Railroad Company "for the consideration
of 500 head of good stock cattle."[8] Here, the matter
rested. The Utah Northern continued its construction
through the reservation and into Montana. A station
was built at the agency.[9] But the Bannock and Shoshoni received no compensation for the right of way.

The Utah Northern Railroad officials probably
would have been content to leave affairs as they were,
had they not contemplated another line from east
to west through the reservation. Realizing that they
would be on safer legal grounds if they obtained the
formal consent of the Indians and the Department
of the Interior to such a right of way, the railroad
directors, through their attorneys, requested the Secretary to make the necessary arrangements for the
granting of the east-west right of way. In compliance
with this request, the Secretary appointed Joseph K.
McCammon, assistant attorney general, as the commissioner to negotiate an agreement with the Indians.[10]

McCammon held a council with the Bannock and

---

[7] *Ibid.*

[8] *Ibid.*

[9] *Report of the Commissioner of Indian Affairs, 1880*, p. 62.

[10] U.S. Congress, House of Representatives, *Agreement with the Shoshone and Bannock Indians*, Ex. Doc. 18, 47th Cong., 1st Sess., Serial No.
2026 (Washington, 1882) , p. 4.

Shoshoni on July 2, 1881, in order to obtain their permission to the running of a preliminary survey of the new road. He informed them that the government thought the new railway would be beneficial to Fort Hall and so wanted them to assent to it. In this conference the Shoshoni chiefs did most of the talking, but both Bannock and Shoshoni agreed to permit the initial survey and to meet with the commission two weeks later for a final "talk" about the right of way.[11]

At the second council, July 18, 1881, the Shoshoni chiefs present were Captain Jim, Pocatello John, Jim Jennings, Gibson Jack, Jack Ballard, Jim Ballard, Nosey Ballard, and Mink. The Bannock were represented by Po-ha-ve (Race Horse), Pagwhite, To-ki-o, Ti-hee, Mo-pi-er, and Horn. McCammon outlined the exact route of the new line along the Portneuf River and then west toward the American Falls of Snake River. The chiefs allowed the commissioner to set the price for the land necessary for the right of way and indicated their satisfaction with the sum of six thousand dollars that he proposed. McCammon then declared that an agreement had been reached and that they would all meet later in the day to sign the papers which he would have drawn up.

Some confusion resulted at this announcement and, when order was restored, the interpreter said,

The Bannock don't agree. They say the Shoshones have done all the talking and they have not had a chance to say anything. . . . They say the whites have settled down there [along the Utah Northern line] and they don't like it. . . .

---

[11] *Ibid.*, pp. 11-12.

They are satisfied about the road going through, but they say they had a talk last year with the Secretary, and the Secretary told them that no whites should come on the reservation. They say they think that is why the troops are here, to look after such things.

McCammon assured the Bannock that he would get the necessary authority to have the trespassers removed. Chief Pagwhite made the most complaint about the matter and said through the interpreter that he would "be better satisfied when he gets the money in his own hands, so that he can handle it himself. . . . He says he supposed you [McCammon] were sent here to look after this railroad business, and see that they were not swindled out of their lands." McCammon reiterated that the railroad would not get the right of way until it had paid the price decided upon. The meeting then adjourned until the afternoon.[12]

Before the agreement was signed by the Indians, Chief Mo-pi-er indicated a desire to address the council, and his speech was translated as follows:

Mo-pi-er, here, says that he had a talk with some white men a good while ago, near Fort Bridger, about this reservation, and he has not forgot it yet. . . . They had a meeting, and the old chief that has since died, Tagee, was among them. They had a council with some white men, and the white men told them that this would be their country—that they could always have this for their land; . . . He says he will sign the agreement, and wishes you to show it to the Great Father; and he wants you to tell the Great Father that he always lives up to his agreements; that he has always been friendly to the whites, and hopes he always will be, and all his people. . . . He says, about this road, he hopes

---

[12] *Ibid.*, pp. 12-13.

it will not be changed in any way; meaning (as the interpreter afterward explained), that he hoped there would not be any change made in the bargain; that they would get the money according to promise, and not be cheated.[13]

After the old chief had finished, the signing was accomplished, 269 Indians assenting to the agreement.

The treaty provided for the cession of a strip of land 100 feet in width (except at the Pocatello station where it was 200 feet) running from the eastern boundary of the reservation for 36 miles to the Utah Northern Railroad, then coinciding with that line north for about 10 miles, then west along the Portneuf River for 8 miles, and finally west from that point for 19 miles to the edge of the reservation. In addition to this right of way, which amounted to 670 acres, the Indians ceded 102 acres for depots, stations, sidings, et cetera. The company was to pay $6,000 for the entire acreage, at the rate of about $7.77 an acre. Claims for any damages or loss of life resulting to the Indians from the construction or operation of the road were to be taken to Idaho courts where the proper United States attorney was to institute action for compensation from the railroad company.[14] The agreement of 1881 was approved on July 3, 1882, and the Utah Northern promptly deposited $6,000 with the Treasurer of the United States to the account of the Bannock and Shoshoni.

According to the terms of the act of July 3, 1882, the east-west right of way through the reservation

---

[13] *Ibid.*, p. 14.

[14] Charles J. Kappler (ed.), *Indian Affairs, Laws and Treaties* (Washington, 1903), I, chap. 268, 199-201.

was granted to the Utah Northern Railroad Company or "its successors or assigns." Apparently there had been an earlier tacit agreement between that firm and the Union Pacific Railroad because, at a meeting of the Board of Directors of the Union Pacific in 1882, and on motion of Jay Gould, as seconded by Russell Sage, the Utah Northern transferred its right of way through the reservation to the Union Pacific subsidiary, the Oregon Short Line Railroad Company. President Sidney Dillon of the Union Pacific informed the Department of the Interior of the change in 1882, although the deed of assignment recording the transfer was not filed until February 4, 1885.[15]

As already indicated, the Bannock and Shoshoni had received no compensation from the Utah Northern Railroad Company for its north-south right of way across the reservation. For three years after 1878, no action was taken on the matter. But on May 10, 1881, officials of the railroad took a step which again focused governmental attention on the line through the Fort Hall reserve. The railway company filed with the Department of the Interior a series of fifteen maps of definite location of its road, from the boundary of Idaho to a point in Montana. The eleven maps concerned with passage through public lands were approved March 6, 1882, but the remaining four were disapproved on the grounds that the con-

---

[15] U.S. Congress, House of Representatives, *Agreement with the Shoshone and Bannock Indians*, Ex. Doc. 140, 50th Cong., 1st Sess., Serial No. 2558 (Washington, 1888), p. 12; U.S. Department of the Interior, "Special Case No. 99" (MS in U.S. National Archives, Washington, D.C.), pp. 12, 20.

sent of the Indians had not been formally obtained for the Fort Hall Reservation right of way.[16]

The Secretary of the Interior wrote Sidney Dillon of the Union Pacific, calling his attention to the fact that no compensation had been made to the Indians for the lands taken under the act of June 20, 1878, and requesting information about the quantity of land taken. He further suggested that Dillon propose a financial settlement which could be presented to the Indians for their ratification.[17]

The next action on the part of the Union Pacific came on June 12, 1884, when its attorneys filed with the Department of the Interior a series of nine maps which included the Fort Hall right of way. Approval was withheld because the necessary affidavits by company officials to authenticate the maps had not been made. The Secretary took this opportunity to revive the matter of nonpayment by the Utah Northern for its right of way through the Indian lands. He estimated that the firm had appropriated about 1,670 acres for the 200-foot strip across the reservation and about 456 acres for eight stations, or a total of 2,126 acres. The Secretary also commented on the "unusual and extraordinary quantity, nearly 300 acres, of land taken by the company for Pocatello station alone."[18] In conclusion, he said that the Bannock and Shoshoni should be compensated for the construction of the north-south road across the lands just as they had been for the east-west grant of a through road.

---

[16] U.S. Congress, Senate. *Report . . . Relative to Failure of the Utah and Northern . . . to Compensate . . . for the Right of Way, op. cit.,* p. 3.

[17] *Ibid.,* p. 4.

[18] *Ibid.,* pp. 4-5.

He directed the Commissioner of Indian Affairs to prepare a history of the case for presentation to Congress. On December 9, 1884, the matter was referred to the Senate Committee on Indian Affairs and began its slow journey through routine legislative channels. In an effort to expedite action, the case was made the subject of an executive message to Congress on December 21, 1885; and, as a result, a bill was introduced to authorize the Bannock and Shoshoni to sell additional land at Pocatello Station to the Utah Northern. The proposed legislation did not even mention a payment to the Indians for the original Utah Northern right of way. Upon the suggestion of the Commissioner of Indian Affairs, the bill was amended to include the matter, and again it was fed into the congressional hopper for action.[19]

Meanwhile, attorneys for the Utah Northern and the Oregon Short Line Railroad filed with the Department of the Interior, on May 24, 1886, an application for additional land at Pocatello, the junction of the two roads. Action on this request was postponed until the above bill was passed, but when congressional approval of the bill was delayed, the attorneys for the two lines renewed their application.[20]

At this juncture, the Department of the Interior decided to resolve the entire problem by sending commissioners to negotiate for the additional lands at Pocatello and for compensation to the Indians for the Utah Northern right of way. The Department then

---

[19] *Report of the Commissioner of Indian Affairs, 1886,* p. xxxii.

[20] U.S. Congress, House of Representatives, *Agreement with the Shoshone and Bannock Indians,* Ex. Doc. 140, 50th Cong., 1st Sess., Serial No. 2558 (Washington, 1888), pp. 11-12.

A commissioner negotiates for additional lands for right of way

planned to introduce new legislation which would include the proposed agreement and thus satisfy both the claims of the Indians and the desire of the railroads for more ground at Pocatello.

Inspector Robert S. Gardner and Fort Hall Agent Peter Gallagher were appointed to the commission and, in a letter of instructions to them on May 16, 1887, the Indian Commissioner reviewed the entire case for their information. He pointed out that in their application for land at Pocatello, the two railways requested a plot of 1,600 acres to add to the 80 acres already granted the Utah Northern at that place. The commissioner considered that amount of land an "unreasonably large quantity . . . to be required for railroad purposes alone at any single point," and added that "within the experience of this office no railroad company has hitherto required such an extent of land for railway purposes on an Indian reservation as is here asked for."[21]

It was his opinion that the two railroads wished to "found a nucleus around which to establish a town at Pocatello," but he thought that there was a more direct way of accomplishing that end which would also be more advantageous to the Fort Hall Indians. Under this plan, agents of the United States would mark off the amount of land needed for the purposes of a town, split up the area into lots, and sell the lots at public auction. The proceeds of the sale would be given to the Bannock and Shoshoni. Inasmuch as there were already 1,100 people residing at Pocatello Station, the *de facto* existence of the town re-

[21] *Ibid.*, p. 13.

quired that some such measures be taken at once, to give its inhabitants legal residence and to stop encroachments on the reservation.[22]

Armed with these instructions and suggestions, Commissioners Gardner and Gallagher convened the Bannock and Shoshoni leaders at Fort Hall on May 27, 1887. Present were the Bannock chiefs Tyhee, Pagwhite, Race Horse, and Ke-o, while the Shoshoni were represented by Gibson Jack, Captain Jim, and Captain Joe. Many other subchiefs and leading Indians attended. Inspector Gardner began the council by explaining that the government wished the Indians' consent to the sale of a townsite at Pocatello and also wanted to agree on terms for the compensation of the Indians for the Utah Northern right of way. Through the interpreter, Gibson Jack said, "The Bannocks claim they have more right to this reservation than the Shoshones, and that they have the best right to talk first."[23]

Three of the Bannock chiefs then addressed the conference through the interpreter:

Pagwhite: I have told all the boys we cannot allow it; What is the reason the white man keeps coming up close on the land all the time? I have been here a long time, and this is my old home and land.

Ke-o: I do not want to sell right off. I want to send a letter to Washington first. We Bannocks have the first right to this land, and we want to stay on it. . . . The reason I do not want to sell is, because this is a small mountain and there is not much land or ground to hunt upon.

Race Horse: We all like the land, and I want to send a

---

[22] *Ibid.,* pp. 14-17.
[23] *Ibid.,* p. 19.

letter to Washington not to sell the land. You must not think hard feelings against us, . . . I do not know the reason Washington wants my little land. . . . God gives us this land, and that is the reason I want my land yet, and it makes us feel bad when you ask us about it.[24]

Following the Bannock leaders, Chiefs Captain Joe and Gibson Jack then spoke for the Shoshoni:

Captain Joe: We like this land and we must not tell stories to Washington. We Indians like this land, and we do not like to hear the white man talk about buying it.

Gibson Jack: I have changed my mind since that meeting two weeks ago [at a preliminary council where he had favored selling the land], because there is so much talk among the Bannocks, and I feel awfully bad about it. When God first put us on this land he gave us only one law to follow, and now you are going to change this law to-day and take a different course. . . .

They told me there [Washington, D.C.] not to go into any trouble with the white man about the land; that if they wanted the land to let them know at Washington first. General Gardner said that the first treaty they made would remain the same and would never change. . . .

The officials of the O.S.L. came to me and asked permission to put their road through this reservation, and they told me that there would not be very many people here at Pocatello; that they only wanted enough land for the railroad and no more. They told me at Washington that if the white men wanted to buy, not to mind them, but to go to the agent first. They also told me to heed all the instructions they had given me and to keep them in my memory. Now, after telling me what they did, it is hard for me to part with any of my land. How is it that you want me to do so?[25]

Throughout the initial stages of the council the

---

[24] *Ibid.*, pp. 19-20.
[25] *Ibid.*, pp. 21-23.

reservation head chief, Tyhee, had remained silent, but now he asked, "How much line of right of way do you want for the O. S. L. on the reservation?" The railroad agent indicated that about 1,800 acres would be sufficient and agreed to pay the Indians $8.00 an acre for it. Gardner said that the money would be credited to the account of the Indians in the United States Treasury. Chief Tyhee replied, "That is satisfactory." Gibson Jack then spoke again, requesting that nothing more be done toward the sale of the land until the matter had been presented to Congress. Agent Gallagher answered, stressing the need of the Indians for money for farming implements and urging the Bannock and Shoshoni to agree to the cession.

Tyhee thereupon addressed the council:

I do not like the way they have been talking here—one one way, and one another; they do not agree, and it does not suit me. When they held a council here the other day, two weeks ago, I thought I was doing what was right for the good of the Indians; I thought they needed money. Now, I want you all to come to one understanding and agree to sell Pocatello, and if you do agree to sell it, send word to Washington and get an answer so as to tell all the Indians right away. The money that we get for this piece of land will not be for our benefit—it will be for the rising generation. That is how I look at it . . . I hope these white gentlemen do not take offense at what the Bannock are saying.

At the conclusion of Tyhee's speech, Gallagher asked what Pagwhite thought of the head chief's remarks. Pagwhite said, "It is all right to give them a little piece of land." Gibson Jack had one other request. "Will the railroad company let the Indians ride on the freight trains and have the brakemen

stop whenever they want to get off?" When assured
on this point, he joined all the others in following
Tyhee's wishes; and, eventually, 311 Indians signed
the agreement of May 27, 1887.

The terms of the pact were as follows: Article 1
provided for a cession of 1,840 acres at Pocatello
which was to be surveyed and laid off into lots and
blocks as a townsite and then sold at public auction
to the highest bidder. The proceeds of the sale were
to go to the Indians. Article 2 stipulated that the
Utah Northern was to pay the Indians $8.00 an acre
for the reservation land used as a north-south right
of way. When the agreement was incorporated into
an act as passed by Congress, the following sections
were added: Sections 2 and 3 provided for the survey of the Pocatello townsite into lots and blocks;
Section 4 directed the Secretary of the Interior to
name three disinterested persons to appraise the lots,
stipulating that no lot should be sold for less than ten
dollars; Section 5 provided for the sale of the lots
at public auction to be held at "Pocatello House,"
Pocatello Junction, and allowed people owning improvements on particular lots to have the first opportunity of purchasing those lots; Sections 6 to 10 dealt
with arrangements for surveying the area, for setting
up the new reservation boundaries around Pocatello,
and for securing irrigation and water rights to the
citizens of Pocatello; Section 11 granted the Utah
Northern the right of way north and south through
the reservation and an additional 150 acres at Pocatello for shops, et cetera—these lands to be paid for
at the rate of $8.00 an acre; Sections 12 and 13 allowed

railway officials to reside on the right of way and required the company to fence the road and provide
crossings where necessary; Section 14 provided for
the payment of damages to the Indians resulting from
claims against the railway; and Section 15 exacted the
promise from the Utah Northern that it would not
attempt to secure any further grant of land from the
Indians.[26]

After the agreement and the bill accompanying it
had been presented to Congress, the usual delay occurred before it was approved. Agent Gallagher took
a delegation of the leading chiefs to Washington, D.C.,
in 1888, in an attempt to advertise the need for ratification of the agreement. In the same year the agent
wrote his superior that affairs were becoming intol-
erable at Pocatello. "These Indians complain and
want to know from me, how it is that the white man
'makes fence, builds house & no pay,' & if the Government is not going to interfere in their behalf."[27]
Gallagher feared that the Indians would take the law
into their own hands. He mentioned a "Western
Saloon . . . accompanied by the gambling den" which
was being set up in the town, and tried to emphasize
how great was the annoyance which Pocatello had
caused the Indian authorities at Fort Hall.

The congressional act embodying the agreement
was ultimately approved September 1, 1888, and the
three disinterested appraisers were appointed. For
its right of way the Utah Northern paid the Indians

---

[26] U.S. Congress, *Statutes at Large of the United States of America
from December, 1887, to March, 1889* (Washington, 1889), XXV, chap.
936, 452-57.

[27] "Special Case No. 99," *op. cit.*, p. 79.

$7,621.04. Three years later it paid $13,182.72 for the additional 150 acres asked for at Pocatello.[28] The latter sum was much larger because, in addition to the right of way price of $8.00 an acre, the company had to pay also "a sum per acre equal to the average appraisal of each acre of town lots outside of the portion so taken."[29]

The appraisal and sale of the lots at Pocatello townsite extended over a period of three years. Final tabulations showed that the Bannock and Shoshoni received approximately $115,000 for this cession of their reservation. By 1891, Pocatello could boast a population of three thousand and was already beginning to protest its isolation in the midst of an Indian reservation. Only a few years later, this restriction was eliminated when the neighboring Indians agreed to cede still another portion of their homeland.[30]

---

[28] *Report of the Commissioner of Indian Affairs, 1889*, pp. 19, 38.

[29] *Report of the Commissioner of Indian Affairs, 1891*, p. 97.

[30] *Ibid.*, p. 230.

Chief Race Horse and the
State of Wyoming

FROM their earliest meeting with the whites to
the turn of the century in 1900, the Bannock
held the reputation of being warlike and untameable.
Through the years their massacres and depredations,
their horse-stealing raids, with the war of 1878 as a
climax, had convinced the citizens of Idaho and neighboring states that rumors of Bannock warriors on
the trail should be heeded until proved false. After
the outbreak in 1878, the Bannock never again took
to the warpath in substantial numbers, but their reputation and occasional threats led to many "scares,"
at least in newspaper headlines. The Bannock would
have concurred with a statement attributed to a Paiute
Indian:

When three or four bad white men stop and rob one
stage, maybe kill somebody, you send one sheriff to catch
three, four bad men, same way when some bad white men
steal some cattle, or some horses, you send one sheriff; but
when three, four bad Injun stop one stage, kill somebody,
steal some horse or cow, you try catch three, four bad
Injun? No; all white men say, "Injun broke out, Injun *on
warpath,*" and then come soldier for to kill everybody.[1]

---

[1] Laurence F. Schmeckebier, *The Office of Indian Affairs* ("Institute
of Government Research, Service Monographs of the United States
Government," No. 48 [Baltimore, 1927]) , p. 82.

During the 1880's, reports that the Bannock had left the reservation to indulge in their age-old occupations of horse stealing and scalp lifting were of common occurrence, although whites acquainted with the Indians did not believe too many of the rumors. In May of 1881, common knowledge that the Bannock were displeased with their agent gave credence to a report that part of the tribe had gone to war. When the facts were established, it was found that a group of cowboys on the reservation, bent on giving a "tenderfoot" among them a little experience with "redskins," had dressed themselves as Indians and had so frightened the "t. f." that he "lit out . . . for the states."[2]

The people of Bruneau Valley, in May of 1883, petitioned the Idaho state officials to protect them from a reported Bannock incursion into their area. However, the *Idaho Statesman* deprecated the fears of the citizens there by saying, "Scares of this kind are rather common in the section named."[3] Perhaps the comment of Agent Peter Gallagher of Fort Hall concerning these "scares" best indicated the unlikelihood of any further outbreaks by the Bannock. When a "false alarm" of an Indian raid was circulated near the reservation in May of 1887, Gallagher said:

The Bannock have given themselves some little notoriety, for a small band, by their love of "heap fight"; but whilst given to deeds of boldness and daring in the past, and as much as going to war more than once, and furthermore put down by my predecessors as an obstreperous and ungovern-

[2] *Blackfoot Register*, May 7, 1881, No. 43.
[3] *Idaho Statesman*, May 1, 1883, as quoted in *Idaho Falls Register*, May 12, 1883, Vol. 3, No. 45.

able kind of human beings—far different from the Shoshones in this respect, and which I think too true—still I must say of them, since my assuming charge they have given me comparatively but little trouble.[4]

The roving nature of the Bannock, and especially their hunting of wild game outside the reservation, tended to lend color to most of the reports of Indian wars. Eventually, a "war scare" occurred which was to deprive them of their right to hunt on the unoccupied lands of the United States, and to confine them to the narrow limits of the Fort Hall Reservation.

In 1893 the citizens of western Wyoming began to send in complaints to government officials that wandering Indians were wantonly destroying game in the mountainous region south of Yellowstone National Park. Other reports were received by the Indian Commissioner from the people of Idaho, Montana, and Utah that Indians were being given passes to make social visits to other reservations; it was charged that, while en route to their destinations, these Indians stopped to slaughter deer and elk. The accusation was made that the game animals were killed for their hides only, and that the carcasses were abandoned. Governor John E. Osborne, of Wyoming, underscored this claim by transmitting to the Commissioner of Indian Affairs and the Secretary of the Interior a petition signed by "almost every settler" in Uinta County "praying for relief from the depredations of wandering Indian tribes." The statement concluded:

---

[4] U.S. Office of Indian Affairs, *Annual Report of the Commissioner of Indian Affairs, 1888* (Washington, 1889) , p. 83.

Your petitioners would respectfully ask you to compel these Indians to remain on their reservations, and thus stop this indiscriminate slaughter of game, running our cattle off their ranges, and insure the safety of our homes, and your petitioners will ever pray.[5]

The commissioner, therefore, directed the agents of these states to convene their Indians in council and instruct them that it was unlawful and contrary to treaty right to kill game for the hides only. Permission to hunt was granted only when the Indians wished to get game to supplement their reservation food rations.[6]

In answer, the agents indicated they would comply with the instructions, but denied that any of their Indians had made a practice of killing deer and elk just for the hides. The agents charged, instead, that white hunters were allowed to hunt without hindrance from government authority and killed twice as much game as did the Indians.[7]

The most vociferous complaints against Indian hunters came from the settlers of the Jackson Hole country in Wyoming. Some of these "settlers" were men who had sought the refuge to be found in

---

[5] John E. Osbourne to Secretary of the Interior, Cheyenne, Wyoming, November 20, 1893. U.S. National Archives, Records of the Bureau of Indian Affairs, Land Division, Letters Received, Record Group 75.

[6] *Report of the Commissioner of Indian Affairs, 1895*, p. 61.

[7] *Ibid.*, p. 62. Two years later, the editor of the *Idaho World* defended the Bannock and other Indians who customarily hunted game in the Jackson Hole country. He cited a report in the *Hailey Times* that a group of citizens of that town had engaged in a contest to see who could kill the most grouse and sage hens, and that, in the resulting holocaust, over three thousand of these game birds were destroyed. The editor commented. "Why should the Bannocks care for the preservation of game when they know that the whites, who enact the laws for its preservation, neither obey nor enforce those laws?" *Idaho World*, August 23, 1895.

such an area, remote from the centers of civilization. Many of them were only nominally ranchers and made their living principally as guides for tourist parties, or "dudes," who came to hunt the wild game of the Rockies. Throughout 1893 and 1894, these settlers continued their charges of wanton destruction of game, and many stated publicly that, if the Indians returned in 1895, the whites would organize and drive them back to the reservations.

Even though the Indian hunters stayed to themselves and harmed no one, the professional guides and settlers of Jackson Hole were determined to stop the continual Indian hunting which was ruining their business. The United States Commissioner at Marysvale, Wyoming, later reported that the citizens of that community made the removal of Indian hunters from Jackson Hole the main issue in the local election of 1894, and only those men who were in favor of banning the Indians from the area were elected to office. Constable William Manning of Marysvale said:

We knew very well when we started in on this thing that we would bring matters to a head. We knew some one was going to be killed, perhaps on both sides, and we decided the sooner it was done the better, so that we could get the matter before the courts.[8]

In September of 1894, the County Attorney of Fremont County complained to the governor of the incompetency of the Indian agent at Fort Washakie and of the "insulting demeanor of these Indians, their

---

[8] *Report of the Commissioner of Indian Affairs, 1895,* p. 76.

refusal to submit to arrest to duly constituted authorities, . . ."[9]

In their opposition to Indian hunters, the Jackson Hole people were backed by most of the Wyoming state officials, headed by the new governor, William A. Richards. He wrote to the Indian Commissioner in June, 1895, to report that Indians from Idaho and Wyoming were killing large game in Uinta and Fremont counties, and to ask that they be forced to return to their reservations. He said, "It is not want that leads to this destruction so much as a depraved appetite. They consider an unborn calf the greatest of delicacies and wantonly kill the mother to obtain it, leaving her carcass to the less fastidious coyote. . . ." Richards added that the poverty-stricken counties were unable to prosecute the Indians arrested "with no possibility of collecting a fine from them if convicted, and to whom a short imprisonment with plenty to eat is no punishment."[10]

The executive included a copy of the Wyoming fish and game laws which he claimed the Indians were violating. Thus, the main issue was brought to the early attention of federal officials: Was the right of the Bannock and Shoshoni to hunt on the unoccupied lands of the United States (as granted them by the Treaty of Fort Bridger) abrogated by the laws of the state of Wyoming which set up "closed seasons" for hunting?

---

[9] Will L. Simpson to John E. Osborne, Fremont County, September 5, 1894. U.S. National Archives, Records . . . of Indian Affairs, Land Division, *op. cit.*

[10] William A. Richards to Hoke Smith, Cheyenne, Wyoming, June 17, 1895, *ibid.*

Governor Richards thought the treaty stipulation was nullified, and so backed the settlers in their demands for removal of the Indians from Jackson Hole. When the local officials of Marysvale determined to arrest any Indians who violated the fish and game laws of Wyoming, the governor wired them, in June of 1895, "to enforce the laws of Wyoming, to put the Indians out of Jackson's Hole, and to keep them out at all costs, to depend upon him for protection, and that he (Governor Richards) would see [them] through. . . ."[11] In view of this later trouble, it was unfortunate that the agreement of 1873 with the Bannock and Shoshoni should have gone unratified. In that treaty the Indians had agreed to give up their right to hunt on the lands of the United States in exchange for a house and a milch cow for each family.[12]

With the support of their governor, the officials of Marysvale resolved to arrest all violators of the game laws and, on June 7, 1895, sent Constable William Manning with twelve deputies to search for trespassers. The group found three Bannock, one of whom had several green hides in his possession. This Indian was fined fifteen dollars and his hides were confiscated. He paid his fine and was released, as were the other two who were so old and nearly blind that it was considered impossible for them to kill an elk. On June 24, Manning and five men came upon a camp of fifteen Bannock who reportedly had forty

[11] *Report of the Commissioner of Indian Affairs, 1895,* pp. 78, 79.

[12] U.S. Congress, House of Representatives, *Bannock and Other Indians in Southern Idaho,* Ex. Doc. 129, 43rd Cong., 1st Sess., Serial No. 1608 (Washington, 1873), pp. 2, 5.

elk hides. The constable told them they were under arrest and instructed them to accompany him to Marysvale. The Indians refused to submit to arrest and said they would kill all the game they wished. Manning then informed them he would summon soldiers to make the arrest; whereupon, the spokesman for the Bannock told the constable that he and "the soldiers might go to hell as they were not afraid of either of us." The deputies admitted defeat and left the hunters. Another expedition under Manning arrested eight Bannock on July 4 at the head of Green River, and took them to Marysvale where six of them were fined seventy-five dollars each and costs —the total amount of the fines and costs being about $1,400. The Indians, unable to pay the fines, were held in jail until the town fathers could get instructions from the county officials. When no instructions were received, the jail guard was relaxed and the prisoners allowed to escape.[13]

This dereliction on the part of their legally elected representatives did not add to the satisfaction of the Jackson Hole settlers and, when Constable Manning and twenty-six deputies started out on July 10 to arrest some Indian hunters, they apparently were determined to take a different course in dealing with such a situation. Three days later the white party came upon a camp of Indians at Fall River, fifty-five miles from Marysvale. The deputies surrounded the camp at daybreak and arrested the nine Indian men, thirteen squaws, and five papooses whom they

---

[13] *Pocatello Tribune*, July 29, 1895, p. 2; *Report of the Commissioner of Indian Affairs, 1895*, pp. 69, 76.

found in the tipis. Putting the squaws and children in the rear of their line of march and placing each Indian brave between two deputies, the constable and his party started for Marysvale. The Indians were roughly treated, and Manning directed his men aloud to shoot only the horses if the prisoners attempted to escape. He also informed the Indians that they would be hung or shot as soon as Marysvale was reached. After an all-day march, while the cavalcade was passing through a grove of timber, the Indians noticed that all the whites were loading their rifles. At sight of this, the squaws began to wail; and the Indian men, now convinced that they were going to be shot down, made a break for the woods. Without warning the deputies fired on the fleeing braves, six of whom were hit. One was killed and another left for dead. The rest escaped. The wounded Indian survived for seventeen days in the mountains until found by a white rancher and nursed back to health. In the melee, also, two of the papooses were jostled from the horses, one afterwards being found and cared for by some Mormon settlers. The other was never found.[14]

As later investigation proved, Manning admitted ordering his men to shoot any Indian who tried to escape, despite the fact that the maximum penalty for the crime with which the Bannock were charged was a fine of ten dollars and three months' imprisonment. Of the Indian who was killed, Manning said,

[14] *Report of the Commissioner of Indian Affairs, 1895*, pp. 67-79; Province McCormick to Commissioner of Indian Affairs, Fort Hall, Idaho, October 6, 1895. U.S. National Archives, Records of the Bureau of Indian Affairs, Record Group 75, *op. cit.*

"The old Indian was killed about 200 yards from the trail. He was shot in the back and bled to death. He would have been acquitted had he come in and stood his trial, for he was an old man, almost blind, and his gun was not fit to kill anything."[15] The Indian officials who investigated the affair were convinced that the deputies deliberately tempted the Indians to try to escape. Manning and his men knew that the Bannock would be released, as had been the other six Bannock who had been arrested and then allowed to escape. The Indian Commissioner said,

The whole affair was, I believe, a premeditated and pre-arranged plan to kill some Indians and thus stir up sufficient trouble to subsequently get United States troops into the region and ultimately have the Indians shut out from Jacksons Hole. The plan was successfully carried out and the desired results obtained.[16]

Evidence to support this contention begins with a telegram sent by officials at Marysvale to Governor Richards, dated July 15:

Nine Indians arrested, one killed, others escaped. Many Indians reported here; threaten lives and property. Settlers are moving families away. Want protection immediately. Action on your part is absolutely necessary.[17]

The telegram was signed by Justice of the Peace Frank H. Rhodes and Constable William Manning.

---

[15] *Report of the Commissioner of Indian Affairs, 1895*, p. 77; Province McCormick to Commissioner of Indian Affairs, Fort Hall, Idaho, October 6, 1895, U.S. National Archives, Records of the Bureau of Indian Affairs, Record Group 75, *op. cit.*

[16] *Report of the Commissioner of Indian Affairs, 1895*, p. 77.

[17] *Ibid.*, p. 63.

Without warning the deputies fired on the fleeing braves

With this initial call for assistance, the war scare began. Governor Richards called for troops and, eventually, five companies of the United States Eighth Infantry were dispatched to Jackson Hole.

Newspaper reports circulated that the Bannock warriors were killing settlers and burning homes to the ground. Appeals from citizens and officials alike poured into Washington, D.C., to "stop the fiendish work of devastation." A rumor gained credence that fifty-nine whites had been murdered and that nine hundred Bannock were headed for Soda Springs, Idaho. According to this report, all residents of the area abandoned their homes and sought the protection of the town. One gentleman arrived in Pocatello with the information that "the Northern Pacific railway can hardly accommodate the tourists who are leaving Yellowstone Park as speedily as possible."[18] Similar movements were recorded as going on throughout most of western Wyoming and eastern Idaho.

The *Idaho Statesman,* at Boise, increased circulation for a few days by printing, in bold type, such headlines as: "Some Alarming Rumors," "Marauding Bannocks," "200 Utes and 400 Lemhi Reported Joining Bannocks," "Country Full of Indians," and, finally, "Absence of Authentic News," the last heading being most nearly the truth. Not only were Idaho newspapers intent on getting the news, but the eastern press took up the scare with gusto. It was reported that a correspondent of *Harper's Weekly* was on his way to the scene of battle "mounted on a 17-pound bicycle and armed with a kodak."[19]

---

[18] *Idaho Statesman,* July 19-30, 1895.
[19] *Ibid.*

Eventually this "newspaper" war came to an abrupt end. The *Pocatello Tribune* reported on August 3: "After two weeks of Massacres on the Atlantic Seaboard the Settlers in the Indian Country Here are Becoming Alarmed."[20] Fred Dubois, United States Senator from Idaho, similarly discounted any great trouble from the Indians and blamed Agent Thomas B. Teter of Fort Hall for the "outbreak," calling him a "carpet-bagger from West Virginia." It was the opinion of Dubois that "the extermination of the whole lazy, shiftless, non-supporting tribe of Bannocks would not be any very great loss."[21]

At the height of the excitement, the Commissioner of Indian Affairs had acted quickly to stop the "war." He directed Agent Teter to proceed to Jackson Hole to investigate, requested military aid from Brigadier General J. J. Coppinger of the Department of the Platte, and instructed the Indian agents of Utah and Wyoming to ascertain the truth of the reports that large bands of Ute and Sioux were in the Jackson Hole area, prepared to unite with the Bannock in a general war. The agents sent word that the reports were false.

Agent Teter discovered the true cause of the furor soon after reaching Wyoming, but advised the sending of troops because two or three hundred Indians had gathered near Fall River and refused to return to the reservation. It was the agent's fear that armed bands of settlers would attack the Indians and cause real trouble. Finally convinced by Teter that they

---

[20] *Pocatello Tribune,* August 3, 1895, p. 1.
[21] *Ibid.*

would be safer at Fort Hall, the Bannock returned to their agency before the troops arrived. Under the headline, "Indians Making a Beeline Back to the Reservation," the *Idaho Statesman* concluded that the Bannock "are more scared now than the white people."[22] Not a person was harmed by the Indians during their removal to the reservation, but the settlers of Jackson Hole freely threatened to hang Teter for attempting to care for the interests of the Bannock.[23]

At the reservation some of the Bannock indicated that they intended to return to Jackson Hole in the fall to hunt game because they could not live on the scanty rations supplied them by the government. The Indian Department, therefore, ordered extra rations sent to Fort Hall to ensure the Indians' remaining at the agency. Nevertheless, the Bannock were in a sullen and angry mood over the murder of one of their number and engaged in several brawls with whites on the reservation and burned signal fires on the mountains at night. To forestall more difficulties, a troop of soldiers was stationed at Fort Hall. The Bannock then demanded the right to send some men to Jackson Hole to recover the possessions of the party arrested by Manning's deputies; and eight braves were finally dispatched, with an escort of soldiers, to perform that mission.[24]

As the truth of the murder in Jackson Hole gradually spread throughout the country, there was a

---

[22] *Idaho Statesman*, August 3, 1895, p. 1.
[23] *Report of the Commissioner of Indian Affairs, 1895*, pp. 63-66.
[24] *Ibid.*, pp. 69-78.

shift of public opinion to the side of the "poor de-
fenceless" Bannock and a rising surge of indignation
which demanded that the perpetrators of the crime
be brought to justice. The Indian Commissioner best
stated the official reaction of the federal government:
"We trust that all the means at the disposal of the
Government will be employed to bring the assassins
to justice."[25] Eastern sentiment was expressed by *The
Illustrated American* of August 17:

> A number of Bannock Indians are arrested on some charge
> or another—anything will do—and are haled off to the town
> jail by some rough-and-ready Western Sheriff and his posse;
> and the Indians, in endeavoring to run away, are shot down.
> It may be set down, that in a community where an Indian
> is esteemed as highly as a wolf that the posse was delighted
> at a legal technicality which afforded them an opportunity
> to give a batch of Bannocks very short shrift; . . .[26]

Agent Teter recommended, on August 2, that the
Office of Indian Affairs request the Department of
Justice to investigate the killing of the Bannock hunter and prosecute "lawless settlers" of Uinta County,
Wyoming. Through Teter, the Indian Commissioner
assured the Bannock that he would use all his influence to bring the guilty parties to justice, and he
asked them to rely on the federal authorities to prosecute the case.

In his report to the United States Attorney General, the commissioner first of all pointed out that
the fourth article of the Treaty of Fort Bridger grant-

---

[25] *Ibid.*, p. 70.

[26] *Illustrated American* (New York), August 17, 1895, p. 207; U.S.
Department of the Interior, *Report of the Board of Indian Commissioners*
(Washington, 1895), p. 9.

ed the Bannock the right to hunt on the unoccupied lands of the United States. Secondly, he cited the decision of the Supreme Court in the case of *Haven-stein* vs. *Lynham:* "If the law of a State is contrary to a treaty it is void," thereby indicating that the Wyoming state officials were acting outside the law in attempting to arrest the Bannock hunters. Not only were the Wyoming officers acting illegally, but they were trespassers on the rights of the Bannock, and the United States was bound to prosecute the violators of the Indian privileges because Article 1 of the Fort Bridger Treaty stipulated:

> If bad men among the whites, or among other people subject to the authority of the United States, shall commit any wrong upon the person or property of the Indians, the United States will, upon proof made to the agent and forwarded to the Commissioner of Indian Affairs, at Washington City, proceed at once to cause the offenders to be arrested and punished according to the laws of the United States, and also reimburse the injured person for the loss sustained.[27]

Acting upon the request of the Indian Commissioner, the United States District Attorney for Wyoming investigated the affair and reported that his department was convinced that "it was a murder perpetrated on the part of the constable, Manning, and his deputies in pursuance of a scheme . . . to prevent the Indians from exercising a right . . . guaranteed to them by treaty."[28] However, the District Attorney added that there were no officials in Jackson Hole—county, state, or national—who would hold any of

---

[27] *Report of the Commissioner of Indian Affairs, 1895,* pp. 73-74.
[28] *Ibid.,* pp. 74-75.

Manning's posse for trial. The Attorney General although approving the findings of the Wyoming District Attorney, informed the Commissioner of Indian Affairs that there was no statute of the United States under which he could prosecute the Wyoming deputies. Nevertheless, on September 24, 1895, the Attorney General decided to take direct action and instructed the Wyoming District Attorney to indict the people concerned and "prosecute the case with vigor."

At the same time the Indian Commissioner dispatched Inspector Province McCormick to Wyoming to confer with Governor Richards. McCormick was instructed to request that the governor concede the right of the Bannock to hunt on those unsettled lands of the United States lying in Wyoming. If the executive refused to do so, then McCormick was to propose that a test case be made so that the matter could be decided by the courts. A Bannock was to be arrested by state officials for hunting out of season. An application would then be brought by the United States District Attorney for Wyoming for a writ of habeas corpus for the release of the prisoner. If the governor were willing to take part in such a test case, and if the Bannock were also willing, then McCormick was to proceed with the necessary arrangements.[29]

As reported later by McCormick, Governor Richards would not concede the treaty right of the Indians, but agreed to aid in the proposed test case. At Fort Hall, the inspector found the Bannock quite willing to submit to a court decision, and two Indians were

[29] *Report of the Commissioner of Indian Affairs, 1896*, pp. 56-58.

chosen, instead of one, to take part in the action, Chief Race Horse being the principal representative of the Indians. In concluding his report, McCormick recommended that, even if the courts found in favor of the Bannock, arrangements should be made to treat with the Indians for relinquishment of their right to hunt on United States lands, because it would be impossible to guarantee them protection from the settlers.[30]

The case was tried in the United States circuit court before Judge Riner on November 21, 1895. The judge decided that the laws of Wyoming were invalid against the treaty rights of the Indians, affirmed their right to hunt on the unoccupied public lands of Wyoming in and out of season, and discharged Race Horse from custody. The Wyoming Attorney General immediately appealed to the United States Supreme Court. On May 25, 1896, in the case of *John H. Ward, Sheriff*, etc., vs. *Race Horse* (Case No. 841), the higher court reversed the judgment of the circuit court and directed the discharge of the writ of habeas corpus and the transfer of the prisoner, Race Horse, to the custody of the sheriff of Uinta County. Only one justice dissented from the opinion.

In delivering the majority view, the Court argued that the point of dispute lay between Article 4 of the Fort Bridger Treaty giving the Bannock the right to hunt on the lands of the United States and the act under which Wyoming was admitted as a state on July 10, 1890. This act provided in part "that the State of Wyoming . . . is hereby declared ad-

---

[30] *Ibid.*, p. 59.

mitted into the Union on an equal footing with the
original states in all respects whatever; . . ." The
act contained no exception or reservation in favor of
or for the benefit of Indians. Wyoming thus had
an equal right with other states to control hunting
on her own public lands. Inasmuch as an act of Congress may supersede a prior treaty, the Supreme Court
therefore held that the Fort Bridger Treaty "giving
the right to hunt on unoccupied lands of the United
States in the hunting districts is repealed in so far
as the lands in such districts are now embraced within the limits of the State of Wyoming. . . ."[31]

After the action of the Supreme Court, Judge Riner
demanded that Race Horse be brought before him
on July 14 to be turned over to the state officers.
The United States Attorney General protested that
because it had been a test case, "this poor Indian
should not be further punished" and so requested
that the chief be allowed "to go without further mo-
lestation." The Indian Commissioner also explained
that, at the time the case was proposed, Race Horse
was at liberty at Fort Hall Reservation and that he
and all the other Bannock accused of trespassing had
been released by the state authorities. In reply, Governor Richards stated that the officials of Wyoming
had no intention of punishing Race Horse under the
statutes of the state. He said that the Bannock had
left the circuit court trial convinced that the state of
Wyoming had no jurisdicion over them and they
would not recognize state authority under the Supreme Court reversal unless Race Horse were brought

---

[31] *Ibid.*, pp. 64-65; *Cheyenne Daily Sun-Leader*, November 4, 1895, p. 1.

back before Judge Riner.[32] The judge was firmly convinced that it was his duty to turn the chief over to the state and said that, if the Indian were not brought before him within a few days, he would issue a bench warrant for his arrest.

Faced with the prospect of further difficulties with the Bannock if Race Horse were arrested, the Indian officials persuaded the chief to give himself up to the Sheriff of Uinta County, who released him on a five-hundred-dollar bond until his appearance before the next district court, September 7, 1896. When Race Horse appeared before the court, he was instructed that it was within the power of the state to imprison him for his crime of hunting contrary to the laws of Wyoming. After assuring himself that the chief and other Bannock were sufficiently impressed that they would have to submit to the jurisdiction of state officials, the judge released Race Horse, and the Bannock and his party returned to their reservation.[33]

Only a few days after the final court action, a Wyoming constable arrested four Bannock whom he had caught unlawfully killing game in Jackson Hole. Agent Teter informed the newspapers that he knew there were Bannock in the Wyoming area who had left the reservation without passes, but he declared that he "did not intend to get shot in the back by some of the outlaws of the Hole by going after them."[34]

To prevent the recurrence of such incidents, the

---

[32] *Report of the Commissioner of Indian Affairs, 1896*, pp. 67-68.

[33] *Ibid.*, pp. 69-70.

[34] *Pocatello Tribune*, September 19, 1896, p. 1.

Fort Hall agent conducted a delegation of Bannock to Washington, D.C., in January, 1897, where the Indians agreed to give up their treaty right to hunt on the public lands of the United States in return for proper compensation. Therefore, in an agreement with the Bannock and Shoshoni, ratified in 1900, a provision was included to pay the Indians $75,000 for the relinquishment of their hunting rights.[35]

But before the Bannock settled down for good on their farms at Fort Hall, their fame as warriors implicated them in one last "Indian scare." On June 28, 1897, the governor of Idaho telegraphed the Office of Indian Affairs as follows: "Three hundred Indians from Fort Hall causing great anxiety among settlers on Camas Prairie. If some are not immediately recalled, trouble will ensue."[36] The information came "from sheriff and settlers." The next day the Idaho executive sent word to United States Senator Henry Heitfield that "complaints continue today. Fences are being burned and cattle killed. Indians come from Lemhi, Umatilla, Fort Hall, and Duck Valley reservations. They must disperse or trouble will soon follow."[37]

The Commissioner of Indian Affairs immediately telegraphed for full reports from the agents at the reservations mentioned. Agent F. G. Irwin of Fort Hall was dispatched to Camas Prairie to make a personal investigation. The War Department, on June

[35] U.S. Congress, Senate, *Fort Hall Indian Reservation in Idaho*, Report No. 60, 56th Cong., 1st Sess., Serial No. 3886 (Washington, 1900), p. 2.
[36] *Report of the Commissioner of Indian Affairs, 1897*, p. 68.
[37] *Ibid.*

30, ordered troops from Fort Robinson, Nebraska, to proceed by the fastest train to the scene of the disturbance.[38] The nation's newspapers were again filled with accounts of a "Bannock War." Dispatches were sent from Boise to eastern journals with the news that "700 or 800 ugly Bannocks on Camas Prairie . . . are threatening to wipe out the town of Soldier."[39]

The *Pocatello Tribune* thought that this scare was the "rankest nonsense. There is no more danger of an Indian uprising than there is of the Chinese declaring war against the United States."[40] Agent Irwin soon confirmed this belief when he reached Camas Prairie. There he found forty-two Indians, most of them from Lemhi Reservation, only two families from Fort Hall, and not one Bannock among them. They were quite peaceable, engaged in "nothing more serious than digging camas roots and chasing ground squirrels, and totally unconscious of the alarm they were supposed to be causing."[41] The *Wood River Times* commented that "all the '*scare*' is away from here," and indicated, from reports of settlers, that the Indians were so happy over the large crop of camas on the prairie that they had indulged in a "grass dance" in honor of the forthcoming harvest.[42] Under the heading of " 'Tis Love Not War," the *Pocatello Tribune* said of the grass dance:

This is an Indian free love feast and bears no relation to

---

[38] *Ibid.*

[39] *Pocatello Tribune*, July 3, 1897, p. 1.

[40] *Ibid.*

[41] *Report of the Commissioner of Indian Affairs, 1897*, p. 69.

[42] *Wood River Times*, July 1, 1897, as quoted in *Report of the Commissioner of Indian Affairs, 1897*, p. 70.

war. . . . It is at these "grass dances" that the dusky brave
wooes the timid Indian maiden and bears her away to his
lodge after having won her by his graceful dancing and
hid out with her for a few nights, under the pale moon and
blinking stars, in some secluded spot among the willows.
'Tis love not war, that fills the hearts of the Indians on
Camas Prairie today.[43]

Following the revelation that there was no cause
for alarm, the troops ordered to duty at Camas Prairie
were given instructions to remain where they were;
Agent Irwin conducted the Lemhi and Shoshoni
back to their respective reservations, and the "Camas
Prairie Scare" was over. One group that was dis-
mayed by the order to return the Indians to their
reservations was a company of Hailey, Idaho, busi-
nessmen who had planned to use the Indians as a
part of their July Fourth celebration.

The responsibility for the initial reports of trouble
was eventually traced to a Camas Prairie rancher,
S. G. Humphrey. When asked by Agent Irwin why
he had started the circulation of petitions and made
the request for troop protection, Humphrey said, "My
wife is gone and won't return as long as the Indians
are around. I want you to take the varmints away;
we do not want them here."[44]

Although the end of the century thus found the
Bannock tamed at last, confined to a reservation, and
no longer privileged to wander at will in search of
game, this last incident proved that their reputation
alone could still cause some trepidation on the part
of many Idaho citizens, and could still furnish ex-
citing copy for the publishers of eastern newspapers.

---

[43] *Pocatello Tribune,* July 3, 1897, p. 1.
[44] *Report of the Commissioner of Indian Affairs, 1897,* p. 70.

Land Cessions and Allotments

THE legal maneuverings of the 1880's and 1890's over hunting rights and the railroad right of way were not the only problems which involved the Bannock and Shoshoni in negotiations with federal authorities. The governmental promise to grant individual allotments of farming land required a long and tedious procedure of councils and congressional legislation before the Indian farms became realities. A parallel process was the gradual whittling down of the reservation as the Indians turned from hunting to farming, and as the clamor of whites for reservation lands reached the ears of officials in Washington.

The Treaty of Fort Bridger, in 1868, was one of the last formal treaties between an Indian tribe and the United States government. The Indian Appropriation Act of 1871 provided that from that time no Indian tribe within the boundaries of the United States should be considered as an independent nation capable of making treaties with the United States. Thereafter, the results of negotiations were embodied in agreements which required ratification by both houses of Congress. This act did not change the individual status of the Indian nor grant him citizenship. In fact, under it he was neither citizen nor alien.[1]

As already noted, the period after 1871 and until the later 1880's was characterized by the attempt of the government to settle the Bannock on their reservation, and by the need for issuing rations for their subsistence until they were able to farm for a living. The unratified agreement of 1873 would have been a partial answer to some of the problems that the shift to reservation life had brought.

Until 1887, Indian lands were held in common, and the rewards of private initiative on the part of individual Indians were sometimes lost in the struggle to provide food for all the tribe. There were constant requests from agent and Indian alike for a change in the law, providing individual allotments of land for farming purposes. In answer to this need, Congress finally passed the Allotment Act of 1887, which made sweeping changes in the relations of the Indian with the government. Under the new law, the President was authorized to issue land allotments in severalty whenever he was convinced that a reservation was suited for agricultural and grazing purposes. The allotments were to be made as follows: "To heads of families, 160 acres; to single persons over 18 and orphan children under 18, eighty acres; and to other single persons under 18, forty acres, with double allotment when the land was valuable only for grazing purposes."[2] The Indian was to select

---

[1] Laurence F. Schmeckebier, *The Office of Indian Affairs* ("Institute of Government Research, Service Monographs of the United States Government," No. 48 [Baltimore, 1927]), pp. 58-65.

[2] *Ibid.*, p. 79.

his own tract of land; but, if he failed to do so, a government official was to be authorized to make the selection for him. The Indian could not sell or dispose of his allotment in any way for a period of twenty-five years or longer, if the President thought it advisable. Those who received allotments were granted full citizenship and were made subject to state and territorial laws. Citizenship was also offered to any Indian who took up residence apart from the tribe and within the borders of the United States. After all allotments had been made, any surplus reservation land was to be sold back to the United States and the proceeds used for the betterment of the Indians to whom it had belonged.[3]

Among those who fought so long for the allotment of land in severalty were the Indians and agents of Fort Hall Reservation. As early as 1879, Governor Mason Brayman of Idaho Territory had declared that the remedy for the existing evils and embarrassments of the Office of Indian Affairs was to make the Indians self-sustaining citizens by giving them "in severalty, the first right of selection upon their own particular relinquished reservations."[4] Brayman questioned that Fort Hall Reservation even existed except as a scrap of paper in the files of the Office of Indian Affairs:

It is a question with some whether Fort Hall reservation is a reservation. A railroad has been constructed across it, White settlers go upon and occupy it. At the Territorial election of 1878, polls were opened, a large number of votes,

---

[3] *Ibid.*, pp. 78, 80.
[4] U.S. Congress, House of Representatives, *Report of the Secretary of the Interior*, Ex. Doc., 46th Cong., 2nd Sess., Serial No. 1911 (Washington, 1879) , X, 423.

including those of some one hundred and fifty native Indians, received and counted. Upon a contest in the general assembly of a seat claimed upon returns including these Indian votes, it was gravely decided upon investigation and report of committees that no such reservation had been legally established.[5]

The question of white settlers encroaching on reservation lands led the next governor, John B. Neil, to suggest that the portion of the reservation occupied by whites be taken from the Indians in return for proper compensation. He merely echoed the belief of most Idaho citizens that the reservation was much too large and that the excess lands should be thrown open to settlement.[6]

Still another problem which involved the Bannock and Shoshoni was the disposition of the Lemhi Indians whose reserve was much too small to accommodate their numbers, if the contemplated allotment plan was to be undertaken. Chief Tendoy had kept his people peaceful during the Nez Perce and Bannock wars, but there was much dissatisfaction over inadequate food supplies and dishonest agents. Captain Edward Ball of the United States Army reported to his superior in April, 1878, that the issues of food were "entirely inadequate to meet the needs of six or seven hundred Indians for that period [one winter] even if they get it all, and if the agent takes out his *percentage* which according to the Indians stories and the opinion of the citizens generally is quite large, they will fare very poorly."[7] In the same month

---

[5] *Ibid.*, p. 424.

[6] *Ibid.*, 3rd Sess., Serial No. 1960 (Washington, 1880), X, 549.

[7] Edward Ball to Acting Asst. Adj. Gen., District of Montana, Horse Prairie, Montana, April 30, 1878. U.S. National Archives, Records of

of 1878, Major James S. Brisbin also visited the
Lemhi Indians and, in an interview with Tendoy,
learned his reasons for leaving the reservation for the
Yellowstone region:

He [Tendoy] said the Agent was a bad man and cheated
them. He had stayed there until he was nearly starved and
had witnessed the sufferings of his women and children until
he could stand it no longer and his heart became sad within
him every day. His people had gone for days without food
and when he had asked for a little calico to make his wife
a dress, although she was almost naked, it had been refused.[8]

Major Brisbin listed the census of the tribe at that
time as 300 Sheepeaters, 190 Bannock, and 450 Shoshoni.

An executive order of January 7, 1879, attempted
to deal summarily with the Lemhi and force them
to move to Fort Hall. Agent John A. Wright made
the necessary arrangements for removing the government property in the spring. But when the main
tribe returned from the buffalo country in May, Chief
Tendoy "bitterly protested against the change," while
the subchief, Peggé, declared he would go to war before submitting.[9]

Because of their aversion to moving to Fort Hall,
the Bureau of Indian Affairs then attempted to place
them on the Crow Indian Reservation in Montana.
A council of the Crow chiefs agreed reluctantly to

the Bureau of Indian Affairs, Idaho Superintendency, Letters Received,
1866-1880, Record Group 75.

[8] James S. Brisbin to Asst. Adj. Gen., Dept. of Dakota, St. Paul, Minn.,
April 1, 1878. U.S. National Archives, Letters Received, Idaho Superintendency, *op. cit.*

[9] U.S. Office of Indian Affairs, *Annual Report of the Commissioner
of Indian Affairs, 1879* (Washington, 1880), p. 54.

allow the Lemhi a place on their reservation, although their agent reported: "The Crows are fearful that their young men might be led into excesses, that the Bannocks might commit crimes that the people would charge upon the Crows."[10] The Lemhi would not accede to this reserve for a home, and the matter remained unsolved.

Faced with the problems of the rebellious Lemhi, the white encroachment on the Fort Hall Reservation, and the desire of the Bannock and Shoshoni for allotments in severalty, the Indian officials of Idaho suggested that a delegation of the leading chiefs of the three tribes be sent to Washington, D.C., to meet with the Commissioner of Indian Affairs in an attempt to resolve these various difficulties. It was hoped that the Indian leaders would be so impressed with the power and strength of the United States that they would not only agree to the proposals of the Indian Commissioner but would also carry back to their people the firm conviction that it was useless to try to oppose the wishes of the government. Among the chiefs chosen to go were Tendoy of the Lemhi, Gibson Jack and Captain Jim of the Shoshoni, and Tyhee of the Bannock.[11]

The result of the conference was an "Agreement with Shoshones, Bannocks, and Sheepeaters, of Idaho" to which all the chiefs assented and which all signed at Washington, D.C., on May 14, 1880. Article 1 provided for the removal of the Lemhi to Fort Hall.

---

[10] A. R. Keller to E. A. Hoyt, Crow Agency, Montana, May 19, 1879. U.S. National Archives, Letters Received, Idaho Superintendency, *op. cit.*

[11] *Report of the Commissioner of Indian Affairs, 1880,* p. xxx.

Article 2 ceded the Marsh Creek portion of the reservation to the United States and, in doing so, established a southern reservation boundary so indefinite that it remained a constant source of trouble to the Indians and their agents. The third article provided that the land cessions would entitle the Lemhi to a compensation of $4,000 a year for twenty years, and the Bannock and Shoshoni to a sum of $6,000 a year for twenty years. Article 4 outlined that allotments of land at Fort Hall would be made as follows: to each head of a family not more than 160 acres of farming land and not more than 160 acres of grazing land; to each single person over 18 years of age, and to every other person under 18 years of age, not more than 80 acres of farming land and not more than 80 acres of grazing land. The individual Indian was to choose his own allotment with the advice of the agent. The fifth article stated that patents of ownership of the lands would be given the Indians as soon as Congress passed the necessary laws.[12]

Almost as soon as the agreement of 1880 was signed, there appeared the first of many obstacles which were to prevent its ratification for several years. When the Lemhi learned of the agreement, they refused to confirm the action of their chiefs, and the Indian Commissioner was forced to recommend to Congress, in 1880, that the portion dealing with the Lemhi be eliminated. But he urged that the remaining provisions be accepted and made law.[13] Again, in 1881, he advised prompt action on the part of Congress,

---

[12] *Ibid.*, p. 278.
[13] *Ibid.*, p. xxx.

Leading chiefs were sent to Washington, D.C.

stating, "The Indians cannot understand the delay, and are impatient to have the agreements carried into effect."[14]

The voluntary removal of thirty-two Lemhi to Fort Hall in 1882 posed a new problem to the Office of Indian Affairs, which passed it on to the Committee on Indian Affairs in the House of Representatives. Should the bill embodying the agreement be modified so that those Lemhi who wished could remove to Fort Hall? At the same time the Indian Commissioner pointed out that the agreement would not be legal until a majority of the adult male Indians had signed it. The signatures of the chiefs only were not sufficient. After much delay, this legal action was accomplished although, by this time, the Bannock and Shoshoni were rather disgusted with the proceedings and doubted that the agreement would ever be ratified.[15]

By 1884 the white settlers in the proposed cession on Marsh Creek were becoming as anxious as the Indians to have the agreement legalized. The Bannock and Shoshoni had never occupied the area and tended to regard the line proposed by the 1880 pact as the reservation border. However, the zigzag course followed by the new boundary caused much anxiety and dissatisfaction to both whites and Indians. Agent A. L. Cook therefore suggested that a new line running straight east and west be adopted which would include all of the fifty families of white settlers with-

[14] *Report of the Commissioner of Indian Affairs, 1881*, p. lxii.

[15] U.S. Congress, House of Representatives, *Agreement with the Shoshone and Bannock Indians*, Ex. Doc. 18, 47th Cong., 1st Sess., Serial No. 2026 (Washington, 1882), pp. 2-9.

in the proposed cession, rather than just a portion of them. He indicated that the Indians would not oppose such action, and the boundary would then be readily discernible to both parties. The recommended new line would increase the part ceded by 100,000 acres, making a total of about 450,000 acres to be given up by the Indians. If the agreement were so amended, the reservation would then be left with 800,000 acres, of which 5,000 acres would be tillable land which could easily be irrigated. Cook also emphasized the need for a survey of the reservation in anticipation of the granting of allotments.[16]

The constant pleas of the officials of the Indian Department for congressional action on the agreement of 1880 were echoed by the delegates from Idaho Territory. F. T. Dubois reported to Congress, in 1888, that the Bannock and Shoshoni still considered the agreement as binding on them and wanted to know why the government had not paid the money promised them under the pact.[17]

During the same year Chief Tyhee held a council with the reservation Indians and then demanded that Agent Peter Gallagher send a letter to Washington requesting permission for Tyhee, with "some of his young men" and perhaps "some of the Shoshonis," to visit the Great Father in Washington, "shake hands and feel good." Tyhee wished to inquire of the "Big Chief" in the capital city why the Indians did not

---

[16] *Report of the Commissioner of Indian Affairs, 1884*, p. 63.

[17] U.S. Congress, House of Representatives, *Agreement with the Shoshone and Bannock Indians*, Ex. Doc. 140, 50th Cong., 1st Sess., Serial No. 2558 (Washington, 1888), p. 17; also *Report of the Commissioner of Indian Affairs, 1888*, p. 83.

"catch" any money in compensation for the loss of their lands. Gallagher recommended that a delegation be allowed to go:

I am free to say that they are feeling rather sore over their disappointment, & whilst I do not agree with others in anticipating trouble, it is well to remember that the past has proven that no small band of Indians care less about work & love fight more than these Bannocks.

Some good might be accomplished by the trip if some of their "young men" . . . "Bannock braves" . . . could see something of the Country & people, & thereby get some of the "heap fight" knocked out of them. I dare say it would have a cooling effect on their ardor.[18]

A month later, Gallagher wrote to a friend that he had heard nothing of his request and had again "to face the music of a pow wow, & not getting 'paper from Washington.' "[19] In time, permission was granted, and Gallagher escorted a delegation of the leading men of both tribes, headed by Chief Tyhee, to Washington.

Perhaps inspired by the Indian visit, Congress at length confirmed the agreement of 1880 on February 23, 1889. It was ratified as originally drawn up, with the addition of three other sections. Section 1 provided for the issue of patents of ownership as soon as the procedure of allotment had been completed. The second section set aside the sum of $12,000 for a survey of the reservation and $5,000 for the expense of moving the Lemhi to Fort Hall. Section 3 said

[18] P. Gallagher to J. D. C. Atkins, Fort Hall Agency, February 7, 1888. U.S. Department of the Interior, "Special Case No. 99" (MS in U.S. National Archives, Washington, D.C.), p. 67.

[19] P. Gallagher to G. E. Hindmarsh, Fort Hall Agency, March 25, 1888. "Special Case No. 99," op. cit., p. 71.

that the portion of the agreement relating to the removal of the Lemhi would not be in force until satisfactory evidence had been presented to the President of the United States that a majority of the adult male members of the Lemhi tribe had accepted the terms of the agreement.[20]

A group of the Lemhi under Chief Tendoy had visited Fort Hall during the winter of 1888 and had signified their willingness to move to that reservation as soon as Congress ratified the agreement of 1880. Despite this apparent anxiety to get to Fort Hall, when Inspector F. C. Armstrong was sent to conduct the necessary negotiations with them in the spring of 1889, not a single vote was cast in favor of the proposed change. The Indian Commissioner, like his predecessors in office, was determined to keep trying and recommended that further negotiations be undertaken to persuade the Lemhi to reconsider their refusal to leave Lemhi Valley.[21]

Not until 1906 did the Lemhi agree to abandon their home in the Salmon River area. In that year, and of their own volition, they decided to make the change. With only three thousand acres of land available for farming, the 78 Bannock, 101 Sheepeaters, and 289 Shoshoni left in the tribe would have had only about six acres each under the Allotment Act of 1887. They were compensated for the improvements they had made on their little farms at Lemhi, and were to receive eighty acres of farming land and eighty acres of grazing land on the Fort Hall Reser-

---

[20] *Report of the Commissioner of Indian Affairs, 1889*, pp. 432-33.
[21] *Ibid.*, pp. 17, 174-75.

vation. In April, 1907, the first group traveled to Fort Hall and, within a few months, the entire tribe had left their old home. One who stayed behind was the old Chief Tendoy, who died May 9, 1907. It was perhaps fitting that he should die in the Lemhi Valley where he had ruled his people so well. The settlers of the area, grateful for his long years of service to the cause of peace between the two races, subscribed about two hundred dollars toward the erection of a suitable monument to mark the burial place of Chief Tendoy.[22]

Throughout the 1880's and the long delay before the distribution of land allotments could get underway, the agents of Fort Hall were cognizant that, without sufficient irrigation water, the proposed farms would fail before they were even started. The Indian Commissioner, in his report for 1887, had said that "next to the expenditure of money for irrigating ditches is the importance of Congressional action in ratifying treaties made by the Indians. . . ."[23] The Indians were informed the following year that work was to be started to build a canal through the reservation, and they were "gratified in the prospect of having pretty soon one irrigating ditch."[24]

A preliminary survey of the proposed canal was begun in 1889. The ditch was to leave Snake River a few miles below the present Idaho Falls, cross Blackfoot and Portneuf rivers, and terminate at American

---

[22] *Report of the Commissioner of Indian Affairs, 1906*, p. 217; *Report . . . 1907*, p. 94.

[23] *Report of the Commissioner of Indian Affairs, 1887*, p. 69.

[24] Gallagher to Atkins, Fort Hall Agency, February 27, 1888. "Special Case No. 99," *op. cit.*, p. 71.

Falls—a distance of about eighty miles. According to the survey, the canal would be 38 feet wide at the bottom, 62 feet at the top, and would carry water to the depth of 8 feet. It was estimated that the canal would irrigate 300,000 acres of land, two thirds of which would be on the reservation. The projected cost was $238,000.[25]

The absolute need for a means of irrigating the Indian farms, if allotments were to be made, was emphasized by Agent S. G. Fisher in 1890:

Until some provisions are made for an increased supply of water it is absurd to ask the Indians to take their land in severalty, from the fact that not one in ten of those willing to farm could get their 160 or even 80 acres covered by water. In most cases their "farms" comprise from 2 to 10 acres, scattered along in the bends of the creeks coming out of the mountains. In many instances 160 acres would take in a dozen or more of their little cultivated patches called farms, including their log cabins and fences.[26]

By an act of March 3, 1891, Congress authorized the Secretary of the Interior to contract with responsible companies for the construction of irrigation canals on the Fort Hall Reservation. The expense of the projects was to be paid out of the money belonging to the Bannock and Shoshoni, which was held in the United States Treasury.[27] The act also authorized the Secretary of the Interior to grant a right of way across the reservation for a canal to carry water to the near-by town of Pocatello. Any surplus water

---

[25] *Report of the Commissioner of Indian Affairs, 1889*, p. 176.
[26] *Report of the Commissioner of Indian Affairs, 1890*, p. 76.
[27] *Report of the Commissioner of Indian Affairs, 1894*, p. 443.

from this ditch was to be reserved for the use of the Indians. The only company to submit a "formal proposition" for such a right of way was the Idaho Canal Company, and a contract was to be granted that company as soon as it had filed a map of "definite location," and had conformed to the other terms of the agreement.[28]

Apparently the contract was never completed, perhaps because the government failed to make the necessary appropriation. By 1895, the Indian Department had decided to employ a superintendent to direct the work of establishing an irrigation system on the reservation. The plan failed because a sufficient supply of water could not be obtained on the reservation; prior appropriations of water rights eliminated this possibility. By this time the Bannock and Shoshoni were becoming somewhat suspicious of the negotiations for a canal and, in a petition to the Indian Bureau, complained that

Our Agent says Washington wants us to pay the White man to make a ditch on our land and pay him for taking care of it, and then buy the water out of a ditch our money has built on our land, and which rightfully should belong to us, we think he is mistaken.[29]

Advertisement was made for bids from private concerns and on January 25, 1896, the same Idaho Canal Company signed a contract to construct a canal from Snake River across Blackfoot River to Ross Fork

---

[28] *Report of the Commissioner of Indian Affairs, 1891*, p. 52.

[29] *Report of the Commissioner of Indian Affairs, 1896*, p. 30; Petition of Bannock and Shoshoni Indians, Pocatello, Idaho, October 1, 1895. U.S. National Archives, Records of the Bureau of Indian Affairs, Education Division, Letters Received, 1881-1895, Record Group 75.

Creek, capable of delivering three hundred cubic feet of water per second at certain points on the reservation to be designated by the Secretary of the Interior. The company also agreed to extend the canal from Ross Fork Creek as far as necessary toward Portneuf River to supply water to the lands in that area as soon as they were opened to settlement. Water was to be conveyed to this land for five dollars an acre, plus an annual charge of seventy-five cents an acre for maintenance. For the construction north of Ross Fork Creek and the delivery of three hundred cubic feet of water through the finished canal, the Idaho Canal Company was to receive $90,000, with an annual maintenance charge of fifteen dollars per cubic foot.[30]

The engineer employed by the government to superintend the construction of laterals suggested some changes in the route of the canal, and Mr. A. P. Davis was sent to investigate the proposed alterations. The upshot of this inspection was the government's execution of a new contract with the Idaho Canal Company which required that two dams be built across Blackfoot River to divert the water of that stream into the reservation canal, part of which had already been constructed. For the four miles of canal completed by late 1896, the company was paid $30,000.

Agent Irwin of Fort Hall reported in July, 1897, that a portion of one of the completed canals had been destroyed by a flood in the early spring and that the canal company had not repaired it. In consequence, the work had to be performed by the gov-

---

[30] *Report of the Commissioner of Indian Affairs, 1896,* pp. 30-31.

ernment. The two diversion dams on Blackfoot River had not yet been constructed, but were to be finished by October of that year.[31] Similarly, no work had yet been done on the main canal across the reservation from Blackfoot River to Ross Fork Creek, a distance of seventeen miles.

At the very beginning most of the Indians had been suspicious of the proposed irrigation project, convinced that they would be defrauded by it, one way or another. Jim Ballard, one of the Shoshoni leaders, had led a group of reservation Indians in signing a petition protesting the building of the canal. The protest was finally dispatched to the Secretary of the Interior. By 1897, however, Agent Irwin noted that there seemed to be no further hostility on the part of the Indians to the canal project.[32]

By December, 1897, the Idaho Canal Company had completed the two diversion dams across Blackfoot River and, as agreed in the contract, were then to receive the second payment of $30,000. The second payment was held up until the company had paid off some $13,944 in liens which had been filed against it. In April, 1899, a Mr. J. H. Brady informed the Interior Department that he had contracted with the Idaho Canal Company to build the canal across the reservation to Ross Fork Creek, and wanted assurance that the final payment of $22,500 would be paid to the Idaho Canal Company immediately upon the completion of construction of the ditch, instead of a year from the date of the second payment as the govern-

---

[31] *Report of the Commissioner of Indian Affairs, 1897,* pp. 30-32.
[32] *Ibid.; Pocatello Tribune,* February 1, 1896, p. 1.

ment contract required. The Department of the Interior refused to change the contract as Brady wished.[33]

Meanwhile, the affairs of the Idaho Canal Company had been placed in the hands of a receiver as a result of $16,887 in liens against the firm, a mortgage of $50,000, and a bonded indebtedness of $300,-000. The company failed to do any work toward the fulfillment of its contract in the summer of 1899, so Inspector W. H. Graves was sent to investigate the condition of the company and to recommend what action the government should take.

During 1899, the receiver of the company was not able to find a responsible firm which would undertake to complete the canal, and the Fort Hall agent said it was difficult to tell whether the receiver was in earnest about finishing the job. The Idaho Canal Company finally arranged to dig the canal, and informed the agent in December, 1899, that the ditch was finished.[34]

W. H. Graves inspected the canal and reported that it was not acceptable according to the terms of the contract. Upon examination, Graves found that the canal was not excavated sufficiently but was a "built-up" channel, made cheaply by scraping up the loose surface material along the outside of the channel. One or two attempts were made to flow water through the ditch but, in each case, the stream broke through the sandy embankments and washed out deep gorges below the canal, covering many valuable acres of land with a deep layer of sand.[35]

[33] *Report of the Commissioner of Indian Affairs, 1898,* pp. 47-48.
[34] *Report of the Commissioner of Indian Affairs, 1899,* pp. 50, 181.
[35] *Report of the Commissioner of Indian Affairs, 1900,* p. 61.

Inspector Graves had sufficient opportunity to observe the Indian reaction to the "government's" fraudulent ditch:

These Indians are so impressed with the idea that this irrigation undertaking is a deception and a fraud and pregnant with so much trouble and disaster for them when they attempt to farm and depend upon the ditch for their supply of water that they will not talk about it nor listen with patience to any explanations concerning the matter. It will take a long time to overcome the prejudice that they have acquired against this company and its ditch system.[36]

As the Department of the Interior acknowledged the failure of the Idaho Canal Company to fulfill its contract, and as the Interior Department sought other arrangements to provide the reservation with an effective irrigation system, the Bannock and Shoshoni had for contemplation a good example of white disregard for honorable contract. Jim Ballard and his fellow tribesmen had rightly diagnosed the Idaho Canal Company as a fraud.

During the 1890's, several factors had focused the attention of the Office of Indian Affairs on the need for a new agreement with the Bannock and Shoshoni. As has been explained, it was necessary to deprive the Indians of their right to hunt on the unoccupied lands of the United States; but the tribes had never received any compensation for the relinquishment of this privilege. Another matter involved encroachments on the neighboring lands by citizens of Pocatello. Also, the reservation embraced large areas which were not occupied by the Indians and not needed

---

[36] *Ibid.*

by them, and white speculators kept up a constant barrage of requests that these lands be thrown open to settlement.[37]

An act of Congress, June 10, 1896, authorized the appointment of a commission to treat with the Indians concerning these matters. Benjamin F. Barge, James H. McNeely, and Charles G. Hoyt were named to the commission in August and these men began negotiations with the Bannock and Shoshoni. An agreement was reached in September, 1897, under which the Indians agreed to cede about 150,000 acres to the government for $600,000. The *Pocatello Tribune* said:

It is a big price that the government is paying, and one that no one but the Indians could ever get from the government. . . . This is the best deal we have ever heard of anyone making with the U. S. Government. The price, $4.00 per acre, is an unheard of price for public lands and we do not believe that Congress would ever approve any such deal, if it were not that the money was to go to the Indian.[38]

The government apparently agreed with the Pocatello newspaper because, although over a dozen of the leading Indians had already signed the pact, the Department of the Interior refused to accept it, wanting a larger cession at a lower price. The chiefs refused to reduce the amount they were asking, and affairs remained at a stalemate for several months.

At length the Indians capitulated to government demands and signed an agreement on February 5, 1898, which gave to the government some 400,000

---

[37] *Report of the Commissioner of Indian Affairs, 1898,* p. 143.
[38] *Pocatello Tribune,* September 11, 1897, p. 1.

acres of land at about $1.25 per acre. The new line of the reservation was to be north of Pocatello, and the only section remaining to the Indians of this south segment was the land along Bannock Creek, where a great number of Indian families had settled. The main cause for the change of attitude on the part of the Indians was a visit by a delegation of them to Washington, D.C., in January, 1899.[39]

After the agreement had been signed, the Fort Hall agent warned his superior that it should be ratified as it was and at once, because "Indians are very suspicious; they have agreed once, and it would be almost useless to ask them to agree again to some different treaty."[40] With unprecedented speed, at least as far as treaties with the Bannock were concerned, the national Congress ratified the agreement on June 6, 1900. For the 400,000 acres ceded, the government agreed to pay the Indians $525,000, with an additional $75,000 as compensation for their surrender of the right to hunt on the unoccupied lands of the United States. Of the total sum of $600,000, $75,000 was to be used in the erection of a new school building on the reservation. The rest was to be given the Indians in ten annual payments: $100,000 for the first payment, $50,000 for each of the next eight payments, and $25,000 for the last payment. An important article of the agreement provided that Indians residing on lands ceded might remain there and receive allotments of the lands occupied and improved

[39] U.S. Congress, Senate, *Fort Hall Indian Reservation in Idaho*, Report No. 60, 56th Cong., 1st Sess., Serial No. 3886 (Washington, 1900), pp. 2-5.
[40] *Report of the Commissioner of Indian Affairs, 1898*, p. 143.

by them, or they might move to the diminished reservation. If the Indian family chose to move, any improvements on the land it had occupied would be appraised and reimbursement would be made to the family. Those Indians who chose to remain outside the reservation were guaranteed water rights for irrigation purposes from the streams located on the ceded portion of the reserve.[41]

The Office of Indian Affairs was disappointed in the financial settlement made to the Bannock and Shoshoni. The office, early in the 1890's, had decided upon a long-range plan which, it was hoped, would provide an efficient irrigation system for the reservation. The Idaho Canal Company had, therefore, been given the contract to carry water to the unused portion of the reserve. After the introduction of irrigation water had thus enhanced the value of this unneeded land, the Indian officials had hoped to sell it at a handsome profit. The sum of money so obtained was to have been used to complete the reservation irrigation system, of which the Idaho Canal Company project was only a part. The Indian Commissioner estimated that $75,000 of the $600,000 granted the Indians would be sufficient to pay for the proposed irrigation improvements.

But, according to the agreement, the entire allotment of $525,000 was to be paid out in cash to the Indians. With a population of about 1,500 at Fort Hall, the disbursement to each Indian from the first cash payment of $100,000 amounted to about $67.00,

---

[41] *Report of the Commissioner of Indian Affairs, 1900,* p. 102; U.S. Congress, Senate, *Fort Hall Indian Reservation in Idaho, op. cit.,* pp. 2-5.

or to about $335.00 for a family of five. The Commissioner of Indian Affairs deplored this plan of cash payments as a detriment to the tribe, and regretted that the $75,000 so badly needed for irrigation works was to be paid out in such small amounts to the individual Indians.[42]

The Bannock and Shoshoni "would not consent to the expenditure of any of said sum for irrigation purposes, nor would they allow any of it to be so placed as to permit the Secretary of the Interior to expend it for their benefit."[43] In these words the Indian Commissioner summed up the opposition of the Indians to any other investments in irrigation projects. The ghost of the Idaho Canal Company still hovered over the reservation, and the Bannock and Shoshoni evidently refused to allow their money to be invested in ditches which would not hold water.

---

[42] U.S. Congress, Senate, *Fort Hall Indian Reservation in Idaho, op. cit.*, pp. 10-12.

[43] *Ibid.*, p. 11.

Reservation Life

THE time from 1871 to 1887 has been characterized as the "Reservation Period" in the policy of the United States government toward the Indians. The dominant features of these years were settlement on reservations, endeavor by the agents to exercise complete control, and issuance of rations in order to provide subsistence and keep the Indians quiet. For the Bannock, this period could well be extended to 1900, because the tardy development of irrigation facilities at Fort Hall precluded the assignment of farming allotments to many families. Bannock reluctance to engage in farming proved to be an additional deterrent to their adaptation to a civilized life.[1]

Soon after the establishment of Fort Hall Reservation, the Idaho Superintendent of Indian Affairs was able to report that several buildings had been constructed at the agency and that a sawmill was in operation. Insufficient appropriations from the federal government curtailed operations of the mill and, in 1872, the agent complained that 123,780 feet of saw logs had been rotting for two years in the mill yard. By that time a flour mill was in use and, the

---

[1] Laurence F. Schmeckebier, *The Office of Indian Affairs* ("Institute of Government Research, Service Monographs of the United States Government," No. 48 [Baltimore, 1927]), p. 66.

following year, a shingle machine was in operation. Homes for the agency employees and warehouses for the annuity goods had been constructed within a few years after the founding of the agency, and the reservation plant was ready to serve the needs of the Bannock and Shoshoni.[2]

The principal activity of the agent, especially in the early years, was the purchase and distribution of rations and annuity goods. Annual contract awards were made to responsible bidders. In 1877, E. S. Newman accepted a contract to deliver 52,500 pounds of flour to Fort Hall for $3.00 per 100 pounds. He also supplied the 400,000 pounds of beef ordered for that year. Another item of issue in 1877 was 35,000 pounds of "hard bread."[3] On one occasion the agent postponed bids for the delivery of beef until he had received one from a group of Texas cattlemen who were approaching the Idaho country with a large herd. The supply of rations decreased as farming became more popular. Comparative figures for the years 1880 and 1885 indicated the trend; the reduction in amounts of the major articles used during the five-year period were as follows: beef—950,000 to 250,000 pounds; flour—200,000 to 100,000 pounds;

---

[2] U.S. Office of Indian Affairs, *Annual Report of the Commissioner of Indian Affairs, 1869* (Washington, 1870), p. 72; *Report . . . 1873*, p. 61; U.S. Congress, House of Representatives, Ex. Doc., 42nd Cong., 3rd Sess., Serial No. 1560 (Washington, 1872), p. 656.

In the opinion of many Idaho citizens, Indian reservations were luxuries, and it was thought that if they were absolutely necessary, they should be situated in areas which would never be fit for white occupation. One newspaper commented: "The Middle Fork [Salmon River] Region has only one redeeming virtue, it would make a splendid reservation for the Indians. They would all tumble off and break their necks." *Yankee Fork Herald* (Bonanza, Custer County, Idaho), August 7, 1879, p. 1.

[3] *Report of the Commissioner of Indian Affairs, 1876*, pp. 157, 160, 165.

sugar—12,000 pounds to 8,000 pounds; and coffee—
8,000 pounds to 4,000 pounds.[4]

The Treaty of Fort Bridger specified certain annuity goods which were to be distributed annually
to the Bannock, and these people developed singular
methods of converting the various articles to their
use. Most of the red flannel issued to the squaws
was taken by the braves for horse trimmings; the
blankets were cut up and fashioned into leggings and
breechcloths; and only a small portion of the articles
was employed for the purpose originally designed.
Most of the goods were resold, at about one fourth
the original cost, to white buyers who thronged the
reservation at the time of distribution. The Indian
men sold their clothing at prices ranging from $2.00
to $5.00 a suit. Agent M. P. Berry recommended
that it would be better for the Indians and the government if ready-made leggings, shirts, skirts, breechcloths, et cetera were issued rather than cloth. He
said, "Those things, with blankets, hats, camp equip-
age, and brown muslin, should be the sum total of
issues to the Bannock until they become permanent
residents of the reserve."[5]

The governmental policy of civilizing the Indians
as rapidly as possible was aimed principally at teaching them how to subsist themselves so that they would
not have to depend on rations and annuity goods.
The agency for transforming the Indians from wards
of the government to self-sufficient citizens was to be
the individual farm. First, however, the Indian had

---

[4] *Report of the Commissioner of Indian Affairs, 1885,* p. 65.
[5] *Report of the Commissioner of Indian Affairs, 1871,* p. 543.

to be shown how to raise crops, and that was accomplished by establishing a reservation farm operated by the agent, with white and Indian labor. Of thirty-five acres planted to seed in 1869, only seven acres of potatoes and turnips were successful, but at least a start had been made.[6] The following year Agent Danilson persuaded the Boise Shoshoni to furnish a daily detail of thirty-three men to work on the reservation farm. The agent requested the male occupants of five Bannock lodges to help on the farm, but they "positively refused to work" and left for the mountains to await the arrival of Chief Taghee. A grasshopper plague destroyed almost the entire crop of 1871; but, by 1872, the agent was able to report 250 acres under cultivation on the government farm and three acres being cultivated by Indian farmers.[7]

With the introduction of individual farms, reservation officials began to request the seeds and agricultural implements promised the Bannock by Article 8 of the Fort Bridger Treaty. But the requisite amount of money was meager and slow in coming. Even appropriations for the reservation farm were discouragingly small.[8]

Despite the lack of funds, the year 1874 proved to be quite successful for agriculture at Fort Hall. The 292 acres cultivated by the government produced 3,100 bushels of wheat, and the agent was able to

---

[6] *Report of the Commissioner of Indian Affairs, 1869,* p. 72.

[7] Danilson to Jones, Fort Hall, May 2, 1870, in Fort Hall Agency Letter Book, Copies of Letters Sent, 1869-1875 (MS at Fort Hall Agency, Fort Hall, Idaho), p. 38; U.S. Congress, House of Representatives, Ex. Doc., 42nd Cong., 3rd Sess., Serial No. 1560, *op. cit.,* p. 790.

[8] U.S. Congress, House of Representatives, Ex. Doc., Serial No. 1560, *op. cit.,* p. 656; *Report of the Commissioner of Indian Affairs, 1876,* p. 42.

report that thirty-two Indians were actually engaged in farming, most of them on the reservation acreage. Only twenty-eight acres were being farmed by individual families.[9]

In an attempt to arouse more interest in the pursuit of agriculture, Agent James Wright held a council with the Bannock and Shoshoni in December, 1874. The majority of those present indicated a willingness to start farming, and Wright immediately requested $3,500 worth of farming equipment for distribution to the Indians interested. Apparently the order was never filled because, during the following year, only five families were engaged in farming forty-two acres of land. A hopeful sign was that one of the number was the head chief, Tyhee, who had built himself a comfortable house and gave every indication of settling down to farm life.[10]

Beginning with 1876 there was a rapid increase in the number of Indians who engaged in farming as an individual occupation. During that year, twenty-four families cultivated 120 acres upon a portion of the reservation farm and raised 500 bushels of potatoes and 2,000 bushels of wheat. The agent said, "They are thoroughly in earnest in this matter, and are constantly at work."[11] Idaho Governor Brayman visited Fort Hall in 1879 and came away with the enthusiastic report that there were then 150 families engaged in agriculture.[12] This account has to be tem-

---

[9] *Report of the Commissioner of Indian Affairs, 1874,* p. 116.

[10] *Report of the Commissioner of Indian Affairs, 1875,* p. 259; *Report . . . 1876,* p. 42.

[11] *Report of the Commissioner of Indian Affairs, 1876,* p. 42.

[12] U.S. Congress, House of Representatives, "Report of the Governor

pered with a later report, in 1893, which listed only 130 families engaged in farming; but it indicates that at least a portion of the two tribes had begun to show an interest in the raising of crops.[13]

The many who refused to farm, or who did so only half-heartedly, depended on "Washington" for their wants and, when the agents told them they would have to work for the things they wanted, they would reply, "No, Washington give Indian all; you no ask him for it."[14] A reduction in rations was the only answer to that attitude; and when such an event occurred in 1882, a group of them purchased three mowing machines, six sulky hay rakes, and two lumber wagons, which were, as the agent said, "The first property, except a pony or gun, they have ever bought for themselves."[15] The same agent described their farming habits during the early 1880's:

But few live in houses, and most of those that do are near the agency. . . . It is their custom to move from their farms in the fall to near Snake River, 8 to 10 miles west of the agency, where there is plenty of scrub cedar and cotton-wood for fuel, and good pasturage near for their ponies. Those that leave houses for the winter generally find doors and windows gone on their return in the spring.[16]

One agency employee was designated as a "farmer," and it was the duty of this man to instruct about 1,500 Indians in the methods of raising crops. The

of Idaho," in *Report of the Secretary of the Interior*, Ex. Doc., 46th Cong., 2nd Sess., Serial No. 1911 (Washington, 1879), p. 424.

[13] *Report of the Commissioner of Indian Affairs, 1893*, p. 135.

[14] *Report of the Commissioner of Indian Affairs, 1882*, p. 49.

[15] *Ibid.*

[16] *Ibid.*

impossibility of his task was well illustrated, in 1887, by the resident agent, who listed the various reservation communities under the charge of the one farmer:

Bannock Creek, 25 miles from agency, with a population of about 300; Port Neuf settlement, distant some 16 miles, with a population of 200 or more; Blackfoot, 13 miles away, with a like population; upper Ross Fork, 12 miles distant, with some 300 souls; and lower Ross Fork, and around agency, between 400 and 500. . . .[17]

Another side to the picture was the incompetency of the reservation "farmers," some of whom "could not harness a span of horses," according to one Indian complaint.[18]

As indicated in a previous chapter, irrigation was a requisite for farming, and the allotment program could not succeed until the government provided a means for bringing water to Indian farmland. Agent Peter Gallagher was, therefore, quite correct in one sense when he referred to Indian farming as a "burlesque on civilization."[19] But to measure Indian farming by the standard of the successful farming operations employed by whites was wholly unfair when it is considered that, during Gallagher's tenure, the Bannock and Shoshoni did not have adequate irrigation facilities.

The agent's report for 1881 included the production statistics of a typical reservation harvest: 3,888 bushels of wheat, 3,200 bushels of oats, 180 bushels

---

[17] *Report of the Commissioner of Indian Affairs, 1887,* p. 67.

[18] Petition of Bannock and Shoshoni Indians, Pocatello, Idaho, October 1, 1895. U.S. National Archives, Records of the Bureau of Indian Affairs, Education Division, Letters Received, 1881-1895, Record Group 75.

[19] *Report of the Commissioner of Indian Affairs, 1886,* p. 107.

of barley, 2,375 bushels of potatoes, 80 bushels of vegetables, and 600 tons of hay.[20] The hay was either sold in the stack or was hauled off by the purchasers. This commodity came to be the most important cash crop produced by the Indians. By 1900, Bannock and Shoshoni farmers occupied 167 dwelling houses and cultivated 2,050 acres of land, figures which reveal just how slow was the process of conversion to sedentary farm life.

The reluctance of the Bannock and some of the Shoshoni to take up agriculture convinced most of the Fort Hall agents that stock raising would not only be more profitable but also more in keeping with the nomadic characteristics of the Indians. J. N. High wrote, in 1872:

. . . the beef purchased for these people is raised and fatted right around them, and with no other cost than herding; $10,000 invested in cattle will, in two years, relieve the Government from ever buying a single pound for this agency, while there was expended during the fiscal year ended June 30, $10,436.68 for beef.[21]

Out of the meager appropriations, the various agents attempted to secure a herd of stock and, from six cattle owned by Indians in 1874, a herd of 580 head had been built up by 1884.[22] By the end of the century, the Indians at Fort Hall were selling over 200,000 pounds of beef each year to the government.[23]

---

[20] *Report of the Commissioner of Indian Affairs, 1881*, p. 63.

[21] U.S. Congress, House of Representatives, Ex. Doc., 42nd Cong., 3rd Sess., Serial No. 1560, *op. cit.*, p. 656.

[22] *Report of the Commissioner of Indian Affairs, 1874*, p. 125; *Report . . . 1884*, p. 64.

[23] *Report of the Commissioner of Indian Affairs, 1899*, p. 181.

There were two principal factors which prevented a more rapid growth of the stock industry. First of all, hunger and improvidence sometimes drove the Indians to kill all their cattle for food. Of 200 head of stock bought for the Indians in 1889, only about 50 head were saved by some of the more enterprising Shoshoni. All the Bannock killed their cattle the first winter.[24] The type of cattle furnished by the government may have had something to do with the lack of success. An Indian petition in 1895 noted:

Washington spent a lot of money for cattle. We know we were to get nice young cows, but in place of getting young cows, we got ones so old and poor they can hardly stand. Quite a number have no teeth and will be dead in the spring and our agent took them and said nothing.[25]

Another obstacle was the natural tendency to keep large herds of horses; and, during most of the period before 1900, there were about three thousand Indian horses pastured on the reservation. The agents attempted to reduce the number but were not very successful.[26]

Throughout the thirty-year reservation period, to 1900, there was a gradual increase in the Indian population of Fort Hall. The census for 1870 listed 520 Bannock and 256 Shoshoni; but the removal of Shoshoni bands to the reservation soon increased the Shoshoni numbers to 521 in 1872. Three years later,

---

[24] U.S. Congress, House of Representatives, *Condition of Indians Taxed and Indians Not Taxed*, Misc. Doc., 52nd Cong., 1st Sess., Serial No. 3016 (Washington, 1891), p. 237.

[25] Petition of Bannock and Shoshoni Indians, Pocatello, Idaho, October 1, 1895, *op. cit.*

[26] *Report of the Commissioner of Indian Affairs, 1880*, p. 62.

the agent reported a total of 897 Bannock: 600 at
Fort Hall, 210 at the Lemhi Reserve, and 87 at
Malheur Agency in Oregon. By 1876, the Shoshoni
outnumbered the Bannock on the Fort Hall Reservation, totaling 964 as compared with 648 for their
neighbors. After the Bannock War of 1878, the census
showed 888 Shoshoni and 331 Bannock, 129 Bannock
being absent from the agency. In 1883, there were
1,085 Shoshoni and 471 Bannock present on the reservation and, from this time until the end of the century
the population of the two tribes remained at about
those figures.[27]

During the early 1870's, the Bannock made no complaint about the increasing numbers of Shoshoni; but
when the rations and annuity goods proved to be
inadequate for all the reservation Indians, the Bannock charged that the supplies furnished for them
under the Bridger Treaty were being given to the
Shoshoni. The Bannock looked upon the other Indians as intruders, and the bad feeling between the
two tribes was one of the causes of the war of 1878.
The jealousy between the two peoples was maintained either deliberately or unwittingly by the various agents. John A. Wright looked upon this rivalry
as an advantage to the government, because the Indian Department could stir up competition by con-
ferring government favors and aid upon the most
deserving tribe.[28]

---

[27] *Report of the Commissioner of Indian Affairs, 1870*, p. 187; *Report
. . . 1872*, p. 51; *Report . . . 1875*, p. 175; *Report . . . 1876*, p. 42; *Report
. . . 1879*, p. 52; *Report . . . 1883*, p. 53; *Report . . . 1894*, p. 130.

[28] *Report of the Commissioner of Indian Affairs, 1878*, p. 49; *Report
. . . 1880*, p. 62.

It was evidently difficult for the agents to maintain strict impartiality, and there is discernible in their reports a leaning to one tribe or the other. Wright said, "The Bannocks as a class being naturally more intelligent than their neighbors, the Shoshones, are the leading Indians in agriculture, in stock raising, in patronizing the school, and in every other enterprise connected with their reservation. . . ."[29] Later, F. G. Irwin commented that the two tribes were still separate and distinct, though having lived together for many years. He said,

The more turbulent and aggressive nature of the Bannock makes that the dominant tribe, although numbering but little more than one-fourth the total population. The Shoshones take kindly to labor and are more disposed to settle down, while the Bannocks are of a roving, idle, and improvident disposition, but little inclined to engage in civilized pursuits. However, those Bannocks who do labor bring to bear more intelligence and persistence, as a rule, than do their Shoshone neighbors. Many of the most prosperous farmers are Bannocks, and their number is constantly growing.[30]

Even those agents who seemed to favor the Bannock admitted that they were harder to control and were more restless and aggressive than the Shoshoni, but Thomas B. Teter was convinced that the Shoshoni were "far more intelligent and progressive than the Bannocks." He was probably influenced in his judgment by an attempt of a group of Bannock to hang him for what they considered wrongs committed

---

[29] *Report of the Commissioner of Indian Affairs, 1880,* p. 62.
[30] *Report of the Commissioner of Indian Affairs, 1897,* p. 127.

against them.[31] The following comments picked at random from the reports of the various agents illustrate the consensus held concerning the different character of the two tribes:

The Bannocks are naturally a turbulent and rebellious people . . . the Shoshones are . . . of a quiet and peaceful disposition. . . .[32]

The Shoshones are an industrious, good-natured, and quiet people; but the Bannocks are restless and roving, and much more difficult to control.[33]

The Shoshones are generally the most docile and easily managed. . . .[34]

The Bannocks, a wild, restless, and nomadic tribe. . . . The Shoshones are . . . more docile and friendly in disposition.[35]

The Bannocks are intractable and very improvident, do not take kindly to any kind of manual labor, adhering to the primitive idea that they were not made to work, resisting stubbornly every effort to induce them to improve their condition. While on the other hand, the Shoshones are more tractable, and as a rule evince a disposition, and in many notable cases an earnest desire, to learn the ways of civilization.[36]

A very natural reaction on the part of most agents was to favor the tribe that was interested and willing to learn how to farm and improve their condition.

---

[31] *Report of the Commissioner of Indian Affairs, 1895,* p. 142.
[32] *Report of the Commissioner of Indian Affairs, 1881,* p. 63.
[33] *Report of the Commissioner of Indian Affairs, 1883,* p. 53.
[34] *Report of the Commissioner of Indian Affairs, 1873,* p. 247.
[35] *Report of the Commissioner of Indian Affairs, 1891,* p. 229.
[36] *Report of the Commissioner of Indian Affairs, 1885,* p. 64.

Because the Bannock preferred "to remember their warrior fathers" and thought it "disgraceful to work," they refused, in the majority of cases, to do any farming whatsoever. Except for the few who raised a little hay, most of the tribe worked hides into gloves, moccasins, et cetera, for sale to whites as a means of earning some ready cash.

The members of the tribe clung to their full Indian dress and refused to adopt white man's clothing. Most of them also retained their Indian names. The Shoshoni, on the other hand, readily adapted themselves to the dress of the white man and adopted American names. While the Shoshoni chiefs soon became Captain Jim and Gibson Jack, the Bannock chiefs were still Tyhee and Mo-pi-er.[37]

A typical representative of his tribe was Chief Bannock Jim, whose actions on one occasion well demonstrated the contempt held by many of the Bannock for white men and their civilization. About 1868, the chief went to Boise to protest to the governor concerning a rumor he had heard that all Bannock who visited Boise were to be shot. A Judge Hollister was among those waiting with Bannock Jim in the anteroom of the executive's office. The chief accidentally dropped a half dollar and, turning to the

---

[37] *Report of the Commissioner of Indian Affairs, 1895*, p. 142; *Report . . . 1890*, p. 77.

Toward the end of the century, many of the Bannock were given white names by agency employees and came to be known by these new appellations, despite any opposition they may have had to them. Some of the more curious combinations were: *Weed-ze-we*, Teton Bill; *Coppe-que-tan*, Coffee Grounds; *We-he-din*, Iron Mouth; *Se-tso Po-ku-wak-i*, Chinaman's family; *Ca-nave*, Johnny Stevens; *Egi*, Little John; *Poh-a-give-to*, Big Mack; *Saw-a-hun*, Little Old Man; and *Pi-ze*, Pit Piper. U.S. Congress, House of Representatives, *Condition of Indians, op. cit.*, p. 54.

judge, said, "Pick it up." The judge stooped and handed the coin to the Indian. Another white man in the room remonstrated with Bannock Jim and explained who Judge Hollister was. "Jim stood upright, looked the judge all over, sniffed at him, and air[i]ly stalked out of the office. In clean-cut impudence and majestic insolence, it was sublime!"[38]

Although the war of 1878 convinced most Bannock of the futility of attempting to resist the spread of white men's laws and customs, turbulent young braves often became involved in serious trouble, not only with the whites, but also with the law-abiding members of their own tribes. In 1883, a young Bannock boy was killed accidentally in the machinery of the agency flour mill. The next morning the mill was burned to the ground by revengeful Bannock, to the great loss of the Shoshoni farmers who had stored 15,000 bushels of wheat and 12,000 pounds of flour in the structure. As was usual at such times, great excitement prevailed for some time among the Bannock, and the agent feared an outbreak.[39] A few years later, two Bannock bucks were arrested by Indian police for stealing horses from the Wind River Reservation. The two killed one of the police and wounded another. A posse of 150 Indians pursued the two bandits and finally had to kill both of them when they refused to surrender. After this affair, Agent A. L. Cook suggested that the whole Bannock tribe be removed from the reservation. He said that the

---

[38] Thomas Donaldson, *Idaho of Yesterday* (Caldwell, Idaho, 1941), pp. 290-91.

[39] *Report of the Commissioner of Indian Affairs, 1883*, p. 53.

refusal of the Bannock to work or farm, while still drawing the same rations as the Shoshoni, set a very bad example and made more difficult the task of persuading the Shoshoni to take up farming.[40]

In defense of the Bannock, it must be noted that sometimes the agents empowered to care for them were not full-fledged angels of mercy. The *Register* of near-by Blackfoot accused Agent John A. Wright of resigning his position and then attempting to make things more difficult for his successor by opening the agency warehouses and telling the Indians to help themselves. The newspaper editor referred to Wright as a "fraud," a "liar," and a "bleary-eyed feature of melancholy and imbecility." When E. A. Stone took over the agency, the *Register* commented that it was "about the same as jumping from the frying pan into the fire," but later admitted that perhaps the new agent would be an efficient administrator.[41]

More serious charges were levelled at Agent Thomas B. Teter in 1895. The Indians became so incensed that they sent a delegation to ask the Idaho governor's influence in having Teter discharged. A petition was also sent to Washington, D.C.:

Our present agent Mr. Teter is afraid of us and we want no one that is afraid for he can do us no good. He carries a pistol and shot himself when he first came here. If he had been away from this agency and killed himself us Indians would have been accused of killing him. We cannot believe him he tells us so many lies. . . .[42]

---

[40] *Report of the Commissioner of Indian Affairs, 1885*, p. 64; A. L. Cook to J. D. C. Atkins, Ross Fork, Idaho, June 25, 1885. U.S. National Archives, Records of the Bureau of Indian Affairs, Education Division, Letters Received, 1881-1895, Record Group 75.

[41] *Blackfoot Register,* May 3, 1881, p. 2; *ibid.,* May 21, 1881, p. 2.

[42] Petition of Bannock and Shoshoni Indians, Pocatello, Idaho, October 1, 1895, *op. cit.*

The *Pocatello Tribune* pointed out, however, that much of the opposition stemmed from the activities of A. W. Fisher, a man who operated a large hay ranch on the reservation and who hoped to become the Fort Hall agent. Apparently Mrs. Fisher was more active than her husband in promoting his candidacy, because the agent took the matter to court, charging that Mrs. Fisher had told the Indians that they would not have to send their children to school, that there would be no canal built on the reservation, and that more rations would be issued them if Mr. Fisher should be assigned to the agency. The Shoshoni leader, Jim Ballard, and some of his followers were so impressed with this propaganda that they threatened Teter in an attempt to get him to resign. The court finally dismissed the case on insufficient evidence but, as already noted, Ballard and his men tried to hang Teter a few months later. Substantiation of part of the Indian charges against the agent came in February, 1897, when he was summarily dismissed as the result of an investigation by officials of the Indian Department.[43]

Other white men, not officially connected with the Fort Hall Agency, were also a source of trouble for the Bannock and Shoshoni. The most serious results came from the occasional incidents in which white men attacked Indian squaws. In 1870, Agent Danilson was forced to request the aid of the military in arresting two drunken white men who had mis-

---

[43] *Pocatello Tribune*, April 20, 1895, pp. 1, 4; *ibid.*, May 4, 1895, p. 1; *ibid.*, January 18, 1896, p. 2; *ibid.*, February 1, 1896, p. 1; *ibid.*, February 27, 1897, p. 1.

treated some Indian women.[44] Fred T. Dubois reported, in 1885, that the Bannock "who have been
quite uneasy for some time, are now very noisy and
threatening" as the consequence of the murder of
one of their women by two cowboys.[45] Another problem concerned the white men who had married Indian women and were living on the rations their
wives drew from the agency. To add to these dis-
turbances, the growth of the town of Pocatello in
the midst of the Indian country brought still more
white people to the reservation and increased the
possibility of difficulties between the two races. One
agent complained that "slaughter pens and food furnished at kitchen doors have induced a number of
the more lazy and trifling families to locate there. . . ."[46]

The army of the United States furnished another
element of discord to reservation life. The military
post at Fort Hall was established on May 27, 1870,
at a site about twenty-five miles from Old Fort Hall
and fifteen miles from the agency. The post was
relinquished to the Department of the Interior for
school purposes on April 26, 1883.[47] Although many
people believed that the military station was necessary to keep the Indians in check, a few would have
agreed with the report of a special commission that
investigated affairs at the reservation in 1873:

---

[44] Danilson to Lieutenant J. B. Smith, Fort Hall, Idaho, November
30, 1870, in Fort Hall Agency Letter Book, *op. cit.,* p. 59.

[45] Idaho, Secretary of State, Miscellaneous Papers (MSS in Statehouse,
Boise, Idaho) , 2/36.

[46] *Report of the Commissioner of Indian Affairs, 1891,* p. 230.

[47] George Crook, *General George Crook; His Autobiography;* ed. and
annotated by M. F. Schmitt (Norman, Okla., 1946) , p. 221.

Your commission cannot refrain from expressing its opinion concerning the effect of the presence of soldiers among the Indians where they are no longer needed to keep them under subjection. They regard the presence of a soldier as a standing menace, and to them the very name of soldier is synonymous with all that is offensive and evil. To the soldier they attribute their social demoralization and the unmentionable diseases with which they are infected.[48]

The commission found that one of the chief objections of the Indians to removal to a reservation was that "we do not wish to give our women to the embrace of the soldiers."

Although the troops also served as an agency for introducing liquor to the reservation Indians, a stronger impetus was given the whisky traffic by white civilians living along the edge of the reserve. Whisky stores at Blackfoot and at Pocatello made good profits by supplying Bannock and Shoshoni with cheap liquor. Most of the troubles involving Bannock men were traceable to the prior drinking of whisky. At the Lemhi Agency, Bannock and Shoshoni bought their spirits regularly from a few Chinese who made that their principal business. A certain "Ah Pew" of Salmon City was arrested, in 1882, and sentenced to a fine of one hundred dollars and thirty days in jail for having failed to evade the law during a liquor transaction with some Lemhi.[49]

Maintaining order among the reservation Indians was a difficult problem in light of the activities of unscrupulous whites and outsiders. Yet Agent Henry W. Reed noted, in 1874, that, despite the lack of laws

---

[48] *Report of the Commissioner of Indian Affairs, 1873*, p. 65.
[49] *Report of the Commissioner of Indian Affairs, 1882*, p. 52.

and regulations, there was little wrongdoing among the Indians.[50] By an act of May 27, 1878, the United States Congress made an initial attempt to deal with reservation law enforcement by providing for a force of Indian police to maintain order and to control the liquor traffic.[51] A few years later, the Fort Hall agent reported that the Indian police had been able to stop the practice of plural marriage on the reservation and had ended the Bannock war and scalp dances.[52] There were certain obstacles, however, to the effectiveness of the police, and the Lemhi agent described one when he said that he had to discharge his force because they refused to do anything against the wishes of Chief Tendoy.[53] A Fort Hall agent met with similar resistance when he attempted to force some Bannock children to attend school. The five Bannock police immediately resigned when told that each had to procure one child for the reservation school. Four Shoshoni police also quit under pressure from the Bannock. But in most instances, the Indian police at Fort Hall did a good service and were quite efficient.[54]

Prior to 1883, the Indian agents had prescribed sentences for minor offenses—either imprisonment in the guard house or withholding of rations. In April, 1883, the Department of the Interior set up Courts of Indian Offenses, composed of members of the tribes and designed to try Indians for the infraction of rules

---

[50] *Report of the Commissioner of Indian Affairs, 1874,* p. 284.
[51] Schmeckebier, *op. cit.,* p. 78.
[52] *Report of the Commissioner of Indian Affairs, 1884,* p. 63.
[53] *Report of the Commissioner of Indian Affairs, 1888,* p. 84.
[54] *Report of the Commissioner of Indian Affairs, 1892,* p. 150.

established by the Office of Indian Affairs. Such minor offenses as polygamy, theft, and certain dances were listed. The courts had no jurisdiction over major offenses, and crimes committed by one Indian against another were still subject to tribal law. A congressional act of March 3, 1885, extended the jurisdiction of the United States courts to include the major crimes committed by reservation Indians.[55] The Fort Hall Court of Indian Offenses was presided over initially by two Shoshoni judges and one Bannock judge, John Mopier. The Bannock judge wore a dark blue suit while sitting in court but reverted to full Indian dress as soon as his official duties were over. The two Shoshoni judges wore "citizens' dress" all the time.[56]

The Bannock seemed to suffer from many of the evils of civilization while not enjoying a full share of its benefits. Their roving habits and constant exposure made them subject to such diseases as influenza, while the more sedentary Shoshoni did not succumb so readily to these ills. According to a report of the Indian Office in 1891, the Shoshoni were increasing slightly in population and, at the same time, the Bannock were decreasing in numbers. The chief reason assigned was that the dissolute habits of the Bannock increased the incidence of venereal disease among them, and hereditary syphilis killed many of their children.[57] The agents' reports well substantiated this assertion.

---

[55] Schmeckebier, *op. cit.*, p. 77.

[56] *Report of the Commissioner of Indian Affairs, 1890*, p. 77.

[57] U.S. Congress, House of Representatives, *Condition of Indians, op. cit.*, p. 237.

For a while, the agency physicians considered building a hospital on the reservation; but Dr. W. W. Miller finally decided against it, in 1890, because he feared that if a patient died in the institution, it would "forever after be tabooed as an infernal machine, a contrivance of the evil spirit for catching poor deluded Indians, and the Indian medicine men would say, 'I told you so,' and that would settle it."[58] Miller, therefore, continued to treat the Indians at their camps, occasionally finding room at the agency for a serious case.

The spiritual welfare of the Fort Hall Indians was not neglected, the most aggressive missionary work being done by the Mormons. Their religious activities among the Bannock and Shoshoni were frowned on by government officials, who tried to keep the Indians from attending Mormon services. During 1875, missionaries from the Utah church established headquarters at Corinne, where they furnished rations to all Indians who would come and listen to their doctrine. Bannock and Shoshoni made clandestine visits to Corinne, and Agent James Wright reported, "They go away in the night and when they return deny that they have been there, and when pressed get mad."[59] A month later, Agent W. H. Danilson wrote, ". . . large numbers [Bannock and Shoshoni] have gone and are still going to Utah to get washed and greased and enrolling themselves in the cause of the Mormons."[60] He accused the Mormon missionaries

[58] Report of the Commissioner of Indian Affairs, 1890, p. 79.

[59] James Wright to E. P. Smith, Fort Hall, June 30, 1875, in Fort Hall Agency Letter Book, 1869-1875, op. cit., p. 284.

[60] W. H. Danilson to E. P. Smith, Fort Hall, July 31, 1875, ibid., p. 290.

of teaching the Indians that if they would be baptized and join the church,

> . . . the old men would all become young, the young men would never be sick, that the Lord had a work for them to do, and that they were the chosen people of God to establish his kingdom upon the earth, etc.; also that Bear River belonged to them, and if the soldiers attempted to drive them away not to go, as their guns would have no effect upon them.[61]

By late summer there were about one hundred and twenty Indians from Fort Hall at the Corinne encampment, and the agent's expostulations were finally answered when troops were dispatched to break up the missionary enterprise and to send the Indians back to the reservation. When the Bannock and Shoshoni returned to Fort Hall, Danilson was pleased to note that they were much "disgusted with the whole proceeding, have lost faith in the Mormons, and say they did not know they were doing anything in opposition to the Government."[62] The agent wrote a letter to the Commissioner of Indian Affairs at the request of Chiefs Tyhee and Gibson Jack which said in part: "The Mormons are all the time making bad talk —they have deceived us in many ways and we will not believe them anymore."[63]

Mormon activity did not cease after the Corinne episode, and Bannock and Shoshoni members of the church became missionaries among their people at

---

[61] *Report of the Commissioner of Indian Affairs, 1875,* p. 258.

[62] *Ibid.*

[63] W. H. Danilson to E. P. Smith, Fort Hall, Idaho, September 15, 1875. U.S. National Archives, Records of the Bureau of Indian Affairs, Idaho Superintendency, Letters Received, 1866-1880, Record Group 75.

The Bannock and Shoshoni returned to Fort Hall

Fort Hall.   Agent Cook wrote in 1883 of the annoyance which Mormon emissaries were causing him with their persistent efforts to convert the Indians. At that time Cook estimated that three hundred of the reservation Indians were members of the Mormon church. He asked the commissioner for help to stop the Mormons from instructing the Indians "in polygamy and other vile doctrines."[64]

The only other religious organization which had much influence among the Bannock and Shoshoni was the Methodist Episcopal Church. Beginning in the early 1870's, the Indian agencies in the United States had been apportioned among "various religious associations and missionary societies," and Fort Hall had been assigned to the Methodists.[65] Apparently this group did not take an active interest in its Indian mission, and Danilson wrote in 1876 that although a Reverend Jameson had been assigned to the agency, he received no compensation from his church. Danilson employed him as the agency teacher. The minister held religious services as well as school classes. The agent concluded his report on missionary activity by saying, "There seems to be an indifference to its [Methodist] obligation and responsibility in this work."[66] Ten years later, Agent Gallagher, reporting on missionary work said, "From what I can learn, nothing has ever been done in this direction."[67] The Indian Commissioner's report for 1900 listed the fol-

---

[64] Report of the Commissioner of Indian Affairs, 1883, p. 53.
[65] Report of the Commissioner of Indian Affairs, 1872, p. 73.
[66] Report of the Commissioner of Indian Affairs, 1876, p. 42.
[67] Report of the Commissioner of Indian Affairs, 1886, p. 108.

lowing statistics for Fort Hall Agency: One male and four female missionaries, sixty Indian church members, and one church building.[68]

Except for Mormon and Methodist proselyting, the Fort Hall Indians were not the objects of intensive missionary work on the part of the Christian churches. The tribal medicine men still exercised great power and, during the late 1880's, a new Indian doctrine swept the reservation. The prophet of this Ghost Dance religion was a Nevada Paiute, Wovoka. He taught such precepts as: "Do no harm to anyone. Do right always. Do not tell lies. When your friends die, you must not cry. You must not fight."[69] Many of the Bannock became converts and played an important part in aiding the spread of the new religion. Their knowledge of the Paiute tongue and their ability to speak Shoshoni made them the mediators between the Paiute prophet and the Plains tribes to the east of the Rockies. When the religious fervor was at its height, in 1889, a Bannock traveled from Nevada to visit the Eastern Shoshoni and Arapaho in Wyoming and to tell them that the "dead people were coming back."[70] Later in the same year, a Cheyenne, Porcupine, visited Fort Hall, was royally received by the Bannock chief, and requested some Bannock interpreters to accompany him to Nevada. The Fort Hall agent issued passes to the group, and the Indians journeyed by train via Salt Lake City to Nevada and

---

[68] *Report of the Commissioner of Indian Affairs, 1900*, p. 641.

[69] James Mooney, "The Ghost Dance Religion and the Sioux Outbreak of 1890" (*Fourteenth Annual Report of the Bureau of American Ethnology, 1892-93*, Part II [Washington, D.C., 1896]), p. 785.

[70] *Ibid.*, pp. 793, 807.

the home of Wovoka. Throughout the duration of the Ghost Dance religion, in the 1890's, the Bannock remained the principal agents for the transmission of the doctrine to eastern Indians.

To counteract the influence of such medicine men and to prepare Indian youth for full citizenship, the Office of Indian Affairs had inaugurated a program of education for them in 1870 when the first general appropriation was made for the support of industrial and other schools at the various agencies. At first there was no attempt to develop a uniform course of instruction but, in 1882, a superintendent of schools was appointed to inspect the educational facilities at the reservations and make suggestions for the betterment of the program. The teachers were appointed by the agents, and "political affiliations had more weight than scholastic attainments."[71]

The Fort Hall School was started in 1874 and enrolled twenty-five students the first year.[72] In 1876 there were twenty-three pupils, seven of whom could read.[73] Agent E. A. Stone was not very impressed with the educational advancement at Fort Hall when he took over the agency in 1881.

Notwithstanding the fact that this school is costing the government some $1,700 per annum for teacher and employes, in addition to food and clothing for the pupils the fact still remains that not one single Indian on the reservation can read a word.[74]

---

[71] Schmeckebier, *op. cit.*, p. 71.

[72] *Report of the Commissioner of Indian Affairs, 1874*, p. 104.

[73] *Report of the Commissioner of Indian Affairs, 1876*, p. 210.

[74] *Report of the Commissioner of Indian Affairs, 1881*, p. 63.

A small mission school was established at Fort Hall in 1887 by the Women's Connecticut Indian Association, under the direction of Miss Amelia Frost. The school was well supported financially, its main purpose being to train Indian girls in the arts of civilization.[75] By 1900, it was reported that 252 Indians could read, which indicated some progress, but also emphasized the slowness with which the Bannock and Shoshoni adapted themselves to new learning habits.[76]

The main hindrance to the operation of a school on the reservation was a deep-rooted Indian superstition that the children who attended classes would die. The Fort Hall agent reported, in 1884, that the Shoshoni were averse to sending their children to school because the medicine men had warned them the children would die if allowed to attend.[77] Agent John Harries of Lemhi Agency encountered the same belief, and often mothers or grandmothers would rush into his school and take the children away, "as if they were removing them from some imminent danger."[78] Harries was able to overcome some of the opposition by enrolling five of his own children in the school.

The Bannock-Shoshoni explained one reason for their aversion to sending their children to school:

We want our children to go to school and the reason some of us don't send them now is, when they are sick we cannot go to see them the distance is too far, for we are not allowed to stay at the school and some of our children died without us seeing them. If when our children are sick we could see

_____

[75] *Report of the Commissioner of Indian Affairs, 1898*, p. 141.
[76] *Report of the Commissioner of Indian Affairs, 1900*, p. 640.
[77] *Report of the Commissioner of Indian Affairs, 1884*, p. 64.
[78] *Report of the Commissioner of Indian Affairs, 1882*, p. 52.

them and take care of them it would be all right. If we take our children out of school when they are sick and they die, if we are satisfied why need anyone care. How would our Father in Washington like for his children to get sick and die and he not to see them. . . .[79]

Unfortunately for the cause of education, the death rate among the children who attended school was much greater than it was among those who continued to live in tipis with their parents. The Indians believed that the practice of burning the children's hair after it had been cut was the principal cause of death.

Although both Bannock and Shoshoni opposed compulsory education for their children, the Bannock were more determined about the matter. When John Mopier presided as one of the judges of the Court of Indian Offenses, he was "not as persistent a worker in procuring children for the school as the other two judges [Shoshoni]."[80] The continued refusal of the Indians to send their children to school at length caused the Office of Indian Affairs to attempt to use force in compelling the parents to obey the law. In January, 1892, the commissioner instructed Agent S. G. Fisher to seize all children of school age who were not in attendance at classes and place them in school. Fisher followed his instructions to the letter and, as he said,

. . . [I] went further than ordered, inasmuch as I was pounced upon on more than one occasion, where a test of strength followed. In one of these encounters I would certainly have been worsted, if not entirely used up, only for the prompt

---

[79] Petition of Bannock and Shoshoni Indians, Pocatello, Idaho, October 1, 1895, *op. cit.*

[80] *Report of the Commissioner of Indian Affairs, 1890*, p. 77.

assistance of Joe Rainey, a half-breed policeman. As it was my clothes were torn, and it became necessary for me to choke a so-called chief into subjection.[81]

It was during this incident that the five Bannock police decided to resign when told they must procure Bannock children for the school. Their decision was prompted by instructions from the Bannock war chief, who also told Fisher to inform Washington that no more Bannock would serve as police. Agent Fisher wrote his superior:

As matters now stand there are but two alternatives. Troops must be sent at once, or it must be admitted that the Bannocks with a few of their Shoshone followers are on top . . . the time is at hand when this wild and lawless element should be made to realize that they will not be allowed to oppose and sneer at orders given them by the United States Government.[82]

Impressed with the seriousness of the matter, the Indian Commissioner sent special agent J. A. Leonard to investigate and offer recommendations concerning how the situation should be handled. Leonard advised the commissioner that certain "non-progressive Indians," mainly Bannock, should be removed from the reservation for a time. The inspector further recommended that troops be brought to the agency where their mere presence would be enough to overawe the Indians. The Bannock had told him that, if the government really wanted their children in school, soldiers would be sent to enforce the compulsory education law.[83] Although no military force was ordered

---

[81] *Report of the Commissioner of Indian Affairs, 1892,* p. 150.
[82] *Ibid.*
[83] *Ibid.,* p. 151.

to Fort Hall, the prejudice against the school had abated somewhat by the next year. But opposition continued, even among some of the most progressive Indians.

A force of cavalry was called to the reservation in 1897 to quiet an insurrection among some of the young braves. The Indian police had seized a fourteen-year-old girl and had taken her to school. The girl had been married the preceding summer, and the husband objected to Agent Irwin that the practice of forcing married women to attend school could not be tolerated. When Irwin insisted that the girl must remain where she was, the Indian gathered some friends and took his bride away from the police by force. Other young bucks joined in the carnival; and, claiming that all the school girls were married, released them from the school, beat the Indian police, and carried on in traditional fashion until the arrival of the soldiers stopped the excitement.[84] In education, as in other aspects of civilization, the Bannock were reluctant to give up their free life for the routine and confinement that white man's ways invoked.

By 1900, the Bannock had shrunk to a population of about 450 and were in danger of being engulfed by the more than one thousand Shoshoni with whom they lived. Although most of them still retained their traditions, customs, and language, some began to adopt the garb of civilization, and intermarriage with the Shoshoni became more common. In his report for 1900, Agent A. F. Caldwell said,

---

[84] *Pocatello Tribune*, September 29, 1897, p. 1.

This is the first time that the Bannock and Shoshoni tribes have been reported together, the population of the two tribes having always been reported separately. They are so intermarried and related to each other that it is nearly impossible to distinguish one from the other, many individuals being the offspring of intertribal marriages.[85]

While the disappearance of the Bannock tribe from the records of the Indian officials did not mean the end of the Bannock people, it marked the end of their history as a tribal entity, and they now became "Fort Hall Indians," members of a reservation group. There are still Bannock at Fort Hall, but they are farmers. The Bannock buffalo hunter and warrior is now only a memory.

---

[85] *Report of the Commissioner of Indian Affairs, 1900,* p. 215.

UNRATIFIED TREATY OF OCTOBER 14, 1863, BE-TWEEN THE UNITED STATES AND THE MIXED BANDS OF SHOSHONE AND BANNACK

Treaty of Peace and Friendship made at Soda Springs in Idaho Territory this fourteenth day of October A. D. one thousand eight hundred and sixty three, by and between the United States of America represented by Brigadier General P. Edward Connor, commanding the Military District of Utah and James Duane Doty, Commissioner, and the under-signed chiefs of the mixed Bands of Bannacks and Sho-shonees occupying the valley of Shoshonee river, as follows—

ARTICLE I. It is mutually agreed that friendly and amicable relations shall be reestablished between the said Bands and the United States; and that a firm and perpetual peace shall be henceforth maintained between the said bands and the United States.

ARTICLE II. The Treaty concluded at Fort Bridger on the 2nd day of July 1863 between the United States and the Shoshonee nation, and also the Treaty concluded at Box Elder on the 30th day of July 1863 between the United States and the Northwestern Bands of the Shoshonee Nation being read and fully interpreted and explained to the said chiefs they do hereby give their full and free assent to all of the provisions of said Treaties and the same are hereby adopted as a part of this Treaty, and the same shall be bind-ing upon the parties hereto, the said Bands sharing in the annuities therein provided for the Shoshonee Nation.

ARTICLE III. The said Bands, in addition, agee [sic] that the roads now used by white men between Soda Springs and the Beaver Head Mines and between Salt Lake and the Boise river mines, as also such other roads as it may be necessary or convenient for the white men to make and use between said places, or between other points within their country, shall at all times be free and safe for travel; and no depre-

dations shall be committed upon white men in any part
of their country. And the said Bands hereby acknowledge
to have received of the United States by its Commissioner at
the signing of these articles provisions and goods to the
amount of three thousand dollars to relieve their immediate wants before their departure to their hunting grounds.

ARTICLE IV. The country claimed by the Said Bands joint-
ly with the Shoshonee Nation, extends, as described by them
from the lower part of Humboldt river, and the Salmon
Falls on Shoshonee river, eastwardly to the Wind river mountains.

Done at Soda Springs this fourteenth day of October A. D.
1863.

In presence of the Undersigned Witnesses—

DAVID BLACK
        Capt. 3rd In'fty C. V.
        Commdg. Camp Connor
HORACE WHEAT
AMES R. WRIGHT   JAMES DUANE DOTY
WILLIS H. BOOTHE   Commissioner
        Special interpreters   P. EDW. CONNOR
                                        Brig. Genl W. S. V.
                                        Comdg. Dist. Utah

Shawowuk	his x	mark
Washetiabo	" x	"
Nawebyo'-gun	" x	"
Mopeeah	" x	"
Goosh' a gund	" x	"
Boo'cwut	" x	"
To'sokwanbenaht'	" x	"
Tahgee	" x	"
Way' geewunah	" x	"
Wonagund	" x	"
Matigund	" x	"
Tee'nitze	" x	"
Tay'be	" x	"[1]

---

[1] U.S. National Archives, Records of the Bureau of Indian Affairs,
"Unratified Treaty of October 14, 1863, between the United States and
the Mixed Bands of Shoshone and Bannock," Record Group 75.

TREATY WITH THE EASTERN BAND SHOSHONI
AND BANNOCK, 1868

Articles of a treaty made and concluded at Fort Bridger, Utah Territory, on the third day of July, in the year of our Lord one thousand eight hundred and sixty-eight, by and between the undersigned chiefs and head-men of and representing the Shoshonee (eastern band) and Bannock tribes of Indians, they being duly authorized to act in the premises:

ARTICLE 1. From this day forward peace between the parties to this treaty shall forever continue. The Government of the United States desires peace, and its honor is hereby pledged to keep it. The Indians desire peace, and they hereby pledge their honor to maintain it.

If bad men among the whites, or among other people subject to the authority of the United States, shall commit any wrong upon the person or property of the Indians, the United States will, upon proof made to the agent and forwarded to the Commissioner of Indian Affairs, at Washington City, proceed at once to cause the offender to be arrested and punished according to the laws of the United States, and also reimburse the injured person for the loss sustained.

If bad men among the Indians shall commit a wrong or depredation upon the person or property of any one, white, black, or Indian, subject to the authority of the United States, and at peace therewith, the Indians herein named solemnly agree that they will, on proof made to their agent and notice by him, deliver up the wrong-doer to the United States, to be tried and punished according to the laws; and in case they wilfully refuse so to do, the person injured shall be reimbursed for his loss from the annuities or other moneys due or to become due to them under this or other treaties made with the United States. And the President, on advising with the Commissioner of Indian Affairs, shall prescribe such rules and regulations for ascertaining damages under the provisions of this article as in his judgment may be proper. But no such damages shall be adjusted and paid until thoroughly examined and passed upon by the Commissioner of Indian Affairs, and no one sustaining loss while violating or because of his violating the provisions of this treaty or the laws of the United States shall be reimbursed therefor.

ARTICLE 2. It is agreed that whenever the Bannocks desire a reservation to be set apart for their use, or whenever the President of the United States shall deem it advisable for them to be put upon a reservation, he shall cause a suitable one to be selected for them in their present country, which shall embrace reasonable portions of the "Port Neuf" and "Kansas Prairie" countries, and that, when this reservation is declared, the United States will secure to the Bannocks the same rights and privileges therein, and make the same and like expenditures therein for their benefit, except the agency-house and residence of agent, in proportion to their numbers, as herein provided for the Shoshonee reservation. The United States further agrees that the following district of country, to wit: Commencing at the mouth of Owl Creek and running due South to the crest of the divide between the Sweetwater and Popo Agie Rivers; thence along the crest of said divide and the summit of Wind River Mountains to the longitude of North Fork of Wind River; thence due north to mouth of said North Fork and up its channel to a point twenty miles above its mouth; thence in a straight line to head-waters of Owl Creek and along middle of channel of Owl Creek to place of beginning, shall be and the same set apart for the absolute and undisturbed use and occupation of the Shoshonee Indians herein named, and for such other friendly tribes or individual Indians as from time to time they may be willing, with the consent of the United States, to admit amongst them; and the United States now solemnly agrees that no persons except those herein designated and authorized to do so, and except such officers, agents, and employes of the Government as may be authorized to enter upon Indian reservations in discharge of duties enjoined by law, shall ever be permitted to pass over, settle upon, or reside in the territory described in this article for the use of said Indians, and henceforth they will and do hereby relinquish all title, claims, or rights in and to any portion of the territory of the United States, except such as is embraced within the limits aforesaid.

ARTICLE 3. The United States agrees, at its own proper expense, to construct at a suitable point on the Shoshonee reservation a warehouse or store-room for the use of the agent in storing goods belonging to the Indians, to cost not exceeding two thousand dollars; an agency building for the residence of the agent, to cost not exceeding three thousand; a residence for the physician, to cost not more than two thousand dollars; and five other buildings, for a carpenter, farmer, blacksmith, miller, and engineer, each to cost not exceeding two thousand dollars; also a schoolhouse or mission building so soon as a sufficient number of children can be induced by the agent to attend school, which shall not cost exceeding twenty-five hundred dollars.

The United States agrees further to cause to be erected on said Shoshonee reservation, near the other buildings herein authorized, a good steam circular-saw mill, with a gristmill and shingle-machine attached, the same to cost not more than eight thousand dollars.

ARTICLE 4. The Indians herein named agree, when the agency-house and other buildings shall be constructed on their reservation named, they will make said reservations their permanent home, and they will make no permanent settlement elsewhere; but they shall have the right to hunt on the unoccupied lands of the United States so long as game may be found thereon, and so long as peace subsists among the whites and Indians on the borders of the hunting districts.

ARTICLE 5. The United States agrees that the agent for said Indians shall in the future make his home at the agency building on the Shoshonee reservation, but shall direct and supervise affairs on the Bannock reservation; and shall keep an office open at all times for the purpose of prompt and diligent inquiry into such matters of complaint by and against the Indians as may be presented for investigation under the provisions of their treaty stipulations, as also for the faithful discharge of other duties enjoined by law. In all cases of depredation on person or property he shall cause the evidence to be taken in writing and forwarded, together with his finding, to the Commissioner of Indian Affairs, whose decision shall be binding on the parties to this treaty.

ARTICLE 6. If any individual belonging to said tribes of Indians, or legally incorporated with them, being the head of a family, shall desire to commence farming, he shall have the privilege to select, in the presence and with the assistance of the agent then in charge, a tract of land within the reservation of his tribe, not exceeding three hundred and twenty acres in extent, which tract so selected, certified, and recorded in the "land-book," as herein directed, shall cease to be held in common, but the same may be occupied and held in the exclusive possession of the person selecting it, and of his family, so long as he or they may continue to cultivate it.

Any person over eighteen years of age, not being the head of a family, may in like manner select and cause to be certified to him or her, for purposes of cultivation, a quantity of land not exceeding eighty acres in extent, and thereupon be entitled to the exclusive possession of the same above described. For each tract of land so selected a certificate, containing a description thereof, and the name of the person selecting it, with a certificate indorsed thereon that the same has been recorded, shall be delivered to the party entitled to it by the agent, after the same shall have been recorded by him in a book to be kept in his office subject to inspection, which said book shall be known as the "Shoshone (eastern band) and Bannock land-book."

The President may at any time order a survey of these reservations, and when so surveyed Congress shall provide for protecting the rights of the Indian settlers in these improvements, and may fix the character of the title held by each. The United States may pass such laws on the subject of alienation and descent of property as between Indians, and on all subjects connected with the government of the Indians on said reservations, and the internal police thereof, as may be thought proper.

ARTICLE 7. In order to ensure the civilization of the tribes entering into this treaty, the necessity of education is admitted, especially of such of them as are or may be settled on said agricultural reservations, and they therefore pledge themselves to compel their children, male and female, between the ages of six and sixteen years, to attend school; and it is hereby made the duty of the agent for said Indians to see that this stipulation is strictly complied with; and the United States agrees that for every thirty children between said ages who can be induced or compelled to attend a school, a house shall be provided and a teacher competent to teach the elementary branches of an English education shall be furnished, who will reside among said Indians and faithfully discharge his or her duties as a teacher. The provisions of this article to continue for twenty years.

ARTICLE 8. When the head of a family or lodge shall have selected lands and received his certificate as above directed, and the agents shall be satisfied that he intends in good faith to commence cultivating the soil for a living, he shall be entitled to receive seeds and agricultural implements for the first year, in value one hundred dollars, and for each succeeding year he shall continue to farm, for a period of three years more, he shall be entitled to receive seeds and implements as aforesaid in value twenty-five dollars per annum.

And it is further stipulated that such persons as commence farming shall receive instructions from the farmers herein provided for, and whenever more than one hundred persons on either reservation shall enter upon the cultivation of the soil, a second blacksmith shall be provided, with such iron, steel, and other material as may be required.

ARTICLE 9. In lieu of all sums of money or other annuities provided to be paid to the Indians herein named, under any and all treaties heretofore made with them, the United States agrees to deliver at the agency-house on the reservation herein provided for, on the first day of September of each year, for thirty years, the following articles, to wit:

For each male person over fourteen years of age, a suit of good substantial woollen clothing, consisting of coat, hat, pantaloons, flannel shirt, and a pair of woollen socks; for each female over twelve years of age, a flannel skirt, or the goods necessary to make it, a pair of woollen hose, twelve yards of calico, and twelve yards of cotton domestics.

For the boys and girls under the ages named, such flannel and cotton goods as may be needed to make each a suit as aforesaid, together with a pair of woollen hose for each.

And in order that the Commissioner of Indian Affairs

may be able to estimate properly for the articles herein named, it shall be the duty of the agent each year to forward to him a full and exact census of the Indians, on which the estimate from year to year can be based; and in addition to the clothing herein named, the sum of ten dollars shall be annually appropriated for each Indian roaming and twenty dollars for each Indian engaged in agriculture, for a period of ten years, to be used by the Secretary of the Interior in the purchase of such articles as from time to time the condition and necessities of the Indians may indicate to be proper. And if at any time within the ten years it shall appear that the amount of money needed for clothing under this article can be appropriated to better uses for the tribes herein named, Congress may by law change the appropriation to other purposes; but in no event shall the amount of this appropriation be withdrawn or discontinued for the period named. And the President shall annually detail an officer of the Army to be present and attest the delivery of all the goods herein named to the Indians, and he shall inspect and report on the quantity and quality of the goods and the manner of their delivery.

ARTICLE 10. The United States hereby agrees to furnish annually to the Indians the physician, teachers, carpenter, miller, engineer, farmer, and blacksmith, as herein contemplated, and that such appropriations shall be made from time to time, on the estimates of the Secretary of the Interior, as will be sufficient to employ such persons.

ARTICLE 11. No treaty for the cession of any portion of the reservations herein described which may be held in common shall be of any force or validity as against the said Indians, unless executed and signed by at least a majority of all the adult male Indians occupying or interested in the same; and no cession by the tribe shall be understood or construed in such manner as to deprive without his consent, any individual member of the tribe of his right to any tract of land selected by him, as provided in Article 6 of this treaty.

ARTICLE 12. It is agreed that the sum of five hundred dollars annually, for three years from the date when they commence to cultivate a farm, shall be expended in presents to the ten persons of said tribe who, in the judgment of the agent, may grow the most valuable crop for the respective year.

ARTICLE 13. It is further agreed that until such time as the agency buildings are established on the Shoshonee Reservation, their agent shall reside at Fort Bridger, U. T., and their annuities shall be delivered to them at the same place in June of each year.[1]

[1] Charles J. Kappler (ed.), *Indian Affairs, Laws and Treaties* (2 vols., Washington, 1903), II, 786-89.

AGREEMENT WITH THE SHOSHONES AND
BANNOCKS, 1873

Whereas the Government of the United States did, on the third day of July, 1868, make a treaty with the Shoshones and Bannocks, which is now in full force between said parties; and

Whereas a reservation was laid off and surveyed for the Bannock Indians and those associated with them under such treaty, and known as the Fort Hall reservation:

And whereas, owing to the increase in the country of the white population, and the scarcity of game for the support of the Indians, it has, in the judgment of the United States Government, become important and necessary that the provision of Article 4 of said treaty of July 3, 1868, shall become the subject of a new agreement between said parties.

ARTICLE 1. It is hereby agreed upon the part of all the Indians interested in said Fort Hall reservation, under the provisions of said treaty of 1868, that a portion of said fourth article of said treaty shall, upon the conditions hereinafter stated, be amended as follows:

The "right," as secured to said Indians by said fourth article of said treaty of 1868, "to hunt on the unoccupied lands of the United States," shall be relinquished, and hereafter the privilege of said Indians to hunt off of the reservation shall be under the written permission of the agent.

ARTICLE 2. It is agreed further that no public highway shall pass through or continue in said reservation without the consent of the Secretary of the Interior; that the Secretary of the Interior shall regulate the rates and amounts of tolls to be charged on that portion of any toll-road or bridge situated in or running through or into said reservation, and not less than one-fourth of such toll shall be paid over and expended under the order of the Secretary of the Interior to aid said Indians in the pursuits of agriculture.

ARTICLE 3. No person whomsoever other than the Indians entitled to homes on the Fort Hall reservation shall be permitted to pasture, herd, or keep on said reservation any cattle, horses, sheep, mules, or other stock whatever, except the stock necessary for the management of the agency, and such as the Government and officers of the military need; nor shall any hay or grass be cut on or removed from said reservation other than for the use or benefit of said Indians, agency, or military.

ARTICLE 4. It is, however, further agreed that the agent may, by agreement in writing, sell grass, hay, or pasture on said reservation, but without detriment to the Indians. Said written agreement, and an itemized statement of the proceeds of such sales and expenditures thereof, which shall be for the benefit of said Indians, shall be reported to the Indian Department.

ARTICLE 5. It is further agreed that the boundaries of the Fort Hall reservation as now surveyed may, by order of the President, be changed as follows: Beginning at a point on the south line of said reservation due west of a point five miles south of a point where the stage-road from Corinne, Utah, to Helena, Montana, now crosses the main branch of the Port Neuf, (near the toll-gate); thence due east past said point until it intersects the south or east line of said reservation; thence following the line of the present survey, and continuing the east line of said reservation due north to the center of Snake River; thence down the center of Snake River to the mouth of the Port Neuf; thence with the line of said survey to the place of beginning.

ARTICLE 6. The provisions of the treaty of 1868 not herein altered or amended shall remain valid.

ARTICLE 7. It is hereby especially agreed that no white person shall be permitted to reside on or remain upon said reservation other than those under the employ and pay of the United States, and the families of such persons, except such other white persons as may be permitted in writing by the agent to remain thereon, all of which shall be binding when confirmed by Congress.

ARTICLE 8. When any head of family or lodge shall have set apart to him, and commenced farming under the pro-

visions of articles 6 and 8 of the treaty of 1868, they shall
then be entitled to have built upon their land so set apart
for them a house under the direction of the Commissioner
of Indian Affairs, and have furnished for him or her a milch
cow.

Concluded and signed at Indian Agency on Fort Hall reservation November 7, 1873.

JOHN P. C. SHANKS
HENRY W. REED
T. W. BENNETT
Special Commissioners

Witnesses:

MILTON SHOEMAKER, M. D.

J. D. BESIER, U. S. Indian Inspector

 Captain Jim, his x mark, Shoshone chief.

 Otter Bear, his x mark, Bannock chief.

 Pagwite, his x mark, Bannock chief.

 Tyee, his x mark, Bannock chief.

 Bocotellah, his x mark, Shoshone chief.

 Pocatellah John, his x mark, Shoshone chief.

 Major George, his x mark, Shoshone chief.

 Gibson Jack, his x mark, Shoshone chief.

 Moshaw, his x mark, Shoshone head-man.

 Aramon, his x mark, Shoshone head-man.

 Louis Leclair, his x mark, interpreter.[1]

[There follow two hundred and thirty signatures of male
members of the Bannock and Shoshoni tribes.]

---

[1] U.S. Congress, House of Representatives, *Bannock and Other Indians
in Southern Idaho*, Ex. Doc. 129, 43rd Cong., 1st Sess., Serial No. 1608
(Washington, 1873) , pp. 4-5.

AN ACT TO ACCEPT AND RATIFY THE AGREEMENT SUBMITTED BY THE SHOSHONES, BANNOCKS, AND SHEEPEATERS OF THE FORT HALL AND LEMHI RESERVATION IN IDAHO MAY FOURTEENTH, EIGHTEEN HUNDRED AND EIGHTY, AND FOR OTHER PURPOSES

Whereas certain of the chiefs of the Shoshone, Bannock, and Sheepeater tribes of Indians have agreed upon and submitted to the Secretary of the Interior an agreement for the sale of a portion of their lands in the Territory of Idaho, their settlement upon lands in severalty, and for other purposes: Therefore,

Be it enacted by the Senate and House of Representatives of the United States of America in Congress assembled, That said agreement be, and the same is hereby accepted, ratified, and confirmed. Said agreement is assented to by a duly certified majority of the adult male Indians of the Shoshone and Bannack tribes occupying or interested in the lands of the Fort Hall Reservation, in conformity with the eleventh article of the treaty with the Shoshones and Bannacks of July third, eighteen hundred and sixty-eight (fifteenth Statutes at Large, page six hundred and seventy), and in words and figures as follows, namely:

FIRST. The chiefs and head men of the Shoshones, Bannacks, and Sheepeaters of the Lemhi Agency hereby agree to surrender their reservation at Lemhi, and to remove and settle upon the Fort Hall Reservation in Idaho, and to take up lands in severalty of that reservation as hereinafter provided.

SECOND. The chiefs and head men of the Shoshones and Bannacks of Fort Hall hereby agree to the settlement of the Lemhi Indians upon the Fort Hall Reservation in Idaho, and they agree to cede to the United States the following territory, namely: Beginning where the north line of township nine south intersects with the eastern line of their reservation; thence west with the extension of said line to the Port Neuf River; thence down and with Port Neuf River to where said township line crosses the same; thence west with said line to Marsh Creek; thence up Marsh Creek to where the north line of township number ten south intersects reservation; thence south and with the boundaries of said reservation to the beginning, including also such quantity of the north side of Port Neuf River as H. O. Harkness may be entitled to under existing law, the same to be conformed to the public surveys, so as to include the improvements of said Harkness.

THIRD. In view of the cessions contained in the above articles the United States agrees to pay to the Lemhi Indians the sum of four thousand dollars per annum for twenty years and to the Fort Hall Indians the sum of six thousand dollars per annum for twenty years, the same to be in addition to any sums to which the above-named Indians are now entitled by treaty, and all provisions of existing treaties, so far as they relate to funds, to remain in full force and effect.

FOURTH. Allotments in severalty of the remaining lands on the Fort Hall Reservation shall be made as follows:

To each head of family not more than one-quarter of a section, with an additional quantity of grazing land, not exceeding one-quarter of a section.

To each single person over eighteen years, and each other person under eighteen years now living, or may be born prior to said allotments, not more than one-eighth, with an additional quantity of grazing land, not exceeding one-eighth of a section; all allotments to be made with the advice of the agent of the said Indians, or such other person as the Secretary of the Interior may designate for that purpose, upon the selections of the Indians, heads of families selecting for their minor children and the agent making allotments for each orphan child.

FIFTH. The Government of the United States shall cause the lands of the Fort Hall Reservation above named to be properly surveyed and divided among the said Indians in severalty and in the proportions hereinafter mentioned, and shall issue patents to them respectively therefor so soon as the necessary laws are passed by Congress. The title to be acquired thereto by the Indians shall not be subject to alienation, lease or incumbrance, either by voluntary conveyance of the grantee or his heirs, or by the judgment, order or decree of any court, or subject to taxation of any character, but shall be and remain inalienable, and not subject to taxation for the period of twenty-five years, and until such time thereafter as the President may see fit to remove the restriction, which shall be incorporated in the patent.

Done at the city of Washington this fourteenth day of May, anno Domini one thousand eight hundred and eighty.

TEN DOY, his x mark.
TESEDEMIT, his x mark.
GROUSE PETE, his x mark.
JACK GIBSON, his x mark.
TI HEE, his x mark.
CAPTAIN JIM, his x mark.
JACK TEN DOY, his x mark.

Witnesses:
J. F. STOEK,
JOS. T. BENDER,
A. F. GENTES,
CHARLES RAINEY, *Acting Interpreter,*
JOHN A. WRIGHT, *United States Indian Agent.*

SECTION 2. That the Secretary of the Interior be, and he is hereby, authorized to cause to be surveyed a sufficient quantity of land on the Fort Hall Reservation to secure the settlement in severalty to said Indians as provided in said agreement. Upon the completion of said survey, he shall cause allotments of land to be made to each and all of said Indians in quantity and character as set forth in the agreement above mentioned; and upon the approval of said allotments by the Secretary of the Interior, he shall cause patents to issue to each and every allottee for the lands so allotted, with the conditions, restrictions, and limitations mentioned therein as are provided in the agreement.

SECTION 3. That for the purpose of carrying the provisions of this act into effect, the following sums, or so much thereof as may be necessary, be, and the same is hereby, set aside, out of any moneys in the Treasury not otherwise appropriated, to be expended under the direction of the Secretary of the Interior as follows:

For the expense of the survey of the land as provided in section second of this act, twelve thousand dollars.

For the first of twenty installments as provided in said

agreement, to be used by the Secretary of the Interior for the benefit of the Indians in such manner as the President may direct: For the Lemhi Indians, four thousand dollars, and for the Fort Hall Indians, six thousand dollars.

For the expense of removing the Lemhi Indians to the Fort Hall Reservation, five thousand dollars.

SECTION 4. That this act, so far as the Lemhi Indians are concerned, shall take effect only when the President of the United States shall have presented to him satisfactory evidence that the agreement herein set forth has been accepted by the majority of all the adult male members of the Shoshone, Bannack, and Sheepeater tribes occupying the Lemhi Reservation, and shall have signified his approval thereof.

Approved, February 23, 1889.[1]

---

[1] U.S. Office of Indian Affairs, *Annual Report of the Commissioner of Indian Affairs, 1889* (Washington, 1890), pp. 432-33.

AN ACT TO ACCEPT AND RATIFY AN AGREEMENT
WITH THE SHOSHONE AND BANNOCK INDIANS FOR
THE SALE OF A PORTION OF THEIR RESERVATION
IN IDAHO TERRITORY REQUIRED FOR THE USE
OF THE UTAH AND NORTHERN RAILROAD, AND
TO MAKE THE NECESSARY APPROPRIATION FOR
CARRYING OUT THE SAME

*Be it enacted by the Senate and House of Representatives
of the United States of America in Congress assembled,* That
a certain agreement made by Joseph K. McCammon, Assistant
Attorney-General, on behalf of the United States, with the
Shoshone and Bannock Indians resident on the Fort Hall
Reservation, in the Territory of Idaho, be, and the same is
hereby ratified and confirmed, subject, nevertheless, to the
conditions hereinafter mentioned. Said Agreement is executed by a majority of all the adult male Indians of the
Shoshone and Bannock tribes occupying or interested in the
lands therein more particularly described, in conformity with
the provisions contained in article eleven of the treaty with
said Indians of July third, eighteen hundred and sixty-eight,
and is in the words following, namely:

This agreement, made this eighteenth day of July, eighteen
hundred and eighty-one, between the Shoshone and Bannock
Indians resident on the Fort Hall Reservation in the Territory of Idaho, represented by their chiefs and head men and
heads of a majority of families, and being a majority of all
the adult male Indians occupying or interested in the lands
hereinafter described, of the one part, and the United States
of America, represented by Joseph K. McCammon, Assistant
Attorney-General of the other part.

Whereas the Utah and Northern Railroad Company has
applied for permission to construct a line of railroad from
east to west through the Fort Hall Reservation, and the said
Indians have consented thereto, and for that purpose have
agreed, for the consideration hereinafter mentioned, to surrender to the United States their title to so much of land
comprised in said reservation as may be necessary for the
legitimate and practical uses of said road:

Now this agreement witnesseth that, for the consideration hereinafter mentioned, the said Shoshone and Bannock Indians do hereby cede to the United States all that part of the present Fort Hall Reservation, in the Territory of Idaho, described as follows, namely:

A strip of land not exceeding one hundred feet in width (except at Pocatello Station, where it is two hundred feet) as will appear on maps hereto annexed, commencing on the eastern boundary of said reservation, striking the south bank of Port Neuf River, until it reaches the Utah and Northern Railroad, already constructed at a point about five miles east of Port Neuf Station, on said road, a distance of about thirty-six miles, more or less; thence following said Utah and Northern Railroad already constructed, a distance of ten and seventy-three hundredths miles, to a point on said road about six miles west of said Port Neuf Station, on said road; thence leaving said road already constructed and proceeding northwestward along the Port Neuf River aforesaid, a distance of eight miles, more or less; thence deflecting from said river westward and continuing to the west boundary line of said Fort Hall Indian Reservation, a distance of about nineteen miles, more or less, from the Utah and Northern Railroad, as shown upon the map or plan thereof hereto attached, marked A; the same being intended to be hereafter used by the said Utah and Northern Railroad Company, its successors or assigns, as a right of way and road bed, and containing by actual survey six hundred and seventy acres or thereabouts.

Also the several pieces or parcels of land situate along and adjoining the said strip of land hereinbefore described as defined in the several plats or maps thereof also hereto attached and marked, respectively, B, C, D, and so forth, the same being intended to be used by the said Utah and Northern Railroad Company, its successors or assigns, for depots, stations, sidings, and so forth, and containing in the whole, by actual survey, one hundred and two acres, more or less.

In consideration of such cession the United States agrees to pay to the Shoshone and Bannock Indians the sum of six thousand dollars, being at and about the rate of seven and seventy-seven hundredths dollars per acre for the lands so ceded, to be deposited in the United States Treasury to the credit of said Indians upon ratification hereof by Congress and necessary appropriation therefor, and to bear interest at five per centum per annum; the same to be in addition to any and all sums to which the above-named Indians are now entitled by treaty.

All provisions of existing treaties not affected by this agreement to remain in full force and effect, and this agreement to be subject to ratification by Congress.

Executed at the Fort Hall Agency, Idaho, the day and year aforesaid.

SECTION 2. That for the purpose of carrying the provisions of this act into effect the sum of six thousand dollars is hereby set aside, out of any moneys in the United States Treasury not otherwise appropriated, to be deposited in the United States Treasury to the credit of the Shoshone and Bannock Indians, and to bear interest at five per centum per annum, such interest to be expended for the benefit of said Indians in such manner as the Secretary of the Interior may direct.

SECTION 3. That the right of way over the land relinquished by said agreement to the United States for the construction of said Utah and Northern Railroad, and the use of the several parcels of land so relinquished intended to be used for depots, stations, sidings, and so forth, for said railroad, are hereby granted to said Utah and Northern Railroad Company, its successors and assigns, for the uses and purposes in said agreement set forth; but the land or any part thereof, relinquished to the United States by said agreement shall not be used for said railroad purposes by or for the Utah and Northern Railroad Company, its successors or assigns, except upon the condition precedent that the said company, its successors or assigns, shall, within ninety days from the taking effect of this act, pay to the Treasurer of the United States said sum of six thousand dollars hereby appropriated to be paid by the United States for the lands relinquished to the United States by said agreement, and shall within the same time, file with the Secretary of the Interior its written acceptance of the conditions of this section. Nor shall said land, or any part thereof, be continued to be used for railroad purposes by or for said Utah and Northern Railroad Company, its successors or assigns, except upon the further condition that said company its successors or assigns, will pay any and all damages which the United States or said Indians, individually or in the tribal capacity, or any other Indians lawfully occupying said reservation, may sustain by reason or on account of the act or acts of said Company, its successors or assigns, its agents or employees, or on account of fires originating by or in the construction or operation of such railroad, the damages in all cases to be recovered in any court of the Territory of Idaho having jurisdiction of the amount claimed, upon suit or action instituted by the proper United States attorney in the name of the United States: *Provided,* That the said United States attorney may accept such sum of money in satisfaction of any such injury or damages as in his discretion may be just; and if so accepted before suit or action is commenced, no suit or action shall be instituted, and if accepted after commencement of suit or action, the same shall be dismissed at the cost of said company, its successors or assigns.

SECTION 4. That all moneys accepted or recovered under the provision of section three of this act shall be covered into the Treasury of the United States, and if accepted or recovered on account of damages sustained by said Indians as aforesaid, they shall be placed to the credit of said Indians in their tribal names, to be expended by the Secretary of the Interior, for the benefit of said Indians, in such manner as he may deem for their best interest, except in the case of an individual Indian, when the amount covered into the Treasury shall be expended for his sole benefit.

Approved, July 3, 1882.[1]

---

[1] Charles J. Kappler (ed.), *Indian Affairs, Laws and Treaties* (2 vols.; Washington, 1903), I, chap. 268, 199-201.

AN ACT TO ACCEPT AND RATIFY AN AGREEMENT
MADE WITH THE SHOSHONE AND BANNACK IN-
DIANS, FOR THE SURRENDER AND RELINQUISH-
MENT TO THE UNITED STATES OF A PORTION OF
THE FORT HALL RESERVATION, IN THE TERRI-
TORY OF IDAHO, FOR THE PURPOSES OF A TOWN-
SITE, AND FOR THE GRANT OF A RIGHT OF WAY
THROUGH SAID RESERVATION TO THE UTAH AND
NORTHERN RAILWAY COMPANY, AND FOR OTHER
PURPOSES

*Be it enacted by the Senate and House of Representatives
of the United States of America in Congress assembled,* That
a certain agreement made and entered into by the United
States of America represented as therein mentioned, with the
Shoshone and Bannack Indians resident in the Fort Hall
Reservation, in the Territory of Idaho, and now on file in
the office of Indian Affairs, be, and the same is hereby, accepted, ratified, and confirmed. Said agreement is executed
by a duly certified majority of all the adult male Indians
of the Shoshone and Bannack tribes occupying or interested
in the lands therein more particularly described, in conformity with the provisions of article eleven of the treaty concluded with said Indians July third, eighteen hundred and
sixty-eight (Statutes at Large, Volume fifteen, page six hundred and seventy-three), and is in the words and figures following, namely:

"Memorandum of an agreement made and entered into
by the United States of America, represented by Robert S.
Gardner, U. S. Indian Inspector, and Peter Gallagher, U. S.
Indian Agent, specially detailed by the Secretary of the Interior for this purpose, and the Shoshone and Bannack
tribes of Indians, occupying the Fort Hall Reservation in
the Territory of Idaho, as follows:

ARTICLE I. The said Indians agree to surrender and relinquish to the United States all their estate, right title, and
interest in and to so much of the Fort Hall Reservation as
is comprised within the following boundaries that is to say:
and comprising the following lands, all in town six (6)
south of range thirty-four (34) east of Boise Meridian.

West one half section twenty-five (25): all of section twenty-six (26); east one-half section twenty-seven (27); northwest quarter section thirty-six (36) ; north one-half section thirty-five (35); northeast quarter of the northeast of section thirty-four (34) ; comprising an area of eighteen hundred and forty (1840) acres, more or less, saving and excepting so much of the above mentioned tracts as has been heretofore and is hereby relinquished to the United States for the use of the Utah and Northern and Oregon Short Line Railways.

The land so relinquished to be surveyed (if it shall be found necessary) by the United States and laid off into lots and blocks as a town-site, and after due appraisement thereof, to be sold at public auction to the highest bidder, at such time, in such manner, and upon such terms and conditions as Congress may direct.

The funds arising from the sale of said lands, after deducting the expenses of survey, appraisement, and sale, to be deposited in the Treasury of the United States to the credit of the said Indians, and to bear interest at the rate of five per centum per annum; with power in the Secretary of the Interior to expend all or any part of the principal and accrued interest thereof, for the benefit and support of said Indians in such manner and at such times as he shall see fit.

Or said lands so relinquished to be disposed of for the benefit of said Indians in such other manner as Congress may direct; and

Whereas in or about the year 1878 the Utah and Northern Railroad Company constructed a line of railroad running north and south through the Fort Hall Reservation, and has since operated the same, without payment, or any compensation whatever to the said Indians, for or in respect of the lands taken for right of way and station purposes; and

Whereas the treaty between the United States and the Shoshone and Bannack Indians, concluded July 3, 1868 (15 Stat. at Large, page 673), under which the Fort Hall Reservation was established, contains no provisions for the building of railroads through said reservation: Now, therefore,

Article II. The Shoshone and Bannack Indians, parties hereto, do hereby consent and agree that upon payment to the Secretary of the Interior for their use and benefit of the sum of ($8.00) eight dollars for or in respect of each and every acre of land of the said reservation, taken and used for the purposes of its said railroad, the said Utah and Northern Railroad Company shall have and be entitled to a right of way not exceeding two hundred (200) feet in width through said reservation extending from Blackfoot River, the northern boundary of said reservation, to the southern boundary thereof, together with necessary grounds for station and water purposes according to maps and plats of definite location, to be hereafter filed by said company with the Secretary of the Interior, and to be approved by him, the said Indians, parties hereto, for themselves and for the members of their respective tribes, hereby promising and agreeing to, at all times hereafter during their occupancy of said reservation, protect the said Utah and Northern Railroad Company, its successors or assigns, in the quiet enjoyment of said right of way and appurtenances and in the peaceful operation of its road through the reservation.

ARTICLE III. All unexecuted provisions of existing treaties between the United States and the said Indians not affected by this agreement to remain in full force; and this agreement to take effect only upon ratification hereof by Congress.

Signed at the Fort Hall Agency, in the Territory of Idaho, by the said Robert S. Gardner and Peter Gallagher on behalf of the United States, and by the undersigned chiefs, headmen, and heads of families and individual members of the Shoshone and Bannack tribes of Indians, constituting a clear majority of all the adult male Indians of said tribes occupying or interested in the lands of the Fort Hall Reservation, in conformity with article eleven of the treaty of July 3, 1868, this twenty-seventh (27) day of May, A. D. one thousand eight hundred and eighty-seven (1887)."

(Here follow the signatures.)

SECTION 2. That the Secretary of the Interior be, and he hereby is, authorized to cause to be surveyed and laid out into lots and blocks so much of the Fort Hall Reservation in the Territory of Idaho, at or near Pocatello Station, on the Utah and Northern Railway, as when the sectional and subdivisional lines are run and established shall be found to be within the following descriptions, to wit: The west half of section twenty-five, all of section twenty-six, the east

half of section twenty-seven, the northwest quarter of west
quarter of section thirty-five, and the northeast quarter of the
northeast quarter of section thirty-four, all in township six
south, of range thirty-four east, of Boise meridian, in the
Territory of Idaho, and containing an area of one thousand
eight hundred and forty acres, or thereabouts; saving and
excepting thereout so much of the above described tracts as
has heretofore been, or is hereby, granted for the use of
the Utah and Northern Railway Company.

SECTION 3. That such survey shall describe the exterior
boundaries of the said town according to the lines of the
public surveys, also giving the name of such city or town,
and exhibiting the streets, squares, blocks, lots, and alleys,
the size of the same, with measurements and area of each
municipal subdivision, the lots in which shall each not exceed four thousand two hundred with a statement of the
extent and general character of the improvements; such map
and statement shall be verified under oath by the party
making the survey; and within one month after making such
verification there shall be transmitted to the General Land
Office a verified transcript of such map and statement; a
similar map and statement shall be filed with the register
and receiver, and a similar copy shall be filed in the office
of the recorder of the county wherein such town is situate.

SECTION 4. That at the time of said survey, the Secretary
of the Interior shall cause the said lots and blocks to be
appraised by three disinterested persons, one of whom shall
be designated by said Indians in open council and the other
two by the Secretary of the Interior, who, after taking and
subscribing an oath before some competent officer to faithfully and impartially perform their duties as appraisers of
said lots and blocks under the provisions of this act, which
oaths shall be returned with their appraisement, shall go
in person upon the ground and determine the value of
each lot and parcel thereof; making lists thereof, particularly
describing each lot, block, and parcel, with the appraised
value thereof, as by them determined, which said list shall
be verified by the affidavit of at least two of said appraisers,
to the effect that said list is a correct list of the said lots,
blocks, and parcels appraised by them, and that the appraise-
ments thereof are the true value of each parcel appraised,

and that the same were determined by them after due and full inspection of each and every parcel thereof; *Provided,* That no lot or parcel shall be appraised at less than ten dollars, and that all improvements shall be appraised separate and distinct from the land.

SECTION 5. That upon the return of said survey, and the appraisement of said lands, if the same shall be approved by him, the Secretary of the Interior shall cause said lands to be offered for sale at public auction, at the door of the "Pocatello House," Pocatello Junction, to the highest bidder, for cash, which sale shall be advertised for at least three months previous thereto, in such manner as the said Secretary shall direct, and shall be conducted by the register of the land office in the district in which said lands are situate, in accordance with the instructions of the Commissioner of the General Land Office. Said sale shall continue from day to day until all of the said lands shall have been sold or offered for sale. The said lands shall be offered in single lots and parcels, and no bid shall be received for any lot or parcel less than the appraised value of the same. All blocks, lots, and parcels of said lands not sold at public sale shall thereafter be subject to private entry at the appraised value thereof: *Provided,* That any person who has been residing upon any of said land, and has made valuable improvements thereon, shall, upon proof to that effect to the satisfaction of the Secretary of the Interior, be permitted to purchase at such sale, for cash, at the appraised value thereof, the lot or parcel so resided upon and improved by him, and in default of his exercising the preference right so conferred upon him by this section, such lot or parcel shall be sold to the highest bidder, for cash, as hereinbefore provided: *Provided further,* That such last-mentioned purchaser shall pay the owner of such improvements the appraised value thereof, as determined under the provisions of this act: *And provided further,* That any right heretofore acquired by the Utah and Northern Railway Company for right of way and the use and occupancy of lands for station and depot purposes, through and upon the lands above described, shall not be affected by this act.

SECTION 6. That the funds arising from the sale of said lands, after deducting the expenses of survey, appraisement, and sale, shall be deposited in the Treasury of the United States to the credit of the Shoshone and Bannack tribes of Indians belonging on said reservation, and shall bear interest at the rate of five per centum per annum; and the Secretary of the Interior is hereby authorized and empowered to expend all or any part of the principal and accrued interest of such fund for the benefit and support of said Indians, in such manner, and at such times as he may deem expedient and proper.

Section 7. That the Secretary of the Interior shall make all needful rules and regulations necessary to carry this act into effect; he shall determine the compensation of the surveyor for his services in laying out said lands into town lots, also the compensation of the appraisers provided for in section four, and shall cause patents in fee simple to be issued to the purchasers of the lands sold under the provisions of this act in the same manner as patents are issued for the public lands.

Section 8. That the sum of five thousand dollars is hereby appropriated, out of any money in the Treasury not otherwise appropriated, for the purpose of carrying this act into effect, which said sum, or so much thereof as may be expended, shall be reimbursed to the Treasury out of the sales of said lands.

Section 9. That the exterior lines of the land by this act authorized to be laid out into town lots and separating the same from the lands of said reservation shall, from the date of the approval of said survey by the Secretary of the Interior, be, and constitute, the line of said reservation between the same and said town.

Section 10. That the citizens of the town hereinbefore provided for shall have the free and undisturbed use in common with the said Indians of the waters of any river, creek, stream, or spring flowing through the Fort Hall Reservation in the vicinity of said town, with right of access at all times thereto, and the right to construct, operate, and maintain all such ditches, canals, works, or other aqueducts, drain, and sewerage pipes, and other appliances on the reservation, as may be necessary to provide said town with proper water and sewerage facilities.

Section 11. That there be, and is hereby, granted to the

said Utah and Northern Railway Company a right of way not exceeding two hundred feet in width (except such portion of the road where the Utah and Northern and the Oregon Short Line Railways run over the same or adjoining tracts, and then only one hundred feet in width) through the lands above described, and through the remaining lands of the Fort Hall Reservation, extending from Blackfoot River, the northern boundary of said reservation, to the southern boundary thereof; and in addition to such right of way, grounds adjacent thereto for station buildings, depots, machine shops, side-tracks, turn-outs, and water-stations, not to exceed in amount of twenty acres for each station, to the extent of one station for each ten miles of its road, according to maps and plats of definite location thereof respectively, to be filed by said company with, and approved by, the Secretary of the Interior, except that at and near its station at Pocatello, in Idaho Territory, said railway company is granted for its use for station grounds, depot buildings, shops, tracks, side-tracks, turn-outs, yards, and for water purposes, not to exceed one hundred and fifty acres, as shown by maps and plats of the definite location thereof; and said company shall pay for said one hundred and fifty acres, in addition to the eight dollars per acre provided in said agreement, a further sum equal to the average appraisal of each acre of town lots in the proposed town-site of Pocatello, outside of said one hundred and fifty acres, provided for in section four of this act, and said eight dollars per acre to be paid within one year from the passage of this act, and said additional sum immediately upon the completion of the appraisement aforesaid: *Provided,* That all lands acquired by said railway company near its station at Pocatello for its use for station grounds, depot buildings, shops, tracks, side-tracks, turn-outs, yards, and for water purposes, as hereinbefore provided, shall, whenever used by said railway company, or its assigns, for other purposes, be forfeited and revert to the United States, and be subject to the other provisions of this act: *Provided further,* That the said Utah and Northern Railway Company shall first pay to the Secretary of the Interior, for the use and benefit of the said Shoshone and Bannack tribes of Indians, the sum of eight dollars per acre for, or in respect of each and every acre of land so taken and used for said right of way and station grounds, in conformity with said maps of definite location, the moneys derived from this source to be deposited in the Treasury of the United States, to the credit of the said Shoshone and Bannack Indians, bearing interest at five per centum per annum, with like power in the Secretary of the Interior, from time to time, to apply all or any part of the principal and accrued interest thereof, for the benefit and support of said Indians in the same manner as is hereinbefore provided with regard to the funds arising from the sale of lands of the Fort Hall Reservation: *And provided further,* That no part of the lands herein authorized to be taken shall be leased or sold by the company, and they shall not be used, except in tenance, and convenient operation of a railway, telegraph or telephone lines, and when any portion thereof shall cease to be so used, such portion shall revert to the tribe or tribes of Indians from which the same shall have been taken, or in case they shall have ceased to occupy said reservation, to the United States; and the construction, maintenance, and operation of said railway shall be conducted with a due regard for the rights of the Indians, and in accordance with such rules and regulations as the Secretary of the Interior may make to carry out this provision.

SECTION 12. That the officers, servants, and employees of said company necessary to the construction and management of said road, shall, while so engaged, be allowed to reside upon said right of way, and station grounds hereby granted, but subject, in so far as the reservation lands are concerned, to the provisions of the Indian intercourse laws, and such rules and regulations as may be established by the Secretary of the Interior in accordance with the said intercourse laws.

SECTION 13. That said railway company shall fence, and keep fenced, all such portions of its road as may run through any improved lands of the Indians, and also shall construct and maintain continually all road and highway crossings and necessary bridges over said railway, wherever said roads and highways do now or may hereafter cross said railway's right of way, or may be, by the proper authorities, laid out across the same.

SECTION 14. That said railway company shall execute a

bond to the United States, to be filed with and approved by the Secretary of the Interior, in the penal sum of ten thousand dollars, for the use and benefit of the Shoshone and Bannack tribes of Indians, conditioned for the due payment of any and all damages which may accrue by reason of the killing or maiming of any Indian belonging to said tribes, or either of them, or of their live-stock, in the construction or operation of said railway, or by reason of fires originating thereby; the damage in all cases, in the event of failure by the railway company to effect an amicable settlement with the parties in interest, to be recovered in any court of the Territory of Idaho having jurisdiction of the amount claimed, upon suit or action instituted by the proper United States attorney in the name of the United States: *Provided,* That all moneys so recovered by the United States attorney under the provisions of this section, shall be covered into the Treasury of the United States, to be placed to the credit of the particular Indian or Indians entitled to the same, and to be paid to him or them, or otherwise expended for his or their benefit, under the direction of the Secretary of the Interior.

SECTION 15. That the said Utah and Northern Railway Company shall accept this right of way upon the expressed condition, binding upon itself, its successors and assigns, that they will neither aid, advise, nor assist any effort looking towards the changing or extinguishing the present tenure of the Indians in their remaining lands, and will not attempt to secure from the Indian tribes any further grant of land or its occupancy than is hereinbefore provided: *Provided,* That any violation of the condition mentioned in this section shall operate as a forfeiture of all the rights and privileges of said railway company under this act.

SECTION 16. That Congress may, at any time, amend, add to, alter, or repeal this act.

Approved, September 1, 1888.[1]

---

[1] U.S. Congress, *Statutes at Large of the United States of America from December, 1887, to March, 1889* (Washington, 1889), XXV, chap. 936, 452-57.

AN ACT TO RATIFY AN AGREEMENT WITH THE INDIANS OF THE FORT HALL INDIAN RESERVATION IN IDAHO, AND MAKING APPROPRIATIONS TO CARRY THE SAME INTO EFFECT
June 6, 1900

Whereas Benjamin F. Barge, James H. McNeely, and Charles G. Hoyt, acting for the United States, did, on the fifth day of February, anno Domini eighteen hundred and ninety-eight, make and conclude the following agreement with the Shoshone and Bannock Indians of the Fort Hall Reservation, in Idaho; and

Whereas Benjamin F. Barge, James H. McNeely, and Charles G. Hoyt, being duly appointed and acting commissioners on behalf of the United States for such purposes, have concluded an agreement with the headmen and a majority of the male adults of the Bannock and Shoshone tribes of Indians upon the Fort Hall Indian Reservation, in the State of Idaho, which said agreement is as follows:

Whereas the aforesaid commissioners were appointed by the Secretary of the Interior, under and by virtue of an act of Congress, approved June the tenth, eighteen hundred and ninety-six, entitled "An act making appropriations for current and contingent expenses of the Indian Bureau of the Interior Department, and fulfilling treaty stipulations with various Indian tribes for the fiscal year ending June the thirtieth, eighteen hundred and ninety-seven, and for other purposes," and by said act were authorized to negotiate with the Bannock and Shoshone Indians, in the State of Idaho, for the cession of part of their surplus lands; and

Whereas the Indians of the Fort Hall Reservation are willing to dispose of part of their surplus lands in the State of Idaho, reserved as a home for them by a treaty concluded at Fort Bridger July the third, eighteen hundred and sixty-eight, and ratified by the United States Senate on the sixteenth day of February, eighteen hundred and sixty-nine, and also by Executive order:

Now therefore, this agreement, made and entered into by and between the aforesaid commissioners on behalf of the United States of America, and by the headmen and a majority of the male adults of the Bannock and Shoshone tribes of Indians, located on the Fort Hall Indian Reservation, in the State of Idaho.

Witnesseth:

ARTICLE 1. That the said Indians of the Fort Hall Reservation do hereby cede, grant, and relinquish to the United States all right, title, and interest which they have to the following-described land, the same being a part of the land obtained through the treaty of Fort Bridger on the third day of July, eighteen hundred and sixty-eight, and ratified by the United States Senate on the sixteenth day of February, eighteen hundred and sixty-nine:

All that portion of the said reservation embraced within and lying east and south of the following-described lines: Commencing at a point in the south boundary of the Fort Hall Indian Reservation, being the southwest corner of township nine (9) south, range thirty-four (34) east of the Boise meridian, thence running due north on the range line between townships 33 and 34 east to a point two (2) miles north of the township line between townships five (5) and six (6) south, thence due east to the range line between ranges 35 and 36 east, thence south on said range line four (4) miles, thence due east to the east boundary line of the reservation; from this point the east and south boundaries of the said reservation as it now exists to the point of beginning, namely, the southwest corner of township nine (9) south, range thirty-four east, being the remainder of the description and metes and bounds of the said tract of land herein proposed to be ceded.

ARTICLE 2. That in consideration of the lands ceded, granted, and relinquished, as aforesaid, the United States stipulates and agrees to pay to and expend for the Indians of the said reservation, six hundred thousand dollars ($600,-000) in the following manner, to wit:

Seventy-five thousand dollars ($75,000), or as much thereof as may be necessary, shall be expended by the Secretary of the Interior in the erection of a modern school plant for the Indians of the Fort Hall Reservation at a point near the present agency, said point or site to be selected by the Secretary of the Interior, and the surplus remaining, if any, of the above seventy-five thousand dollars ($75,000) may be expended by the Secretary of the Interior for the educational needs of said Indians.

One hundred thousand dollars ($100,000) shall be paid in cash pro rata, share and share alike, to each man, woman, and child belonging to and actually residing on said reservation, within three months after the ratification of this treaty by the Congress of the United States. The remainder of said sum total shall be paid pro rata in like manner, as follows:

Fifty thousand dollars ($50,000) one year after the first payment.

Fifty thousand dollars ($50,000) two years after the first payment.

Fifty thousand dollars ($50,000) three years after the first payment.

Fifty thousand dollars ($50,000) four years after the first payment.

Fifty thousand dollars ($50,000) five years after the first payment.

Fifty thousand dollars ($50,000) six years after the first payment.

Fifty thousand dollars ($50,000) seven years after the first payment.

Fifty thousand dollars ($50,000) eight years after the first payment.

Twenty-five thousand dollars ($25,000) nine years after the first payment.

The deferred payments shall bear interest at the rate of four (4) per centum per annum, said interest to be placed annually to the credit of said Indians, and shall be expended for their benefit by the Secretary of the Interior at such times and in such manner as he may direct.

Provided, That none of the money due to said Indians under this agreement shall be subject to the payment of any claims, judgments, or demands against said Indians for damages or depredations claimed to have been committed prior to the signing of this agreement.

ARTICLE 3. Where any Indians have taken lands and made

homes on the reservation and are now occupying and cultivating the same, under the sixth section of the Fort Bridger treaty hereinbefore referred to, they shall not be removed therefrom without their consent, and they may receive allotments on the land they now occupy; but in case they prefer to remove they may select land elsewhere on the portion of said reservation not hereby ceded, granted, and relinquished and not occupied by any other Indians; and should they decide not to move their improvements, then the same shall be appraised under direction of the Secretary of the Interior and sold for their benefit, at a sum not less than such appraisal, and the cash proceeds of such sale shall be paid to the Indian or Indians whose improvements shall be sold.

ARTICLE 4. So long as any of the lands ceded, granted, and relinquished under this treaty remain part of the public domain, Indians belonging to the above-mentioned tribes, and living on the reduced reservation, shall have the right, without any charge therefor, to cut timber for their own use, but not for sale, and to pasture their live stock on said public lands, and to hunt thereon and to fish in the streams thereof.

ARTICLE 5. That for the purpose of segregating the ceded lands from the diminished reservation, the new boundary lines described in article one of this agreement shall be properly surveyed and permanently marked in a plain and substantial manner by prominent and durable monuments, the cost of said survey to be paid by the United States.

ARTICLE 6. The existing provisions of all former treaties with the Indians of the Fort Hall Reservation, not inconsistent with the provisions of this agreement, are hereby continued in force and effect; and all provisions thereof inconsistent herewith are hereby repealed.

ARTICLE 7. The existing main traveled roads leading from McCammon to Blackfoot and from McCammon to American Falls are declared public highways, and the proper use of such is hereby granted to the general public.

ARTICLE 8. The water from streams on that portion of the reservation now sold which is necessary for irrigating land actually cultivated and in use shall be reserved for the Indians now using the same, so long as said Indians remain where they now live.

ARTICLE 9. This agreement shall take effect and be in force when signed by the commissioners and by a majority of the male Indians of the Fort Hall Reservation over eighteen years of age, and ratified by the Congress of the United States.

Signed on the part of the United States Government by the commissioners aforesaid and by the following Indians of the Bannock and Shoshone tribes, residing and having rights on the Fort Hall Indian Reservation.

> BENJAMIN F. BARGE, Commissioner.
> JAMES H. MCNEELY, Commissioner.
> CHARLES G. HOYT, Commissioner.

FORT HALL INDIAN AGENCY,
Ross Fork, Idaho, February 5, 1898.

(1) Jim Ballard (x); witness, Mary W. Fisher. (2) Pocatello Tom (x); witness, Chas. M. Robinson. (3) Kunecke Johnson (x); witness, Mary W. Fisher. (And 247 others.)

*   *   *   *   *   *   *   *   *   *

We certify that we interpreted the foregoing agreement with the Bannock and Shoshone Indians and that they thoroughly understood the entire matter; that we truly interpreted for the commissioners and the Indians at all the councils held to discuss the subject and to individual Indians.

> J. J. LEWIS,
> KENNEKE (his x mark) JOHNSON,
> Interpreters.

Witness:
CHAS. M. ROBINSON.
J. H. BEAN.
ALBERT W. FISHER.
ROSS FORK, IDAHO, February 5, 1898.

FORT HALL AGENCY, IDAHO, February 5, 1898.

I hereby certify that two hundred and twenty-seven (227) Indians constitute a majority of male adult Indians on or belonging on the Fort Hall Indian Reservation, Idaho.

> F. G. IRWIN, Jr.,
> First Lieutenant, Second Cavalry, Acting Indian Agent.

Therefore,

Be it enacted by the Senate and House of Representatives

of the United States of America in Congress assembled, That the said agreement be, and the same hereby is, accepted, ratified, and confirmed.

SECTION 2. That for the purpose of making the first cash payment stipulated for in article two of the foregoing agreement, and for the purpose of a new school plant, as provided in the same article, the sum of one hundred and seventy-five thousand dollars be, and the same is hereby, appropriated, out of any money in the Treasury not otherwise appropriated.

SECTION 3. That for the purpose of surveying, establishing, and properly marking the western and northern boundaries of the tract ceded by the foregoing agreement, as required by article five thereof, and for field examination and necessary office work in connection therewith, the sum of one thousand dollars, or so much thereof as may be necessary, be, and the same hereby is, appropriated, out of any money in the Treasury not otherwise appropriated.

SECTION 4. That before any of the lands by this agreement ceded are opened to settlement or entry, the Commissioner of Indian Affairs shall cause allotments to be made of such of said lands as are occupied and cultivated by any Indians, as set forth in article three of said agreement, who may desire to have the same allotted to them; and in cases where such Indian occupants prefer to remove to lands within the limits of the reduced reservation, he shall cause to be prepared a schedule of the lands to be abandoned, with a description of the improvements thereon, and the name of the Indian occupant, a duplicate of which shall be filed with the Commissioner of the General Land Office.

Before entry shall be allowed, as hereinafter provided, of any tract of land occupied and cultivated as above and included in the schedule aforesaid, the Secretary of the Interior shall cause the improvements on said tract to be appraised and sold to the highest bidder. No sale of such improvements shall be for less than the appraised value. The purchaser of such improvements shall have thirty days after such purchase for preference right of entry, under the provisions of this Act, of the lands upon which the improvements purchased by him are situated, not to exceed one hundred and sixty acres: *Provided,* That the proceeds of the sale of such improvements shall be paid to the Indians owning the same.

Any Indian electing to abandon the land occupied by him as aforesaid shall have reasonable time, in the discretion of the Secretary of the Interior, within which to remove the improvements situated upon the land occupied by him.

SECTION 5. That on the completion of the allotments and the preparation of the schedule provided for in the preceding section, and the classification of the lands as provided for herein, the residue of said ceded lands shall be opened to settlement by the proclamation of the President, and shall be subject to disposal under the homestead, townsite, stone and timber, and mining laws of the United States only, excepting as to price and excepting the sixteenth and thirty-sixth section in each Congressional township, which shall be reserved for common-school purposes and be subject to the laws of Idaho: *Provided,* That all purchasers of lands lying under the canal of the Idaho Canal Company, and which are susceptible of irrigation from the water from said canal, shall pay for the same at the rate of ten dollars per acre; all agricultural lands not under said canal shall be paid for at the rate of two dollars and fifty cents per acre, and grazing lands at the rate of one dollar and twenty-five cents per acre, one-fifth of the respective sums to be paid at time of original entry, and four-fifths thereof at the time of making final proof; but no purchaser shall be permitted in any manner to purchase more than one hundred and sixty acres of the land hereinbefore referred to but the rights of honorably discharged Union soldiers and sailors, as defined and described in sections twenty-three hundred and four and twenty-three hundred and five of the Revised Statutes of the United States, shall not be abridged, except as to the sums to be paid as aforesaid.

The classification as to agricultural and grazing lands shall be made by an employee of the General Land Office under the direction of the Secretary of the Interior.

No lands in sections sixteen and thirty-six now occupied, as set forth in article three of the agreement herein ratified, shall be reserved for school purposes, but the State of Idaho shall be entitled to indemnity for any lands so occupied: *Provided,* That none of said lands shall be disposed of under the town-site laws for less than ten dollars per acre: *And provided further,* That all of said lands within five miles of the boundary line of the town of Pocatello shall be sold at public auction, payable as aforesaid, under the direction of the Secretary of the Interior for not less than ten dollars per acre: *And provided further,* That any mineral lands within said five mile limit shall be disposed of under the mineral land laws of the United States, excepting that the price of such mineral lands shall be fixed at ten dollars per acre instead of the price fixed by the said mineral laws.[1]

---

[1] U.S. Congress, Senate. *Fort Hall Indian Reservation in Idaho.* Report No. 60, 56th Cong., 1st Sess., Serial No. 3886 (Washington, 1900), pp. 2-5.

MANUSCRIPT SOURCES

BEATTIE, H. S. "The First in Nevada." Bancroft MS, dictated in 1884. Bancroft Library, University of California, Berkeley, California.

BYBEE, ROBERT L. "Dictation." MS in L.D.S. Church Historian's Office, Salt Lake City.

Church of Jesus Christ of Latter-Day Saints. "Journal History." MS in L.D.S. Church Historian's Office, Salt Lake City.

DAINES, W. H. "Journal." MS in L.D.S. Church Historian's Office, Salt Lake City.

Fort Hall Agency. Letter Book, Copies of Letters Sent, 1869-1875. MS at Fort Hall Agency, Fort Hall, Idaho.

Idaho, State of. "Secretary of State Miscellaneous Papers." MSS in State-house, Boise, Idaho.

MOORE, DAVID. "Salmon River Mission, Journal." MS in L.D.S. Church Historian's Office, Salt Lake City.

——. "Salmon River Mission Record." MS in L.D.S. Church Historian's Office, Salt Lake City.

PARRY, JOSEPH; MCQUARRIE, ROBERT; and HALL, JOSEPH. "Report of the Committee on Pioneers." MS in L.D.S. Church Historian's Office, Salt Lake City.

REES, JOHN E. "Bannock Petroglyphs Along the Blackfoot River." Un-published MS, Public Library, Blackfoot, Idaho.

U.S. Department of the Interior. "Special Case No. 99." MS in U.S. National Archives, Washington, D.C.

U.S. National Archives. Records of the Bureau of Indian Affairs. MSS in the U.S. National Archives, Washington, D.C.

    Education Division, Letters Received, 1881-1895. Letter, A. L. Cook to J. D. C. Atkins, Ross Fork, Idaho, June 25, 1885. Record Group 75.

——. Petition of Bannock and Shoshoni Indians, Pocatello, Idaho, October 1, 1895. Record Group 75.

Idaho Superintendency, Letters Received, 1866-1880, Record Group 75.

Land Division, Letters Received, Record Group 75.

Montana Superintendency, Letters Received, 1867-1868, Record Group 75.

Oregon Superintendency, Letters Received, 1848-1873.

    No. 3, Copies of Letters Received and Sent, 1850-1853.

    "Report of the Oregon Superintendency of Indian Affairs, 1848-73, Letter Books," No. 10, D.

    "Report of the Oregon Superintendency of Indian Affairs, 1848-73, Letter Books," No. 10, F.

    No. 16, Copies of Letters Received, 1858.

Utah Superintendency, Letters Received, 1868, Record Group 75.

Washington Superintendency, Flathead Agency, Letters Received, No. 22.

Wyoming Superintendency, Letters Received, 1869-1870, Record Group 75.

PRINTED SOURCES

Official:

KAPPLER, CHARLES J. (ed.). *Indian Affairs, Laws and Treaties.* Compiled to December 1, 1902. Compiled and edited by Charles J. Kappler, clerk of the Senate Committee on Indian Affairs. Washington: Government Printing Office, 1903.

U.S. Congress. *Statutes at Large, Treaties and Proclamations of the United States of America from December, 1867, to March, 1869.* Edited by George P. Sanger. Vol. XV. Boston, 1869.

——. *Statutes at Large of the United States of America from December, 1887, to March, 1889.* Vol. XXV, chap. 936. Washington, 1889.

——, House of Representatives. *Agreement with the Shoshone and Bannock Indians,* Ex. Doc. 18, 47th Cong., 1st Sess., Serial No. 2026. Washington: Government Printing Office, 1882.

——. *Agreement with the Shoshone and Bannock Indians,* Ex. Doc. 140, 50th Cong., 1st Sess., Serial No. 2558. Washington: Government Printing Office, 1888.

——. *Bannock and Other Indians in Southern Idaho,* Ex. Doc. 129, 43rd Cong., 1st Sess., Serial No. 1608. Washington: Government Printing Office, 1873.

——. *Condition of Indians Taxed and Indians Not Taxed,* Misc. Doc., 52nd Cong., 1st Sess., Serial No. 3016. Washington: Government Printing Office, 1891.

——. *Depredations and Massacres by the Snake River Indians,* Ex. Doc. 46, 36th Cong., 2nd Sess., Serial No. 1099. Washington: Government Printing Office, 1860.

——. Ex. Doc., 42nd Cong., 3rd Sess., Serial No. 1560. Washington: Government Printing Office, 1872.

——. Ex. Doc. 1, 45th Cong., 3rd Sess., Serial No. 1843. Washington: Government Printing Office, 1878.

——. Ex. Doc. 381, 38th Cong., 1st Sess., Serial No. 1182. Washington: Government Printing Office, 1863.

——. *Fort Kearney, South Pass, and Honey Lake Wagon Road,* Ex. Doc. 63, 36th Cong., 2nd Sess., Serial No. 1100. Washington: Government Printing Office, 1860.

——. *Indian Depredations in Oregon and Washington,* Ex. Doc. 29, 36th Cong., 2nd Sess., Serial No. 1097. Washington: Government Printing Office, 1860.

——. Misc. Doc. 123, 44th Cong., 1st Sess., Serial No. 1702. Washington: Government Printing Office, 1875.

——. "Report of C. H. Miller," in *Report of the Secretary of the Interior on Pacific Wagon Roads,* Ex. Doc. 108, 35th Cong., 2nd Sess., Serial No. 1008, March 1, 1859. Washington: Government Printing Office, 1859.

——. *Report of the Commissioner of Indian Affairs,* Ex. Doc., 32nd Cong., 1st Sess., Serial No. 636. Washington: Government Printing Office, 1851.

——. "Report of the Governor of Idaho," in *Report of the Secretary of the Interior,* Ex. Doc., 46th Cong., 2nd Sess., Serial No. 1911. Washington: Government Printing Office, 1879.

——. *Report of the Secretary of the Interior,* Ex. Doc., 46th Cong., 2nd Sess., Serial No. 1911. Washington: Government Printing Office, 1879.

——. *Report of the Secretary of the Interior,* Ex. Doc., 46th Cong., 3rd Sess., Serial No. 1960. Washington: Government Printing Office, 1880.

——, Senate. Ex. Doc. 42, 43rd Cong., 1st Sess., Serial No. 1580. Washington: Government Printing Office, 1873.

——. Ex. Doc. 42, 36th Cong., 1st Sess., Serial No. 1033. Washington: Government Printing Office, 1860.

——. *Fort Hall Indian Reservation in Idaho*, Report No. 60, 56th Cong., 1st Sess., Serial No. 3886. Washington: Government Printing Office, 1900.

——. *Military and Indian Affairs in Oregon*, Ex. Doc., Vol. I, No. IV, No. 11, 32nd Cong., 1st Sess., Serial No. 611. Washington: Government Printing Office, 1851.

——. "Report of B. F. Ficklin," in *Report of the Secretary of War*, Ex. Doc., II, No. 1, Part II, 35th Cong., 2nd Sess., Serial No. 975. Washington: Government Printing Office, 1859.

——. *Report of the Commissioner of Indian Affairs*, Ex. Doc., 31st Cong., 2nd Sess., Serial No. 587. Washington: Government Printing Office, 1850.

——. *Report of the Commissioner of Indian Affairs*, Ex. Doc., 33rd Cong., 1st Sess., Serial No. 690. Washington: Government Printing Office, 1853.

——. *Report of the Commissioner of Indian Affairs*, Ex. Doc., No. 10, 27th Cong., 3rd Sess., Serial No. 414. Washington: Government Printing Office, 1842.

——. *Report of the Commissioner of Indian Affairs Relative to the Failure of the Utah and Northern Railroad Company to Compensate Certain Indians for Right of Way*, Ex. Doc. 6, 48th Cong., 2nd Sess., Serial No. 2261. Washington: Government Printing Office, 1885.

——. *Report of the Secretary of War*, Ex. Doc., 36th Cong., 2nd Sess., Serial No. 1079. Washington: Government Printing Office, 1860.

——. *Report of the Secretary of War*, Ex. Doc., II, No. 1, Part II, 35th Cong., 2nd Sess., Serial No. 975. Washington: Government Printing Office, 1859.

U.S. Department of the Interior. *Report of the Board of Indian Commissioners*. Washington: Government Printing Office, 1895.

——, Office of Indian Affairs. General Files, Idaho, W1028/1878 and W1004/1878.

U.S. Government Records. *The War of the Rebellion; a Compilation of the Official Records of the Union and Confederate Armies.* Series I, Vol. L, Part I. Washington, 1897.

U.S Office of Indian Affairs. *Annual Reports of the Commissioner of Indian Affairs*, for the years 1851 to 1907. Washington: Government Printing Office, 1852-1908.

Private:

AKIN, JAMES, JR. "The Journal of James Akin, Jr.," edited by Edward Everett Dale. (*University of Oklahoma Bulletin*, New Series No. 172, University Studies No. 9.) Norman, Okla.: University of Oklahoma, 1919.

BLUTH, JOHN V. "The Salmon River Mission," *Improvement Era* (Salt Lake City), III, No. 11 (September, 1900), 911.

BROWN, JOHN E. *Memoirs of a Forty-Niner. Journey Across the Plains to the Pacific;* edited by his daughter, Mrs. Katie E. Blood. New Haven, Conn., 1907.

BRUFF, JOSEPH GOLDSBOROUGH. *Gold Rush; The Journals, Drawings, and Other Papers of J. Goldsborough Bruff, 1804-1889;* edited by Georgia Willis Read and Ruth Gaines. 2 vols.; New York: Columbia University Press, 1944.

Church of Jesus Christ of Latter-Day Saints. *Doctrine and Covenants.* Salt Lake City, 1920.

CLYMAN, JAMES. *James Clyman, American Frontiersman, 1792-1881; the*

Adventures of a Trapper and Covered Wagon Emigrant as Told in His Own Reminiscences and Diaries; edited by Charles L. Camp. San Francisco: California Historical Society, 1928.

COKE, HENRY J. *A Ride Over the Rocky Mountains to Oregon and California.* London: Richard Bentley, 1852.

COX, ROSS. *Adventures on the Columbia River, including the Narrative of a Residence of Six Years on the Western Side of the Rocky Mountains.* New York: J. and J. Harper, 1832.

CRAWFORD, LEWIS F. (ed.). *Rekindling Camp Fires, the Exploits of Ben Arnold (Connor); an Authentic Narrative of Sixty Years in the Old West as Indian Fighter, Gold Miner, Cowboy, Hunter and Army Scout.* [Cedar Rapids, Iowa, 1926.]

CRAWFORD, MEDOREM. "Journal of Medorem Crawford, an Account of His Trip Across the Plains with the Oregon Pioneers of 1842," edited by F. G. Young, in *Sources of the History of Oregon,* Vol. I, No. 1. Eugene, Ore.: Star Job Office, 1897.

CROOK, GEORGE. *General George Crook; His Autobiography;* edited and annotated by Martin F. Schmitt. Norman, Okla.: University of Oklahoma Press, 1946.

Daughters of Idaho Pioneers. *History of the Development of Southeastern Idaho.* [1930]

DAVENPORT, T. W. "Recollections of an Indian Agent," *Oregon Historical Society Quarterly* (Portland, Ore.), VIII (December, 1907).

DeSMET, P. J., S.J. *Letters and Sketches; with a Narrative of a Year's Residence Among the Indian Tribes of the Rocky Mountains* [Philadelphia, 1843]. Reprinted in *Early Western Travels, 1748-1846,* Vols. XXVII and XXVIII, edited by Reuben Gold Thwaites. Cleveland: The Arthur H. Clark Company, 1906.

DICKSON, ALBERT J. *Covered Wagon Days; a Journey Across the Plains in the Sixties, and Pioneer Days in the Northwest; from the Private Journals of Albert Jerome Dickson;* edited by Arthur Jerome Dickson. Cleveland: The Arthur H. Clark Company, 1929.

DRANNAN, WILLIAM F. *Thirty-One Years on the Plains and in the Mountains; or, The Last Voice from the Plains; an Authentic Record of a Life Time of Hunting, Trapping, Scouting and Indian Fighting in the Far West.* Chicago: Rhodes, 1900.

ELLIOTT, T. C. (ed.). "The Peter Skene Ogden Journals, Snake Expedition, 1825-1826," *Oregon Historical Society Quarterly,* X, No. 4 (December, 1909).

———. "The Peter Skene Ogden Journals, Snake Expedition, 1827-1828," *ibid.,* XI, No. 4 (December, 1910).

———. "Journal of John Work, Covering the Snake Country Expedition of 1830-31, *Oregon Historical Society Quarterly,* XIII, No. 4 (December, 1912), 369-71.

FARNHAM, THOMAS J. *Travels in the Great Western Prairies, the Anahuac and Rocky Mountains, and in the Oregon Territory.* New York: Greeley, 1843.

FERRIS, W. A. *Life in the Rocky Mountains . . . from February, 1830, to November, 1835;* edited by Paul C. Phillips. Denver: Old West Publishing Company, 1940.

Franklin County (Idaho) Historical Society. *The Passing of the Redman.* Preston, Idaho, 1917.

FREMONT, JOHN C. *Memoirs of My Life.* Chicago and New York: Belford, Clarke & Company, 1887.

GOVE, JESSE A. *The Utah Expedition, 1857-1858; Letters of Capt. Jesse Augustus Gove, 10th Inf., U.S.A.;* edited by Otis G. Hammond. (New

Hampshire Historical Society "Collections," Vol. XII.) Concord, N.H., 1928.

HAMBLIN, JACOB. *Autobiography.* Salt Lake City, 1858.

HAMILTON, WILLIAM T. *My Sixty Years on the Plains, Trapping, Trading, and Indian Fighting;* edited by E. T. Sieber. New York: Forest and Stream Publishing Co., 1905.

HEWITT, RANDALL HENRY. *Notes By the Way; Memoranda of a Journey Across the Plains from Dundee, Ill., to Olympia, W.T., May 7 to November 3, 1862.* Olympia, Wash.: Washington Standard, 1863.

HOPKINS, SARAH WINNEMUCCA. *Life Among the Paiutes; Their Wrongs and Claims;* edited by Mrs. Horace Mann. Boston: Cupples, 1883.

IRVING, WASHINGTON. *The Adventures of Captain Bonneville.* New York: J. B. Miller & Co., 1885.

KELLY, LUTHER S. *"Yellowstone Kelly"; the Memoirs of Luther S. Kelly,* edited by Milo M. Quaife, with a foreword by Lieutenant-General Nelson A. Miles, U.S.A. New Haven, Conn.: Yale University Press, 1926.

LEFORGE, THOMAS H. *Memoirs of a White Crow Indian,* as told by Thomas B. Marquis. New York: D. Appleton-Century Company, Inc., 1928.

MILES, NELSON A. *Personal Recollections and Observations of General Nelson A. Miles, embracing . . . the Story of His Indian Campaigns, with Comments on the Exploration, Development and Progress of Our Great Western Empire.* Chicago, New York: The Werner Company, 1896.

MITCHELL, S. AUGUSTUS. *Accompaniment to Mitchell's New Map of Texas, Oregon, and California, with the Regions Adjoining.* Philadelphia: S. Augustus Mitchell, 1846.

MUNGER, ASAHEL. "Diary of Asahel Munger and Wife," *Oregon Historical Society Quarterly,* VIII (1907), 400.

OWEN, JOHN. *The Letters and Journals of Major John Owen, Pioneer of the Northwest, 1850-1871;* edited by Seymour Dunbar, and with notes to Owen's text by Paul C. Phillips. 2 vols.; New York: Edward Eberstadt, 1927.

PALMER, JOEL. *Journal of Travels Over the Rocky Mountains to the Mouth of the Columbia River, 1845 and 1846.* Reprinted in *Early Western Travels, 1748-1846,* Vol. XXX, edited by Reuben Gold Thwaites. Cleveland: The Arthur H. Clark Company, 1906.

ROLLINS, PHILIP A. (ed.). "Wilson Price Hunt's Diary of His Overland Trip Westward to Astoria in 1811-12," in *The Discovery of the Oregon Trail, Robert Stuart's Narratives. . . .* New York: Charles Scribner's Sons, 1935.

ROSS, ALEXANDER. *Adventures of the First Settlers on the Oregon or Columbia River* [London, 1849]. Reprinted in *Early Western Travels, 1748-1846,* Vol. VII, edited by Reuben Gold Thwaites. Cleveland: The Arthur H. Clark Company, 1904.

———. *The Fur Hunters of the Far West; a Narrative of Adventures in the Oregon and Rocky Mountains.* 2 vols.; London: Smith, Elder & Co., 1855.

RUSSELL, OSBORNE. *Journal of a Trapper; or, Nine Years in the Rocky Mountains, 1834-1843.* 2nd. ed.; Boise, Idaho: Syms-York Co., Inc., 1921.

SCHOOLCRAFT, HENRY R. *Archives of Aboriginal Knowledge.* Philadelphia, 1860. Vol. I.

SIMPSON, J. H. *The Shortest Route to California, Illustrated by a History of Explorations of the Great Basin of Utah with Its Topo-*

graphical and Geological Character and Some Account of the Indian Tribes. Philadelphia: J. B. Lippincott, 1869.

STUART, GRANVILLE. *Forty Years on the Frontier; the Journals and Reminiscences of Granville Stuart, Gold-miner, Trader, Merchant, Rancher and Politician;* edited by Paul C. Phillips. ("Early Western Journals," No. 2.) Cleveland: The Arthur H. Clark Company, 1925.

TALBOT, THEODORE. *The Journals of Theodore Talbot, 1843 and 1849-52; with the Fremont Expedition of 1843 and with the First Military Company in Oregon Territory, 1849-52;* edited with notes by Charles H. Carey. Portland, Ore.: Metropolitan Press, 1931.

THWAITES, REUBEN GOLD (ed.). *Original Journals of the Lewis and Clark Expedition, 1804-1806.* 7 vols. and atlas; New York: Dodd, Mead and Company, 1904-5. Vol. II, Part II.

TOWNSEND, JOHN K. *Narrative of a Journey Across the Rocky Mountains to the Columbia River, 1832-1834.* Reprinted in *Early Western Travels, 1748-1846,* Vol. XXI, edited by Reuben Gold Thwaites. Cleveland: The Arthur H. Clark Company, 1905.

WALKER, MARY RICHARDSON. "The Diary of Mary Richardson Walker, June 10-December 21, 1838," edited by Rufus A. Coleman, in *Sources of Northwest History,* No. 15, edited by Paul C. Phillips, as reprinted from *The Frontier,* XI, No. 3, p. 8.

WILLIAMS, JOSEPH. *Narrative of a Tour from the State of Indiana to the Oregon Territory in the Years 1841-2.* New York: Cadmus Book Shop, 1921.

NEWSPAPERS

Blackfoot (Idaho) *Register,* May 3, 7, 21, 1881.
Boise (Idaho) *Semi-Weekly Democrat,* August 1, 1868, p. 3.
Cheyenne (Wyoming) *Daily Sun-Leader,* November 4, 1895.
Deseret News (Salt Lake City, Utah), 1858-60, 1862-63.
Idaho Falls (Idaho) *Register,* May 12, 1883.
Idaho Statesman (Boise, Idaho), 1864-1900.
Idaho World (Idaho City, Idaho), August 23, 1895.
Pocatello (Idaho) *Tribune,* 1895, 1896, 1897.
Sacramento (California) *Union,* 1862, 1863.
Salt Lake (Utah) *Tribune,* 1878.
San Francisco (California) *Bulletin,* May 5, 1863.
Wood River Times (Hailey, Idaho), July 1, 1897.
Yankee Fork Herald (Bonanza, Custer County, Idaho) August 7, 1879.

PERIODICALS

Army and Navy Journal, XV, No. 47 (June 29, 1878), 758.
Harper's Weekly, October 31, 1857, p. 649.
Illustrated American (New York), August 17, 1895, p. 207.

MONOGRAPHS

BAILEY, ROBERT G. *River of No Return (The Great Salmon River of Idaho), a Century of Central Idaho and Eastern Washington History and Development.* Lewiston, Idaho: Bailey-Blake Printing Co., 1935.

BANCROFT, HUBERT HOWE. *History of Utah*. San Francisco: The History Company, 1890.

——. "Wild Tribes," in Vol. I, *Native Races of the Pacific States of North America*. 5 vols.; San Francisco: A. L. Bancroft & Co., 1882.

BERREMAN, JOEL V. *Tribal Distribution in Oregon* ("Memoirs of the American Anthropological Association," No. 47.) Menasha, Wis., 1937.

BONNER, T. D. (ed.). *The Life and Adventures of James P. Beckwourth*. ("Americana Deserta.") New York: Alfred A. Knopf, 1931.

BRIMLOW, GEORGE F. *The Bannock Indian War of 1878*. Caldwell, Idaho: The Caxton Printers, Ltd., 1938.

BROSNAN, CORNELIUS J. *History of the State of Idaho*. New York: Charles Scribner's Sons, 1935.

CHITTENDEN, HIRAM MARTIN. *The American Fur Trade of the Far West;* with introduction and notes by Stallo Vinton and sketch of the author by Dr. Edmond S. Meany. 2 vols.; New York: The Press of the Pioneers, Inc., 1935.

DAVID, ROBERT BEEBE. *Finn Burnett, Frontiersman; the Life and Adventures of an Indian Fighter, Mail-Coach Driver, Miner, Pioneer Cattleman, Participant in the Powder River Expedition, Survivor of the Hayfield Fight, Associate of Jim Bridger and Chief Washakie*. Glendale, Calif.: The Arthur H. Clark Company, 1937.

DEFENBACH, BYRON. *Idaho; the Place and Its People; History of the Gem State from Prehistoric to Present Days*. 3 vols.; Chicago and New York: American Historical Society, 1933. Vol. I.

DONALDSON, THOMAS. *Idaho of Yesterday;* introduction by Thomas B. Donaldson. Caldwell, Idaho: The Caxton Printers, Ltd., 1941.

FEE, CHESTER ANDERS. *Chief Joseph; The Biography of a Great Indian;* with a foreword by Charles Erskine Scott Wood. New York: Wilson-Erickson, Incorporated, 1936.

HAFEN, LEROY R. *The Overland Mail 1849-1869; Promoter of Settlement, Precursor of Railroads*. Cleveland: The Arthur H. Clark Company, 1926.

HAILEY, JOHN. *The History of Idaho*. Boise, Idaho: Syms-York Company, Inc., 1910.

HAINES, FRANCIS D. *Red Eagles of the Northwest; the Story of Chief Joseph and His People*. Portland, Ore.: Scholastic Press, 1939.

HEBARD, GRACE RAYMOND. *Washakie; An Account of Indian Resistance to the Covered Wagon and the Union Pacific Railroad Invasion of their Territory*. Cleveland: The Arthur H. Clark Company, 1930.

HODGE, FREDERICK WEBB (ed.). *Handbook of American Indians North of Mexico*. (Smithsonian Institution, Bureau of American Ethnology, Bulletin 30.) Washington: Government Printing Office, 1912.

HOWARD, OLIVER OTIS. *Nez Perce Joseph; An Account of His Ancestors, His Lands, His Confederates, His Enemies, His Murders, His War, His Pursuit and Capture*. Boston: Lee and Shepard, 1881.

HULBERT, ARCHER B. (ed.). *The Call of the Columbia; Iron Men and Saints Take the Oregon Trail*. ("Overland to the Pacific," Vol. 4.) Denver, Colo.: Stewart Commission of Colorado College, 1934.

LITTLE, JAMES A. *Jacob Hamblin*. Salt Lake City, 1881.

McCONNELL, WILLIAM JOHN. *Early History of Idaho, by W. J. McConnell, ex-U.S. Senator and -Governor, who was Present and Cognizant of the Events Narrated*, Published by Authority of the Idaho State Legislature. Caldwell, Idaho, 1913.

MOONEY, JAMES. "The Ghost Dance Religion and the Sioux Outbreak of 1890." In *Fourteenth Annual Report of the Bureau of American*

Ethnology, 1892-93, Part II. Washington, D.C.: Government Printing Office, 1896.

MUMEY, NOLIE. *The Life of Jim Baker, 1818-1898; Trapper, Scout, Guide and Indian Fighter*. Denver: World Press, 1931.

RAY, VERNE F. "Tribal Distribution in Eastern Oregon and Adjacent Regions," *American Anthropologist*, XL (Menasha, Wis., 1938), 405.

REES, JOHN E. *Idaho Chronology, Nomenclature, Bibliography*. Chicago: W. B. Conkey Company, 1918.

ROGERS, FRED B. *Soldiers of the Overland; being Some Account of the Services of General Patrick Edward Connor & His Volunteers in the Old West*. San Francisco: Grabhorn Press, 1938.

SCHMECKEBIER, LAURENCE F. *The Office of Indian Affairs*. ("Institute for Government Research, Service Monographs of the United States Government," No. 48.) Baltimore: Johns Hopkins University, 1927.

SHIMKIN, D. B. *Wind River Shoshone Ethnogeography*. ("Anthropological Records," Vol. V, No. 4.) Berkeley, Calif.: University of California Press, 1947.

SJODAHL, JOHN M. *An Introduction to the Study of the Book of Mormon*. Salt Lake City, 1927.

SMITH, DeCOST. *Indian Experiences*. Caldwell, Idaho: The Caxton Printers, Ltd., 1943.

SMITH, JOSEPH. *History of the Church*. Salt Lake City, 1902.

STEWARD, JULIAN H. *Basin-Plateau Aboriginal Sociopolitical Groups*. (Bureau of American Ethnology, Bulletin 120.) Washington: Government Printing Office, 1938.

——. *Culture Element Distributions, XXIII; Northern and Gosiute Shoshoni*. ("Anthropological Records," Vol. VIII, No. 3.) Berkeley, Calif.: University of California Press, 1943.

STEWART, OMER C. *The Northern Paiute Bands*. ("Anthropological Records," Vol. II, No. 3.) Berkeley, Calif.: University of California Press, 1939.

TEIT, JAMES A. "The Salishan Tribes of the Western Plateaus." In *Forty-Fifth Annual Report of the Bureau of American Ethnology*. Washington: Government Printing Office, 1928.

TOPPING, E. S. *The Chronicles of the Yellowstone; An Accurate, Comprehensive History of the Country Drained by the Yellowstone River, its Indian Inhabitants, its First Explorers, the Early Fur Traders and-Trappers, the Coming and Trails of the Emigrants*. St. Paul: Pioneer Press, 1883.

TULLIDGE, EDWARD W. *History of Salt Lake City, and Its Founders*. Salt Lake City: The Author, 1886.

VESTAL, STANLEY. *Jim Bridger: Mountain Man; A Biography*. New York: William Morrow & Company, 1946.

VICTOR, FRANCES FULLER. *The River of the West; Life and Adventures in the Rocky Mountains and Oregon; embracing Events in the Lifetime of a Mountain-Man and Pioneer; with the Early History of the North-Western Slope*. San Francisco: A. L. Bancroft & Co., 1870.

VINTON, STALLO. *John Colter, Discoverer of Yellowstone Park; an Account of His Exploration in 1807 and of His Further Adventures as Hunter, Trapper, Indian Fighter, Pathfinder and Member of the Lewis and Clark Expedition*. New York: Edward Eberstadt, 1926.

FLATH

Salmon River

NEZ PERCE

Idaho

Weiser River

Middle Fork

Lemhi River

Oregon Trail

Lost River

Malheur River

Payette River

◦ Fort Boise

Owyhee River

Boise River

SHOSHO

Snake River

S

O

Camas Prairie

Bruneau River

Salmon Falls Creek

B

A

Shoshone Falls

C

Oregon

Idaho

Nevada

Goose Creek

Humboldt River

California Trail

Nevada

Utah

SHOSHONI

PAIUTE